Trials
AND
TRIBULATIONS

VEERSEN BHOOLAI

1

Dedicated to Ramprasad Bhoolai

Table of Contents

CHAPTER 1

Return to Reading Hall

As our father's old Vauxhall slowly made its way up the bumpy, steep hill, my sister and I could barely contain our excitement. This was the most exciting moment of our lives.

It was December of 1977 – our school Christmas holidays. For years we had been dreaming of visiting him at his home in Caigual. It was a rural area, part of the town of Sangre Grande, eastern Trinidad.

My parents had divorced five years earlier and my mother had thought the dense bush and lack of electricity was not safe enough for my sister or I at a very young age. When I was seven, she thought that was a good age but didn't want my sister to get jealous so we had to wait for little Leila to get older.

As we slowly made our way up the hill – savannah to the right of us and a sloping hill with trees to the left, we were literally jumping. I had spent fantastic visits here with my grandfather as a youngster. Leila had more vague memories. But our grandfather and this estate were both legendary.

My paternal grandfather, Rampersad Darsan had been born in Penal in the deep South of Trinidad. Penal, (pronounced Peenaal) by the locals.

His parents had come over from India in 1900. The classic indentured laborers, they had put in their five years on the sugar plantations and then got their five acres of land. Like the other East Indians who had been brought over starting in 1845 to replace the freed black slaves who had demanded higher wages, Rampersad's family saved their earnings, worked their land and slowly bought more arable land.

The Indians in Trinidad were famous for their ability to save despite an apparently simple economic appearance. My grandmother, Geeta Mahabir, was born on June 5, 1910, one month before my grandfather. She had been born in the extremely rural area of Guyaguayare. Her family-owned land in both Guyaguayare and Penal.

Rampersad, was an extremely popular young man. Charismatic, handsome, amiable, six feet tall and a sturdy 200 pounds, he was well liked, especially by the ladies.

Like many rural Indians of his generation, he stopped going to school at the age of 10, to work and help sustain the family. He became a plantation labourer working the cocoa and coffee plantations in the deep South. By the age of 22, he was an overseer, this meant he was the foreman of the plantation he worked on. He was given his own house – the quarters being bigger than those of the average worker.

Tall, strapping, handsome, with a full head of beautiful thick hair, Rampersad had a proliferation of lovers – both married and unmarried. He met my father's mother whilst tapping rubber trees with the labourers on a plantation. I would never know quite how it happened but despite she being married with two children, she and Pa became an item. What I can say is that two years later Geeta left her husband and married Rampersad.

My grandfather had been offered a job as an overseer in Sangre Grande. He took Geeta and together they relocated – minus her children. As a child, I could never understand how she had been able to leave her two sons behind. I found out about these men only when I was about 12

2

years old. I tried to question my father about them but he seemed to feign ignorance and apparently had no interest in his brothers.

I did find out however, that in their youth they would visit her and spend holidays at Reading Hall. Decades later, visiting her family in Penal and trying to understand my roots, I spoke to her nephews and nieces at her parents' home where she had grown up. They were much more liberal with information than my father had ever been. They explained that my Ma was a member of the Pooran family. There were seven girls and one brother. When she left her discombobulated husband, her father reached out to him.

"Don't worry. She gone but look we have a next one here for you."

He offered up Ma's younger sister Liloutie. They were duly married and had two children of their own.

I remember expressing my shock that my great aunt had been put forward like glorified livestock. However, as her niece put it, "That is how it was in dem days. Your parents say so and you do it."

I was also informed that Ma did not visit the family home for years, afraid of her father's wrath. She would visit relatives in the area making sure to avoid her father's peripheral vision. However, more than a decade later and early into Pa's prosperous years, she asked permission to see her ailing mother. And only then did she start making regular visits.

My Grandparents on both sides were staunch Hindus. My parents were brought up in the traditional way and like their parents could speak Hindi fluently. In our family we referred to my father's parents as Pa and Ma; however, with my mother's family we used the traditional terms for your mother's parents; Nana for our grandfather and Nani for our grandmother.

The Darsans arrived in Sangre Grande in 1938 and shortly after had their first child – a son - who was still born. Wasting no time, my Uncle Basdeo was born in 1939 and 13 months later on November 1, 1940, my father, Vijay, arrived.

It would be another nine years until they had their third child, my Aunt Shanti, born on July 2, 1949.

Upon their arrival in Grande (as the locals called it), Rampersad, did what he did best, oversee the basic operations of the Estate. Coffee and cocoa were the staple but there was an abundance of oranges, coconuts, honey and rubber tapped from trees. Not only was the rubber tapped but processed as well on the plantation in the "Smoke House." There were a variety of other crops that were also harvested.

Reading Hall Estate had been created in the early 1880s by Michael Reading, a white man from Liverpool, England. The Readings had had only one son, Peter, born in 1885. In late 1946, Peter, in his early sixties, widowed and childless decided that he would spend his final years in Port of Spain. Other than about six families living at the bottom of the hill and a handful of neighbours about a mile away, he had no one around him. The isolation was not how he wanted to spend his final years.

Reading Hall was a massive plantation house built of wood. Almost 90 years later, at the death of my grandfather in 1973, it was still standing strong.

However, widowed and alone in 1946, Peter decided he would sell. Five of the laborers, my grandfather included, decided they would collectively purchase the land – as individually – it was far too expensive. Rampersad borrowed from a few friends and used what little savings he had. He would pay back every cent borrowed, sadly, years later as a wealthy landowner, he had many debtors who dodged him until the day he died.

Peter Reading asked the princely sum of 2000 dollars for his four hundred acres, taking into consideration the house, barns, smoke house and cocoa house, in addition to five residences that were rented out to estate workers.

It was decided amongst the group that as the Overseer, Rampersad, should have the house. Consequently, he got a portion of land that had quite a few buildings already on it as they had been built in close proximity to the house, e.g., the barns, cocoa house, etc. Rampersad's portion was 500 dollars, more than half borrowed.

Thus, at the age of six, my father and the rest of the family moved into the majestic Reading Hall. Situated on a hill, it was literally a step up for the family as they had to take the private road, all 120 meters of it to get up there.

Reading Hall was a sight to behold. A sprawling rectangular structure, there were three bedrooms, a study; a living/dining room that was approximately 108 square meters, bigger than a lot of homes in Trinidad, a massive kitchen connected to a storage room and an underground Roman bath and flushing toilet. At the back of the kitchen was a hearth for cooking and a yard for slaughtering animals that were going to be subsequently cooked. If one stood with your back to the house, there was a garage about 30 metres away, beyond the garage were the barns and smoke house and beyond the smoke house out of sight were the bees. There was a beautiful lawn in front of the house and a sloping lawn at the back that was the crest of the hill. With no proper running water, there were tanks galore. Almost adjacent to the Smoke House, was a super tank and another one beside the house. Both of these were about 22 feet high and a hundred feet in circumference, made of solid concrete. There were two smaller ones, one behind the house and the other near to the kitchen. They collected rainfall and during my holidays at various times, there never seemed to be a shortage of water. I remember a goblet located next to the sink in the dining room. It was always full of rainwater and it was the sweetest water I had ever tasted in my life. I used to call it "the nectar of the Gods."

Halfway down the hill, to the left, you would see a savannah, with a Cocoa house, where harvested cocoa was sunned and processed. The Overseer's house was right next to it. At the foot of the hill, on the main road, were four more houses belonging to the Estate where a worker and his family could live.

By 1949 after a few harvesting seasons, Pa was now a wealthy landowner. He had slowly bought out some of his original partners. He had bought a Ford Club Coupe and with his new economic status to accompany his dashing good looks, he had become a "real sweet man," with the ladies. Decades later, as a young boy, I would hear rumours of his alleged children produced out of wedlock.

Thus, by his seventh year, my father was no longer a little country bookie,[1] running around bare back with no shoes. With the passing of each year as Pa's prosperity rose, my father, and his siblings enjoyed a very comfortable lifestyle. There was never any shortage of clothes or food. Uncle Basdeo was given a car on his fifteenth birthday. Absolute rubbish in any generation, however, by then, Pa was one of the wealthiest landowners in Trinidad and a Member of the Trinidad & Tobago Parliament. So respected was my family in Sangre Grande that the authorities simply looked the other way.

Pa kept in touch with Mr. Reading who together with his sister moved to a house in Morne Coco, a hillside area on the outskirts of Port of Spain. As the Manager of the estate Pa got along well with Reading. He liked Pa's charismatic, bold, confident manner. Pa later borrowed ten thousand dollars from him to purchase more land in Caigual. They would continue to see each other as Pa would pay courtesy calls on his visits to Port of Spain. When Reading died in 1950, Pa carried his two sons with him to pay his respects. Whilst there, he told Ms. Reading, that he would pay the balance of the ten thousand owed at the end of the year.

Ms. Reading responded: "Oh no Rampersad you don't owe anything."

"No. Actually, if you look in the safe, you will see an IOU made out by me to Mr. Reading."

"That's quite alright Rampersad. Peter said that if he ever died, you would owe nothing."

Reading's respect towards my Pa had continued even in death.

---

[1] *Country bookie*: an unsophisticated person from the countryside.

My mother's family story was a little less spectacular, although she did have her fair share of adventures. My Nana was born Inshan Rambarran in Plum Mitan, Sangre Grande in 1902. The son of Indian immigrants; collectively both his parents had over 200 acres of land. Some in Sangre Grande, some further up North in Blanchicheusse and to the far North-West of the island, 30 odd acres in Diego Martin. Nana's father sold the land in Diego Martin as he considered it too far away. Ironically 70 years later that is where my mother would move us and I would spend my best childhood years there.

Nana and his wife Kamala had thirteen children, two dying shortly after birth. Of the surviving 11, my mother was seventh.

The Hindu way is for the daughter to use her father's first name as her surname. Thus, Mummy was born Cintra Inshan on July 21, 1942. However, living in a British system, girls having different surnames from the rest of the family was too confusing for officials, especially with the issuing of ID and inheritance of property. So, my mother like most Indian girls had to adapt and use her father's surname to satisfy the local civil service.

Cintra was one of those people destined for success. As kids my sister and I would hear the stories that all parents deliver to their children, letting them know how lucky they were and how tough life was back in the day.

She had originally lived in a house made of tapia, a solid sort of mud. Nana later built a more solid three-bedroom house. For the first 11 years of her life, the concept of a toilet was foreign to her as both her parents and the school in Plum Mitan had latrines.

Plum Mitan was about five miles from the centre of Grande. You had to take a side road and travel for another three miles to get to Nana's house. My mother had to get up at 5 am to do chores. However, being naturally studious, she would get up at four, study for one hour and then do the chores. "I had to walk five miles to school barefoot because I was too poor," was the drone we would hear repeatedly. "But it was both ways

7

so that was really ten miles. I had no school bag. My books were in a rice sack. One day I was rude to my mother and she slapped me so hard that her hand printed out on my face. I had to spend the whole day in school with that handprint on my face. You all have it too easy."

Forty years later, those stories were like a recording in my head.

My mother was always a top student. At age 11, all students wrote the Island Exhibition, where the top hundred would have the high school of their choice. My mother would always state that she missed out on the top hundred by three marks.

She went to Sangre Grande College, where she would meet my father.

A slim, beautiful girl, she had been proposed to by her teacher at age 12. She turned him down.

Her entrance to SG College, inadvertently led to a better economic and social life. Realizing that the trek from Plum Mitan to central Grande would be a bit too much for her. My Nani asked her brother who lived in Grande to please host her during the week. Vinaya Madosingh was Mum's Mamoo (Uncle). He had no problem with the request. By this time it was 1952, Vinaya, along with my Pa was one of the wealthier businessmen in Grande. He had started off with a trucking business and later built a cinema next to his house on Eastern Main Road. His house itself was a massive two-story structure. His wife contrary to Indian custom was a French Creole woman by the name of Valerie Boucad. She was the daughter of a wealthy local white plantation owner Jean Boucad, from rural Blanchicheusse. Fifteen years her senior, Vinaya had met a 14-year-old Valerie, at a party in Sangre Grande. A covert courtship commenced and ten months later he asked her father for Valerie's hand in marriage. Jean Boucad, saw no reason why this successful Grande businessman would not be a good prospect for his Valerie. He wasn't white but he was a handsome, rich Indian who agreed that Val would be allowed to continue her Roman Catholic faith and that her children to be would follow. By no means was Aunt Val white, in racial terms the locals would refer to her as "red skin," though mulatto would be the more comprehensible terms amongst the British. Her mother was also red skin and Val like her mother was a striking beauty. By the time Mum had entered her house, Val was now in her late 20s. Married at 15, she had had five children; two boys and three girls. The first four were all around the same age as Mum so she got along well with them.

Aunt Val was as kind as she was beautiful. She treated my mother no differently than her own kids. My mother lived in an opulent four-bedroom-house. Because the majority of Val's kids went to high school in Port of Spain (Trinidad's capital), they boarded there on weekdays and came home on weekends. My Mum basically had her own room. Uncle Vinaya's cinema was next door. So, she saw many a double feature for free. Strangely, she never seemed to mention that in her stories of a dire childhood.

Both Uncle Basdeo and Dad were good cricketers and played for SG College. My parents met at SGC with Mum two years behind Dad. When she entered high school Dad was already going out with his homeroom teacher. He was 14 and she 19.

My father was the spitting image of Pa at that age. He was almost as tall, naturally lean and skinny. As handsome as he was my dad never expected his teacher, Ms. Bissoondath to flirt with him.

As an MP and someone responsible for building schools in the area my Pa was well respected. If my father and his brother were late for school (which was almost every day) or missed a few days – let's just say they staff looked the other way.

It was the norm for Pa to take some of his racehorses to Guyana if ever there was a break in the schedule in TT. The horses had to go by boat and this was a two-day trip. Dad and Uncle Basdeo would usually miss about a week of school. They had no problem with this.

Returning from one of his Guyana sojourns, Dad was in class, chatting away with his best friend Sachin during Ms. Bissoondath's English class.

This was her first class with my father. Aware that he had been away for a week, she pointed him out: "Obviously you are unaware of the reading Vijay."

Unbeknownst to her, Vijay loved English and would avidly read his Literature books well ahead of class. The book at hand was *Kidnapped* by Robert Louis Stevenson. Without missing a beat, he stood up: "If you have a question about the reading, all you have to do is ask," he said with a sly smile. Naturally, he knew the reading well.

As the weeks rolled by, he was shocked as she would stand behind him in class and as the other students did their work, she would rub her leg on the back of his calf.

On his fifteen birthday, Vijay was in school enjoying the usual extra attention from friends that comes on such a day. As the class jetted out into the yard for their lunch, Ms. Bissoondath called out to him: "Vijay, stay back please."

Naturally, he was curious. She approached him with a soft smile. "I'm aware that today is your birthday. Here." She extended her right hand and there was a green coloured envelope in her palm."

Vijay – for once – was without words. "Thanks Miss," he managed to reply. He accepted the envelope, with his head bowed, quite surprised by this attention.

As he exited, Sachin was waiting: "What happen to she? You in trouble?"

"Nah boy, I get a present."

They both simultaneously dashed to the toilets. Pretending to go use a toilet, they entered a stall and locked the door. Vijay opened the envelope and pulled out a card.

Written on the inside was: *Have a happy birthday dearest Vijay, best wishes and lots of love, Indra.*

"Wait nah. Her name is Indra!" exclaimed Sachin.

Vijay checked in the envelope and saw a circular object. He tilted the envelope and a ring fell into his hand, silver with a diamond shaped head.

"I get ring too boy!" shouted Vijay.

My father was not quite sure how to process this event. Sure, he was popular with the girls his own age but this was a teacher. Seeing that he saw her only in the confines of the school, surrounded by teachers and students, he saw no proper avenue for him to proceed, so he dismissed the matter. But Indra Bissoondath, had no intentions of the matter being dropped.

She would continue to smile and give Vijay a seductive look in the corridors. As students would read out from the books, she would walk around the class and inevitably find herself at his desk; her hand brushing his shoulder and the customary caressing of his calf with her leg.

In our house there was an old black and white photo of her in an archaic album from my father's youth. Indra was short, slim, dark with very average looking features and very black hair that went halfway down her back. I would always be confused as to the attraction my father had to her.

Two weeks later, on a Friday afternoon, Vijay was on his way out of the school gate. He and his schoolmates were extra hyper as they were every Friday afternoon with the prospect of the weekend ahead of them.

"Hold on Vijay," Ms. Bissoondath called out.

"Steuuppss," with a loud sucking of the teeth. "She serious?"

Vijay trudged his way towards her. "Yes Miss."

"Vijay, I need some help with some boxes. Come please."

They made their way towards one of the classes. There on the teacher's desk was a box full of novels.

Vijay looked towards her expecting to be given instructions on what to do with the box. However, she calmly asked "So what are your plans for this weekend?"

"Well Ms. Bissoondath, I plan to study and maybe go to the cinema."

"Which movie?"

"I think *To have or have not*, starring Humphrey Bogart."

"Well, I was thinking of seeing that as well. Do you want to come with me Vijay?"

Vijay paused for a moment and swallowed. This was virgin territory for the sweet boy from Caigual. "OK Miss."

"Very well, the movie starts at 4:30 pm on Saturday. Meet me at the front by the lamp post at 3:45 because there will be a crowd."

"Yes Miss. OK."

"Good. See you then," she said with the sweetest of smiles and walked out of the class.

Apparently, the books were no longer an issue.

As Vijay exited the school gates still trying to comprehend what the hell had just happened, his ever-present sidekick, Sachin, stood waiting.

"What de hell she want? She had a next present for you?"

"No boy. I get invite to the cinema," responded Vijay, with a proud smile.

"That woman off or what Vijay? I can't get a 13-year-old schoolgirl. How the hell you managing a teacher!?"

Vijay confessed his confusion as well but concluded he must now be amongst the elite sweet men of Sangre Grande College, possibly of all Sangre Grande; a 15-year-old being courted by his teacher!!!!

During the next few weeks, the courtship continued. By the second date they were firmly holding hands in the cinema. As the weeks progressed, both the students and teaching body slowly realized what was happening. The private dates to the cinema, walks in the park and candle lit dinners at the local restaurants. Normally there would have been a reprisal by the Principal. However, this was Rampersad Darsan's son. The biggest landowner in Grande, a Member of Parliament and the man responsible for building numerous roads, bridges, schools and financial donations to various charities. Many in Grande still depended on agriculture. Rampersad was President of the Citrus Fruit Growers Association of Trinidad, the Cocoa Growers Association, the Coffee Growers Association, the Rubber Producers Association and the Beekeepers' Association. As local MP he was the one largely responsible for providing the school with all its resources both physical and financial. Romeo Lalla, the school Principal simply decided to look the other way.

Indra was no beauty and many were surprised that Vijay would settle for her. He did "settle" in a manner of speaking. He managed to find the odd girlfriend outside of Grande College and enjoyed a virile love life.

Two years later Indra received a scholarship to study for her degree in Education in Ireland. She and Vijay were engaged with the understanding that they would be married upon her return. An engagement party was held at the Reading Hall Estate house. It was a small affair with just immediate family and close friends.

Indra left in July of 1957 on the steamboat *Lady of the Seas*. She would stop off at London and then hop on another boat bound for Dublin. There was a grand farewell at the Port of Spain Wharf. Rural Indians were capable of making quite a production of farewells at either a wharf or airport. Her departure was no different. No less than 30 members of her family were there as she set off to Trinidad's "Motherland." My father, Uncle Basdeo and friends on both sides totalled 10. After the tsunami of hugs, the flood of tears and about a hundred well wishes, she was off.

Vijay's next conquest would be my mother, Cintra Rambarran. It would not be easy. Before him many had come and few if any had succeeded. She was short and petite with a bewitching smile. She had fair skin and should length black hair. Even one of her teachers had proposed to her when she was 12 years old.

He himself was not too shabby. He was a tall, slender, handsome youth, with fair skin and thick, black hair combed to the side. Many a young girl in Sangre Grande had fawned over him but now it was Cintra who had caught his eye.

About six months before Indra's departure Vijay had already commenced his courting of Cintra. There would be the obligatory smiles and greetings as he passed her in the corridor or schoolyard. As he was an extremely handsome young man, my mother couldn't help but notice him. Many of the girls did. However, she was well aware of his relationship with their teacher and she had no intentions of taking him seriously.

As the months rolled by Vijay became bolder with Cintra as now there was no Indra to hinder him. He would walk up to her on the lunch break and engage her and her friends in conversation. He was certainly charming and a conversationalist.

If she was playing cricket and she hit a good shot, he would say to the lads around him – loud enough for her to hear – "Good shot. I taught her that shot you know."

He would offer to carry her books after class. Or more slyly simply become very friendly with her girlfriends, aware that she would join the group and he would look less obvious as he chatted with the other girls.

The friendly conversations slowly broke her down. About a month after Indra's departure he invited her to go to the Palace cinema with a group of his friends. As she lived next door to the Palace which belonged to her uncle, this was easy enough. It also meant she didn't have to pay.

He then mentioned they would be meeting for a snack before the movie and coyly suggested she join them. These "dates" became a semi regular occurrence over the next few months and Cintra found herself quite captivated by this well-spoken and extremely handsome man. Her girlfriends and Aunt Val's daughters thought he was incredibly handsome, more handsome than any of the Indian movie stars they had seen. A high compliment indeed.

As both of them had common friends in Grande, they found themselves at the same weddings from time to time. If you've never been to a Hindu wedding, it's quite a sight. It's basically an all-day affair. The major activity takes place at the bride's house. There's a huge ceremony

14

with the Bride, Groom, Pundit and other players. A live orchestra is a must and the food is simply amazing. In fact, the food is so good that as a kid I never realized that no meat is ever served.

With a lot of people and a lot of food, there's a lot of cooking behind the scenes. As my mother was often close or related to the family of the wedding, she along with many other women would be involved in some kind of cooking or preparation of food. My Mum was not yet then the cook she would one day become. She would usually be cutting carrots or peeling potatoes. My father in his bold attempt to spend time with her, would simply walk up, pick up a knife and begin to assist her.

It was uncommon for men to be involved in this endeavour. Surrounded by about ten other women, tables of seasoned meat, vegetables, a variety of spices, and about six pots on the go, he would make small talk while they worked.

One of Mum's aunts would walk up to my father and with a stern look ask, "What are you doing here?"

"I'm just helping her."

"She doesn't need any help."

"I don't mind."

"She doesn't need any help. Go."

And my father would walk off, satisfied with the 15 minutes he had been allowed to invest with Mum.

This went on for about three months. My mother at one point asked about Indra and my father unhesitatingly responded that she was an old woman and his parents would kill him if he were to continue showing an interest in her.

My mother not knowing any better was finally worn down.

Thus, before 1958 had ever come around Vijay and Cintra were now a couple. Most of the small town of Sangre Grande would not have known as they behaved in a proper manner in public. Their more intimate behaviour was in the park or to steal kisses either in or behind her Uncle Vinaya's cinema.

Cintra was smitten. Her best friend at school was a black girl by the name of Anastasia Greene. Anastasia or Ana to her inner circle was the daughter of a local school principal, Mr. Hollis Green. A very well-respected member of the Grande community. Ana and Cintra both raved about handsome Vijay was.

"Girl!" commented Ana to Cintra one day at school: "That boy is as handsome as Harry Belafonte."

They made a noticeable couple indeed. However, my father had never actually severed his relationship with Indra. They continued to correspond and she was due home during the summer holidays of 1958. Vijay had calculated that Cintra should be in the backwoods of Plum Mitan, with her parents and he could manoeuvre Indra throughout Grande appropriately. He would have to find a way to dodge the Palace cinema next door to Cintra's relatives. Discretion was of the essence.

Vijay received a letter in early December of '57 from Indra.

Earlier that day he and Uncle Basdeo had had a disagreement which led to a mini fight. Basdeo had borrowed Vijay's shirt. A tall, burly fellow with a bit of baby fat on him, Vijay explained that he didn't appreciate his shirt being stretched. The fight itself was nothing serious, just a little pushing and shoving and the odd punch that missed its target.

However, it was just after the arrival of the letter that matters intensified. In her letter, Indra described her experiences in Dublin: school, new friends, the rather different Irish culture and their apparent fanaticism for a pint. She said that in the cold weather people would eat more meat as the extra fat would protect them from the cold. This is something that the portly Basdeo might like. Vijay thought it funny and tapped Basdeo on the shoulder to tell him. Basdeo, thinking the fight was still on, swung around and in one motion propelled his elbow across Vijay's jaw knocking him out instantly.

Basdeo was mortified: "Pa!! Pa!! Look Vijay dead!!"

"You sons of bitches!! You're fighting again!" Pa walked into the boys' room and saw his unconscious son on the floor. In an obvious state of shock, he said, "He's dead. OK, wrap him up in a white sheet and we'll take him to the hospital."

Actually, Vijay was far from dead. When Basdeo hit him, his head swung sharply and a vein in his neck got "locked." It basically cut off the flow of blood to his brain and he became unconscious; yet, even in that state he could hear what was happening around him. As he lay on the floor, deep in the black recess of his mind he could hear the conversation around him. "You mean I'm dead and that's how calm they are. Wrap me in a white sheet?" Years later he would still tell the story in disbelief.

Together, Basdeo and Pa put Vijay (all wrapped up in a white sheet) into the trunk of the car – all the while his mother bawling and pulling at her hair. Pa shoved her into the back seat and with Basdeo behind him, made his way to the Sangre Grande General Hospital.

The staff quickly ascertained that Vijay was not dead and a massaging of the neck and some smelling salts quickly revived him.

Nineteen fifty-seven quickly became 1958 and the romance between Vijay and Cintra was in full swing. Handsome, eloquent, rich and the son of the most powerful man in Sangre Grande, Vijay, was quite a catch. Vijay in turn admired Cintra's obvious academic brilliance and her incredibly organized manner. She managed her time excellently and if she set her mind on something, it got done.

Indra returned to Trinidad in July of that year. She was all excited and was eager to discuss her future wedding with Vijay.

Vijay, as planned, manoeuvred her around Grande, trying to avoid any areas where my mother's friends or family might see them together. It worked for almost a month; however, during her fourth and final week, Aunt Val, saw them walking in front of her house. When Cintra came by to visit, she lost no time in telling her. Visibly upset, she immediately had a letter delivered to Vijay's house explaining that they were now finished.

Indra had two days left in Trinidad. Vijay explained that he had a dying aunt in Penal and had to leave town. He remained for those two remaining days in the sanctuary of Caigual's deep bush.

With Indra's departure, Vijay lost no time in trying to woo Cintra once again. He explained that he was simply walking with her on the street. They were going in the same direction. Had her aunt seen any inappropriate behaviour? Of course not.

He made it clear, Indra had never been invited to his home. He had not visited hers. He even lied about leaving town as to avoid her during her last two days. His family could "vouch for this." However, he did see her on the street and they had a civilized conversation as any two adults would.

She wanted to believe this; however, she had pride and needed to save face. Vijay was given the cold shoulder for another two weeks. He duly ate some humble pie and continued to plead his case. He would write letters to her and have her cousins at Aunt Val's house give it to her. On one occasion whilst writing to her late at night, he killed a mosquito and wiped the blood on the letter. "Look, I've cut myself for you." Cintra was incredulous. Her cousins and Ana found him to be full of shit.

However, by the end of the school summer holidays they were an item again. Cintra's siblings had seen the pair in public and it was obvious what was going on. Her brothers wasted no time in informing their parents. They did not approve of the Darsan boy courting their daughter. "That boy family is too rich," said her father. "Break it off."

Cintra had met the love of her life. She was the envy of many a girl at SG College. She had no intentions of breaking anything off. After two months of pressure from her parents, the matter came to a head. Fed up with the constant haranguing, she packed her bags and left a letter for her parents saying that she was going to live with relatives in the south of Trinidad.

In reality, she had very little clue of what she was going to do. She hitched a ride to Ana's house. They spent the next two hours moving her bag from room to room as so Ana's parents wouldn't notice. However, Mr. Greene, was not exactly stupid. He had a small house and the two girls were not the most subtle in trying to hide Cintra's suitcase. Not only was he Ana's father but also a school principal, a status that commanded immediate respect from the young people around him. He sat the two down and demanded to know why Cintra had a suitcase in his house.

Once informed he explained to Cintra that she was a young girl with a lot to learn about life. "You think you are in love but this is really infatuation. Do not be carried away by your emotions." Ana and my mother dutifully listened to Mr. Green, as to interrupt or talk back would lead to a *buff*.[2]

It was agreed that the matter should then be taken to her Uncle Vinaya, whose house on the Eastern Main Rd. was much closer and accessible to Cintra's. As her guardians in central Grande Vinaya and his wife would be an acceptable option.

Six foot tall, a lean 175 lbs and deadly serious when he wished to be, Cintra did not relish the prospect of facing him. However, she had Aunt Val as a buffer.

Uncle Vinaya listened to Mr. Greene, thanked him for his concern and intervention. He then told Cintra to have her beau show up at 2 pm the next day.

Vijay, nervous, hands sweating, dutifully appeared at the appointed time. His eyes widened noticeably when he saw Cintra's father standing next to Uncle Vinaya. Oh Lord, he thought to himself. He called her father.

He did his best to appear calm. Rural Indians were known to go a bit ballistic if they had a disagreement. It was even worse if they thought their family had been harmed in some way. Living off the land, they could use a cutlass as well as some city folk cold use a knife and fork.

Vinaya took the lead: "So! What are your intentions young Darsan.?"

"What does that mean?"

"Don't be stupid boy!" bellowed Vinaya. "What are your intentions towards Mr. Rambarran's daughter?"

---

[2] *Buff: to scold someone.*

"Well Mr. Madosingh, I am courting her and my intentions are honourable."

At this point my Nana chipped in: "My daughter ran away from home because of you."

"I didn't ask her to run away." My father could feel himself cringe on the inside the moment he opened his mouth. He knew he had to tread carefully but the natural impertinence within him was revealing itself.

"Well we have to talk to old man Darsan," said Vinaya. "Tell your father Mr. Rambarran and I will be there tomorrow after lunch to speak to him."

Vijay arrived home that day mumbling and apparently ill. He complained of a terrible headache. His mother who was always close to him put him to bed. She began massaging his head with *limacol* to soothe him.

My father always claimed that he was his father's "backside child." He believed that Basdeo was given greater favour as he was the oldest and because Shanti was the youngest and only girl, she was well spoilt. There was no denying that the two were overly spoilt by Pa. Ma realizing what was going on and sympathizing, would give him extra attention to make up for it. Ironically, years later, he would have no problem doing the same exact thing to my sister Leila.

Later, after sufficiently soothing Vijay, Ma communicated to Pa that he would be having visitors that day. My grandfather, prone to a quick temper, could only shake his head. There always seemed to be a problem with his children, there seemed to be no end to their escapades. Basdeo, was constantly being caught stealing money from his father's pockets. Unlike Vijay who would only steal a handful of dollars as not to be noticed, Basdeo would take fifty dollars or more and be stupid enough to hide them in his own pants making it reasonably easy to catch him.

Vinaya and my Nana arrived the next day with my mother's farewell letter to her parents in tow. My father was too scared to face them so he sat in the bedroom with his mother. My Aunt Shanti, only eight, would run to the back of the porch area that stretched across most of the house and eavesdrop. She would then run back to report.

The conversation lasted about 15 minutes.

"Vijay," Pa called out.

"Yes Pa."

"Come here boy. You will marry that Rambarran girl next April. Ok."

"Yes Pa."

And thus, it was done, the marriage of my parents had been agreed upon. I hesitate to say arranged because they had been courting for about nine months.

The wedding was set for April 19, 1959, just a few months shy of Cintra's seventeenth birthday. Vijay had already graduated high school and Cintra would do the same three months after the wedding.

Two weeks prior to the event Pa invited Nana and his family to dinner at Reading Hall. My Nana had quit drinking in his early twenties. However, Pa, being a bit of an idiot cajoled him into "taking one."

"Come nah man. We is family now. We have to celebrate the moment."

Nana not wishing to appear rude to the local MP in his house "took two."

Within minutes his words were slurring and his children were a bit embarrassed.

Pa watched him with an amused smile for the rest of the night. However, my mother was not impressed and made it clear that none of that would be repeated at the wedding.

My father told him the next day, "You had your fun. Now leave the man alone. Don't embarrass Cintra on her wedding day." And Pa duly complied.

Cintra was giddy with excitement, this would be a grand affair. It was the first wedding amongst Rampersad Darsan's children and he would spare no expense.

Four thousand people were invited, Pa built five outhouses in the front yard and the whole wedding cost five thousand dollars. Indian weddings literally take an entire day. It starts off at the bride's house. There's a lot of live music, prayers by the Pundit and various acts by family members as the bride is given away. Later that day the entire procession then makes its way to the groom's house as she will be living there in the future. It can be an exhausting affair. Alcohol is not allowed, however, to get around this the men have it situated in their car trunks outside of the house. Thus, the consumption of alcohol never actually takes place on the premises. Not surprisingly, the alcohol-free Hindu weddings in Trinidad are rampant with drunken men and occasionally violence.

The affair at Vijay's house ended at around 3 a.m. the next day. There was dancing, singing, eating and a lot of hand shaking. They spent that night in one of the guest rooms. The following morning after a sumptuous brunch of buljol, roti, eggs, bacon, sausages and curried aloo (potato), they were off to the Pegasus Hotel for two days and then Grenada for their one-week honeymoon.

Sadly, despite all the planning and expense, there were very few photos of the wedding. A photographer from the Trinidad Sentinel (the local daily) had been hired, yet curiously most of his photos were unable to be developed. I asked as to how such a professional could be so useless and my father in his usual nonchalant manner shrugged his shoulders.

Vijay had decided that he would study law. My mother coming from a modest economic background decided that because she was good in Spanish, she would study further and become a translator for the United Nations.

However, Pa would make a decision that would have a profound effect on her life as well as that of my sister and me. Rampersad Darsan could be a hard-headed, short tempered man but he also had a huge streak of kindness and generosity in him. He liked Cintra. She was well mannered; strikingly beautiful, well-spoken and intelligent. "I'm sending him to study law. Why don't you do it as well, I'll pay for it."

Cintra was stunned. Never in her life had she expected to have such an opportunity. The last few months had been head spinning indeed: living in one of the grandest houses in East Trinidad, a member of the wealthiest family in Sangre Grande and now the opportunity to study law in England!

It was agreed that they would depart for England in 1960 to commence their studies. She spent the next year teaching at a local primary school. My father spent it, *liming*[3] and playing pool with friends.

What about Indra Bissoondath? Realizing that he would be marrying Cintra, Vijay sent a letter to her explaining that the engagement was off as he would prefer to be with someone closer to his own age. He simply dodged her family in Grande until they figured it out. He was lucky that Pa was such an important man or her father may have come looking for him to preserve the family pride.

Vijay and Cintra migrated to London on July 5, 1960. They would return five years later, a well-groomed, beautiful couple and the first married lawyers in the history of Trinidad & Tobago. The Press was there when they returned in 1965, after all they weren't just a graduating legal couple but one was the son of former MP, Rampersad Darsan.

There was a great photo of my parents, taken in the VIP Lounge; my father well dressed in his suit and tie, my mother in a beautiful black dress, cut an inch above the knee and a stylish bonnet on her head. The following week there was another photo of Cintra, with the cutline, "She's 23 and a lawyer." It went on to explain that she was former MP Darsan's daughter-in-law and destined for great things as one of the few female lawyers in the country.

My sister and I could barely contain ourselves as the car wound its way up the rough, steep hill. This was the most exciting moment of our lives. Little did we know it but we would never be the same again. It was the beginning of the end of our innocence.

---

[3] To lime: to be with friends and have a good time.

CHAPTER 2

The End of Innocence

As we walked towards the house, we could see the glow of lanterns amidst the incredible darkness and thick forest that surrounded us.

We had heard of our father's girlfriend, Neelam. We'd also heard that they had a daughter. However, this was only due to eavesdropping on my mother's conversation with friends. My father finally mentioned them as we were driving up the hill. We entered the house and there they were – Neelam and their daughter Sunita. To my surprise my Aunt Shanti was there with her two sons, Kavi and Varun.

Reading Hall had all the makings of a classic haunted house in any horror movie. Old, wooden, enveloped in darkness and surrounded by forests and grassland, this could be a foreboding place at night. Even my father who had lived there for most of his life, refused to sleep alone in that house.

Aunt Shanti was in the process of a divorce and was staying with my dad. Unable to cope with the primitive nature of the house, she had bought a generator. Not only were there lights but she possessed a colour TV. We would really appreciate her contribution and on later holidays miss it terribly.

During my initial years at the estate there were a variety of individuals I had come to identify with – all black – all from Grenada. There was Robert, a tall muscular man who would give me piggy-back rides around the property during my grandfather's time. Old man Joe – as the name suggested an old fellow who had been employed as a teenager in 1918. Ms. Clara, an old woman, who was missing the first and second toes on her right foot but the bones were still there. And then there was the irrepressible Ms. Lizzie, a character that I would remember until the end of my days.

Robert no longer worked on the estate, however, in later holidays we would see him in passing and greet him. He was now still strapping and fit but bald. As a toddler watching the 1970 World Cup on TV, much to my family's amusement, I would point to the Brazilian Pele, convinced that he was Robert.

Ms. Clara had already died by the time of our visit. Old Man Joe was in his late seventies, half blind and being cared for by his children and grandchildren.

Ms. Lizzie, also in her late 70s was basically retired. As a youngster I had mistakenly assumed that she was one of Pa's servants, as the only black people there had been under the family's employment. However, my father would later explain to me that 'Ms. Lizzie was nobody's servant.' She had her own land, about 10 acres on which she grew cocoa and coffee. She was a family friend and unlike any other black woman I would ever meet.

A lean woman, she always had a head wrap on something that many of the black women of the older generation used to wear – a style that is still popular in Africa today. She had a piece of cloth wrapped around her waist and a smoking pipe tucked between the cloth and her dress. She would occasionally have a cutlass strapped to her side if she had to tend to her land that day. Her husband had died in a stick-fighting incident in 1945.

Stick fighting is exactly what it sounds like – a form of martial arts brought to TT by the African slaves in the 1700s, it became even more popular after the abolition of slavery in 1834. The freed Africans then took it to the streets during Carnival where it was referred to as *Kalinda*. It was a rhythmic sort of battle as their bodies swayed to the beating of the drums and the chanting of the crowd. They used a piece of wood also known by the French word *bois*. Thus, the fighters were known as stick-fighters or bois men. This was an extremely dangerous art form; eyes were lost and people were knocked unconscious or killed. It was eventually banned by the colonial masters in 1882. It was reintroduced in the late 1930s as a form of dance which was exhibited during the Carnival celebrations. Despite the ban, stick-fighting continued to thrive, especially in the small towns. It captured the public's imagination for two reasons, the excitement and the betting. People would bet on the fighter of their choice, the competitors would also bet on themselves. The freed blacks had no intentions of letting the Colonist tell them whether or not they could practice their culture especially one that was as vibrant and as exciting as this.

Ms. Lizzie's husband, Charles, was a fighter of some note. Handsome, broad shouldered and muscular due to years of labour in the cocoa/coffee plantations he was a legend in the Caigual area. He had once gone undefeated for two years in Grande. His favourite arena was in front of Mike's Bar on Eastern Main Road. However, he tried to tackle a well-known fighter who had come from Manzanilla (about 15 minutes from Grande) and inebriated from about five shots of rum, he was struck in the head and died at the Sangre Grande hospital five days later.

Ms. Lizzie never remarried and eventually her two daughters settled down and had their own children. However, what set Ms. Lizzie apart from many of the blacks in Caigual was her command of Hindi and great affection for the Indian culture. It was not uncommon for Afro Trinis who had grown up in areas heavily populated by Indians to socialize with them and adopt many of their ways, e.g., love for Indian music, singing and Indian dancing. It was normal that they would pick up smatterings of Hindi and in some cases as with Ms. Lizzie, speak it fluently.

She would often be seen liming in the company of Indians at their homes or gatherings. When in a state of excitement, she would start babbling in Hindi, get up, dance as a traditional Indian for about five to 10 seconds and then resume speaking. This might happen two to five times a day, more if she were at a party, Indian gathering or wedding. I never questioned her behaviour, I grew up with her and it was normal to me. It was only when I was about the age of six, my mother went to her cousin's house party in Grande and took along our neighbour, a black woman by the name of Joyce. She observed Ms. Lizzie babbling away, doing her Indian dance and her Hindi dialect whenever she got excited. Joyce would watch this woman with an amused expression and just the hint of a smile. It was obvious this was not the kind of black woman that she was used to. For the first time I was aware of what Ms. Lizzie looked like to outsiders.

These Grenadians had all played a part in my childhood whilst visiting the estate in my adolescence. They played with me and tolerated me as I bothered them doing their chores. All except Ms. Clara, as I was afraid of her due to the skeletal bones sticking out of her foot, I gave her as much of a berth as I could.

I looked forward to seeing the others now that I was visiting again.

The first four or five days went along smoothly enough. We got to know Sunita and played with our cousins. We would visit the odd family member in Grande and of course we could watch TV at night.

Although my father had cheated on our mother with Neelam and later had a daughter with her, we had no animosity towards either of them. We were getting along with Sunita. However, we were about to see an incredibly nasty side to Neelam and the end of any harmonious relationship we had with our father.

Neelam, was a tall, slim, attractive woman. When my father had met her back in 1971, she stood five feet, ten inches tall, with waist length black hair and was a lean 135 pounds. She could've easily been a model had she wanted to. My father had been visiting a friend in Curepe, where she lived with her family. As she walked by, he started off the conversation with "Hello, how are you?"

Years later, after she and my father had broken up, her friends would ask her what kind of man was this that could "talk the clothes off your back."

Fast forward seven years later, she was still slim and attractive but now with short hair, just above her shoulders. She had come from a large family of seven kids. Her father was a hardworking man whose strictness with his children was legendary. Despite growing up in such a household, it didn't stop her from setting up house with a married man. Her father had refused to speak to her for two years; he was aghast that any daughter of his could shame his family in such a way.

The first few days with Neelam went along smoothly enough. However, she would do silly things. She would make jokes that as a baby she would beat me when my mother's back was turned and that I would cry and she would laugh. My father would sit back and laugh at this. Apparently neither of them aware of how silly it looked to harass a child. She would encourage Sunita to harass or hit us and then not allow us to defend ourselves. We would look at our father for some sort of support and he would just laugh. One night while driving back to the Estate, she wouldn't stop interrupting my conversations and telling me stupid things to irritate me. After three weeks of this I had had enough. I let out the worst curse words I could think of just to shut her up.

"Fuck off!! Yuh schupid fucking cunt!!

My father immediately stopped the car. He was wearing shorts with no belt. So, he stripped a tree branch and gave me a whipping right there on the road. His style of beating was always the same. He would pin my hands behind my back and beat me on the back of my thighs. That is a soft area and not the best place for a prolonged whipping. I would cry for about an hour and need another few hours just to sleep it off. Neelam's harassment and the ensuing beatings would happen twice more before I returned home and her conscience never bothered her.

It was incredibly hurtful to me that my father would allow this woman to treat us like that. It was basically impossible for a ten-year-old to compute.

During our childhood Leila and I had literally worshipped the ground that our father walked on. We had heard our mother in moments of desperation complaining that despite our adoration of him, he gave her no assistance in terms of child support. It was she who had to bear the brunt of groceries, clothing for us and school fees. We could sometimes see her frustration. This was evident in the lack of toys we would sometimes receive few opportunities to go to the cinema and poor Leila having to suffer the indignity of wearing my hand me downs. She may have looked strange wearing boys' clothes but my mother did the best she could whilst our father maintained his lifestyle in an unperturbed and unfettered manner.

When we lived on his work route we would seem him semi regularly. However, when my mother moved to the North-West of Trinidad to Diego Martin, those visits dwindled down to three or four times a year. We lived for those visits. He would usually bring us comics as he knew I was a comic fanatic. He would occasionally visit me on my birthday and I would receive a present. Despite Leila's birthday being on the same day as his, he never once visited her. Sadly, I never saw him give her a birthday gift. However, if he brought me comics, he would bring some for her as well. It was almost as if she did not exist.

Having adored him to such a degree it was extremely hurtful to see him silently support Neelam's pettiness and cruelty.

Leila and I didn't know it but far worse was yet to come. The man who had visited us, cooked for us and played with us would show us a side of him that would make him the most repulsive man I would ever know.

CHAPTER 3

The Early Years and the Divorce

After our Christmas holidays had finished, we returned home to Cascade Falls in Diego Martin.

The last two days in Caigual had been fun. My Dad cooked whatever we wanted, which turned out to be curried goat, rice and dhal (Lentil peas).

On the way home, he was charming, chatted with us and even played little games such as "I spy with my little eye," to help pass the time away.

For the next few days we missed him terribly, willing to forget the horrors of our mistreatment.

I would live in a few neighbourhoods during my time in TT. But it would be "the Falls," that would provide the core part of my childhood.

After my parents' separation, we lived for about six more months in Curepe before moving to Maracas Valley only a few miles away. "The Valley" was located in the rich green hills of the Northern Range. We would live there for about two years.

A lot of my time there was a bit boring as I would have no kids my own age to play with.

Although "the Gardens" bore the majority of my "boy days," I had distinct memories of the two previous neighbourhoods. Certain incidents that both my parents and I would never forget and would prove the foundation of many an anecdote in the years to come.

I spent the first two and a half years of my existence living on Easter Main Road, Sangre Grande. My parents had decided to live in the town rather than on the Estate. It was really due to my mother's cajoling. She had had enough of her mother-in-law. My father and his mother were close, extra close. Realizing that his father had doted a little more on the older son and the only girl, Ma had doted on my father during both his childhood and adulthood. His five years in England had been hard on her. He and my mother had only come home three times in that period with my grandfather visiting once, whilst visiting London with the TT government as our country negotiated its independence. She would chide my mother on how to cook for him or serve him:

"You need to cut those tomatoes smaller."

"But he's fine with it that way," my mother would patiently respond.

"YOU telling ME! For more than twenty years I feeding this boy. You go tell me how he like it?"

She would say nothing, showing the proper respect one did to older family members. However, after five years of a liberal life in London and one of the few female lawyers in the country, my mother wasn't in the mood to be suffocated in the dense bush of Caigual.

Vijay knew his mother meant well, however, he was sympathetic to Cintra's plight. They made up a reason about needing to go out on their own and starting a life as a couple. They were careful to be as humble as possible as not to offend his parents too much. Pa was understanding. They were only about a twelve-minute drive away and he would drive past their house every day.

Escaping Caigual around July 1966, I was born a year later – November 11, 1967. I was the third grandchild on my dad's side of the family. Uncle Basdeo had already had two kids by this time with a third on the way.

Not too long after my second birthday we moved to Curepe. This would be the first home that I would remember. The house was located on Old Southern Main Road. If you went right, you would be at Curepe Junction about 200 metres after. A left turn would take you all the way to Southern Trinidad; the first major intersection was at the Churchill-Roosevelt Highway – with the Drive-in Cinema on the right. This was in the days when outdoor cinemas were still the rage. People would park their cars next to a speaker, attach it to the window if they wished or go to a covered stand to watch their movie on a massive screen. And it was truly massive. Two hundred metres away in someone else's house, you could still see the movie but of course with no sound.

My earliest memories were nice ones. I was the only child for a while and got great attention and was spoilt. If I wasn't visiting my Pa or Uncle Basdeo's family, I was going out with my parents. However, these were West Indian parents and I would occasionally get a massive whipping from my father – with a leather belt. I can't remember what the 'licks" was for but I had in their eyes misbehaved. I do remember however, not being able to stop screaming. Sounds terrible by today's standards. However, in the seventies in the West Indies and for decades later this would be the norm. Many years later as a student in Canada, I would be amazed at the non-beating policy by North America and wonder why that hadn't been the case during my youth in Trinidad.

As all boys are, I was a bit naughty. An only child with no neighbours' kids to play with, I had to make my own fun. Around the age of four, I crawled under the house and was playing with the dirt. I heard my parents calling but just didn't feel like answering. Some time later, I saw two police officers come to the house. About ten minutes later they left. When I had exhausted my interest in the dirt, I went back inside.

My father's eyes opened wide: "Where were you?"

"I was under the house."

"Didn't you hear us calling you?"

"No."

"Oh my God!" shouted my mother running towards me. "Boy! We called the police! We have them looking for you!"

I just looked up at them.

"But how you didn't hear us calling you?" asked my father with an incredulous smile on his face.

"I don't know. I didn't hear anything."

It would be many decades before I revealed that I had just been plain naughty. I got no whipping that day but they would both make up for it in the future.

My father shouted next door to our neighbour Joe Brown. "Joe we find him boy! The little scamp was playing under the house."

Joe just shook his head and laughed. A black man, about five feet, ten inches and well built. He had saved my life soon after moving into the house. My father had been taking a nap and mother was cooking lunch.

I crawled out of the house and right onto the main road. This was a very busy road. Joe, sitting in his porch saw me. He dashed out and scooped me up with a truck bearing down on me a mere thirty metres away.

My mother jumped when she saw this stranger entering the house with her baby in his arms. When Joe explained himself, she broke down in tears.

She woke my father up, who at the time shouted at her for not keeping an eye on me. They thanked him a number of times and he became a family friend. My mother would send over some curry for him whenever she cooked as she knew how much his family liked it.

Whenever Joe saw me, he would give me a smile and there would be a look on his face as if to say Yes, you're a little terror.

About six months before my fifth birthday, my parents separated. My father's ongoing affair with Neelam had progressed and he had left.

His leaving was traumatic for me to say the least. My mother had become aware that his late nights had a lot more to do with just having a drink with the boys. A colleague of hers at work lived on the same street as Neelam's sister and had seen my father's car parked there for hours. She had also seen the two of them walking on the street intimately. My mother was trying her best to handle it and save her marriage.

We had come home from the cinema and I remember my father saying: "I'm going out for a drink."

My mother grabbed his car keys and said "No! not tonight. You're always going out for a drink."

"Give me the keys!"

"No!"

He grabbed her and they both fell to the ground and began rolling as he shouted and she screamed.

I looked at them in confusion and then horror. How was a four-year-old supposed to compute this? I began to cry.

My mother trying to sway him cried out: "Look Sunil is crying."

My father wrested the keys from her and stormed out. Never even bothering to look at me.

My mother stayed on the floor crying and I looked at her, crying as well, trying to understand what the hell had just happened.

The next few months were confusing and hurtful for me. My father had disappeared and NO ONE would explain why. I would ask my mother and her only answer was "I will tell you when you get older."

Daddy would come over to visit from time to time. I would ask him where he was and he would say that he lived elsewhere.

During the Christmas of 1972, he came over to visit. My mother had bought some presents for him and written *from Sunil*.

We smiled and had a good time. I made him guess what the presents were and he did every time. As they were T shirts, it wasn't too difficult.

When it was time to go, I begged him not to.

"Daddy don't go."

"I have to but I'll come back and visit you."

"Daddy please don't go. I miss you. I want you to stay."

He just gave me a kind smile and said he had to go. I cried but he left any way.

Neither of my parents had ever thought to sit me down and try to explain what was happening. I was just expected to adapt.

Many years later I would discover that my father had actually left us once before for Neelam but then asked to come back. My mother acceded "for the sake of the children." However, just a month later, she realized that some of his calls to the house saying that his vehicle had broken down were just bad excuses to renew ties with Neelam.

At this point even Pa became fed up. "What the hell you doing? You going, you coming. What de ass wrong with you?"

One day, he called my father saying, "Let's meet for lunch. There is a matter I want to discuss with you."

Meeting in POS, he calmly came to the point. "Look this thing you doing eh right. Did you ever think just to have two wives?"

My father looked at him as if he had lost his marbles. "What?"

"Well you know my father had two wives."

Daddy just stared at him, "No."

"Yes, your grandfather had two wives. My mother was the first, of course I was the only child. But then with the second, he had two more."

"You serious!"

"Yes. So, you could do the same."

Daddy had to explain that such a scenario would not be possible.

More than a century after Pa was born, I would visit the area where both he and Ma's family had lived. I was shocked to have someone point out Neepaul St. roughly two hundred metres from Ma's house.

Despite Pa's father having two wives, it appeared that his mother was the boss of the house and all the land had been in her name. Her family's name had been Neepaul and she did not hesitate to name that street in honour of them.

After that conversation, my father never again heard of his father's siblings and never saw them.

I was a rambunctious and hyperactive child. Some people just termed me as "naughty."

There were two incidents that took place in Curepe that led me to believe in later years that I might have been slightly mentally challenged as a boy and just outgrew it.

The first took place about a year before we left Curepe. I saw two red Congo peppers in the fridge and got the mental image of rubbing them in my eyes. So, I did.

Not surprisingly, I started to scream. My mother sprinted towards me and I simultaneously grabbed a bottle of cold water and poured it into my eyes.

I cried and screamed and she kept pouring water into my eyes. When her friends heard the story, they just looked at me and shook their head.

The second had taken place just a few months before when my parents were still together. My cousin Vinaya, Uncle Basdeo's son had come to visit. Aunty Shanti was on what would be one of many separations from her husband Surujnath. My Dad's cousin Padmini was also there.

My parents were at work and everyone that day was in the porch chatting. I was on my tricycle. I looked at the big red steps and wondered what it would be like if I cycled down them. So, I did.

Not surprisingly the tricycle crashed down the steps, I hurtled forward and the underside of my bottom lip crashed against the concrete step. My mouth was covered in blood. My aunt screamed and they all rushed towards me. Many years later as an adult, I would still have a scar under my bottom lip.

When my parents came home, they were in a state. My mother was practically in tears. My father in true Vijay Darsan fashion started shouting at my aunt and Padmini.

"Allyuh right there and this happen?"

My aunt did her best to explain: "How is it our fault. He just decided to ride down the steps. That is OUR fault?"

"But you right there. How could three people be right there. He right in front of you and you let that happen?

That is carelessness and *dotishness*."[4]

My aunt, realizing that she had neither the volume nor ignorance to match her older brother, let the matter drop.

---

[4] *Dotish: to be stupid.*

CHAPTER 4

The Servants

With my father gone, my mother needed help with the children. We would go through a proliferation of servants during the next decade. In the seventies the world *servant* was considered acceptable vernacular, we were later taught to use more appropriate terms such as maid, later housekeeper and finally my mother said just call them by their name. However, that process took 15 years to culminate.

Not too soon after Daddy's departure, we had a Guyanese maid, who was a few years older than my mother. She would walk around in shorts with her butt cheeks hanging out. My mother explained that was not appropriate in her house and to dress appropriately while working for her. She lasted a week.

We then had an old woman who always seemed to have a scowl on her face. On some occasions she would come with her fifteen-year-old daughter who would help her. Sometimes if alone in the room with her daughter, we would hug and kiss. They were French kisses and I rather enjoyed them. When her mother entered the room, I would stop. She allowed me to kiss her and seemed fine with it. Because her mother would interrupt our kissing sessions, I decided I did not like her.

Eventually, the daughter stopped coming to the house. I liked her mother even less now.

One afternoon, she was working as she usually did and decided to use the restroom. There was a lock on the outside and I locked it. She shouted at me to open the door but I said "No, I'll open it when my mother comes home."

"Boy! Open the door. Open the door!"

I repeated my original response.

"Murder! Murder! Somebody help me. HELP!!!

MURDER! MURDER! MURDER!"

Eventually the neighbours heard the screaming. They looked at me over the fence and shouted out as to what was happening. I explained the situation and when she would be released.

The man rushed over and opened the door. The woman was hysterical. "This child is a demon. He needs a cut ass. I leaving this house. As soon as his mother comes home. All o' dem could hull dey ass!!!"

"What kind of mad child is this?"

My poor mother, after a hard day's work and an hour of rush hour traffic, arrived home only to be confronted by a manic woman who was in no mood to be reasoned with.

"You know what this blasted child do?" she exclaimed hysterically gulping for air. "He lock me up in the toilet and refuse to let me out! What the hell kind of child is this? I was in the TOILET for 10 minutes!! This little bitch had me like a prisoner!! "

She packed her bag, her hands trembling and screamed: "Miss Lady, I gone. Please pay. I never want to see this house or this mad ass child EVER!!!"

My mother quietly wrote out a check. We could hear her screaming as she exited the yard, something about "mad ass house and mass ass child."

My mother then got a belt and gave me a severe whipping. I screamed and cried as I would throughout the beatings of my childhood.

I stayed with a family friend until my mother could find a replacement which came approximately two weeks later. Her name was Usha. She was a pretty, 17-year-old girl with long black hair from Caroni in central Trinidad.

She had been recommended by another housekeeper working for a friend of my mother's. My mum had conducted the interview at her home in Caroni. Her mother sat beside her and basically controlled the interview. The salary and working conditions were agreed upon. Her mother finished by saying "If she doh behave, hit she, she need a good lash now and again." This statement would have an emphatic result on our household.

My mother was not an easy woman to work for, whatever the capacity. She was as unpopular with the secretaries at the Ministry as she was with just about any housekeeper we ever had. She was a perfectionist and whether it was cleaning the house or writing a report, it was done meticulously. Whenever our home

had been cleaned, she would walk around wiping the furniture with her finger and say to the poor person, "dust." She would make sure to check the underneath of tables and chairs and show them her finger, "dust."

They would give her a look as if to say is this woman serious? I now have to do it again? But as the help was expected to do at that time, they kept silent.

Being a young child, I did not know exactly what fault my mother had with Usha but she found many. She would chastise her and slap her. This happened more than once. Usha would be quiet and the tears would flow down her face. Even as a four-year-old, I found myself feeling sorry for her. I couldn't understand why my mother was hitting such a big person.

Aunty Shanti was staying with us at this time. While she and my mother were at work, Leila and I would occupy ourselves. A few months before my parents' separation, my mother had gone to Texas on business for the Ministry of Petroleum. My Dad and I had had a wonderful time as he took care of me, cooked for me, took me to the cinema and many other things. He had even taught me a popular children's song at the time: *This little piggy went to market.* I was only four and it was the first song I had ever learnt. I would sing it about 50 times a day. Unbelievably, my father never got fed up or asked me to stop.

Upon my mother's return from Texas, I was presented with a variety of toys including two white handled guns complete with a red belt and holsters. I was a great fan of Westerns and every day I would walk in the front yard in my underwear with two guns strapped around my waist, shooting at passers-by and visitors.

Usha would often try to get us to take an afternoon nap but Leila and I were in no mood. We would ignore her and continue playing. When my mother came home, Usha would complain about us not listening to her and not wanting to take a nap. My mother would listen and then scold us for not obeying.

One day Usha said to us to go and sleep. I remembered my mother's words: "When she says to go and sleep you all must do it. Don't give her a hard time."

On this day I decided to abide. "Come on Leila, let's go sleep."

I got up a few hours later. I walked out into the corridor but could not see Usha. I started shouting her name. I walked to the back of the house and tried to open the door but a table had been pressed against it from the outside. I simply was not strong enough to push it open.

I continued to shout her name but she wouldn't answer me. I checked every room. Finally, as I made my way to the living room, Aunty Shanti entered. She saw me shouting for Usha but showed no emotion. She walked past me to the telephone, read a note and then made her way to my mother's room.

"Aunty Shanti, I can't find Usha." But she continued to show no interest in me.

She opened Mummy's closet, "Hhm, she take yuh mother bra and all boy."

It was beginning to dawn upon me that Usha had left us. Aunty Shanti surveyed the house and did an inventory of what was missing. She then made a call to my mother, followed by one to the police.

I was about to make a startling discovery. In the back room, where Usha slept, was where my parents had kept my toys. They were kept in a suitcase including the newest additions from Texas. Usha had taken the ENTIRE suitcase of toys.

My beautiful white handled guns and belt were gone. My four-year-old mind was crushed. How could she steal all my toys? Why? Those guns and belt were my pride and joy. I had been in seventh heaven, walking around the front yard, they strapped around my waist and pretending to be one of the cowboy characters I had seen on TV.

It was obvious to me at least, that she had been planning this caper for weeks but our refusal to go to sleep had forced her to delay her plans.

The police came later that day and with my mother and Aunty Shanti went through the house together to see what was taken.

"You mean this little bitch tief my bras. She gone off."

A day later my father came by and discussed the matter. The police were sent to her house. But according to her mother, she had not seen Usha in weeks.

I never did get my toys back. I would mourn that two-gun holster for years.

Upon reflection, I must say my mother's attitude towards Usha was surprising. She may not have been perfect but she was not a cruel person. She would go out of her way for people who were in need. She sympathized as she herself had come from humble beginnings. I could understand Usha's retaliation but would always be a bit confused as to why she had to take my toys as well.

CHAPTER 5

Maracas Valley

In early 1973 my mother moved us to Maracas Valley, St. Joseph, less than 10 miles away.

She was struggling as a single mother and only with the assistance of a maid and Pa's constant financial aid as a result of my father's laziness was she able to basically hold it together.

Pa realizing her plight, stepped forward being the pillar of strength in response to my father's phlegmatic manner.

"Why don't you come to Caigual to live? I will hire a driver for you and the children to go to Port of Spain."

However, my mother could not bear the idea of the torturous rush hour traffic both ways.

So, there we were, nestled in the hills of the Northern Range. There was no crazy Southern Main Road, but rather a private road for the neighbours, surrounded by greenery and rivers. Years later, living in Canada, I could appreciate the natural beauty that had surrounded me at that time. But back then it was just a neighbourhood.

There was a local white family next door with two daughters, one my age and the other Leila's. Two blond pretty girls, we naturally gravitated towards them and would play with them on the road in front of our houses.

One day, our servant at the time, a young Indian girl by the name of Sunita was standing at the side of the house and chatting with the father. She was bad mouthing my mother saying what a difficult woman she was. "She always complaining, nothing is ever good enough for her. She like to get on like she is a damn princess. She eh know she is a *coolie* just like me.[5] Hull she ass!"

"I know," responded the father. "I could hear her mouth sometimes from next door. She look like she is a pain in de ass."

"I cah stand she, it's a relief when she goes to work." She pointed at me: "I sure he will go and tell her what I saying."

"Doh worry, I right here." He then looked at me: "Keep yuh little ass quiet eh."

"Fuck you!" was my response.

He ran to the fence, leaned over and slapped me three times across the back of my head. I immediately started crying.

"I will tell my mummy what you did when she comes home!"

"Tell her nah, you think I fraid dat bitch. I living right here. Tell her!"

That day when my mother came home, I promptly reported what had happened. I do not know why but I did not tell her about the maid's gossiping. Perhaps the fact that she had said I would, worked some sort of psychology on me, I really don't know. I did however, tell her that the neighbour had cursed at me and hit me behind the head.

My mother immediately went over and knocked on the door. There was an intense discussion between him and my mother. His wife tried to get into the conversation but he quickly told her to "shut up."

---

[5] *Coolie*: name for the indentured labourers who worked the sugar plantations of the West Indies. These labourers came from India. However, after indentureship was over, coolie was a crude term referring to Indians.

I looked on from the blocks in the wall on our staircase. After about five minutes, my mother returned and made it clear that I was not to speak to him, go over to his house or have anything to do with his children.

Luckily for him, my father never found out. He was from the old school of Indians who took their family honour very seriously. It was something that not all the more urban folks were aware of. My father was about six feet tall and a very lean 144 lbs. The neighbour was about two inches shorter and 10 lbs heavier. However, you would find that in such confrontations, size differential made very little difference with the country Indians. They usually had a cutlass, swiper and a rifle or shotgun.[6] And they were not hesitant to use it.

My father's uncle had resorted to such means in 1967. His daughter, Marla had qualified as a nurse in London and married a fellow Trini there some years earlier.

Unknown to her family, Marla's husband was prone to fits of rage and would beat her from time to time. She had kept it to herself as she was too embarrassed for her family to know. After a few years of financial struggles in London, her father suggested that they come home. He had land and a few properties in the area of Penal where he lived and life would be easier for them.

They returned to Trinidad in 1966 and it was not too long before the family began noticing the bruises and swellings. Marla's father warned his son-in-law more than once to refrain from "damaging" his daughter.

On June 1, 1967, Marla came running into her father's house. Her face covered in blood, she was babbling hysterically. In between the sobs, she explained that her husband Ramkee, had gotten up that morning and decided she talked too much, therefore, he was going to sew her mouth shut with a piece of wire. She had tried to calm him down. But he cut off a piece of fence wire and proceeded to sharpen it. Marla tried to take it

---

[6] *Swiper:* looks like a cutlass but the handle and blade are longer. The blade is at a 45-degree angle and grass is cut in a swiping motion.

from him and throw it away but three consecutive right hands dropped her to the ground. Ramkee then proceeded to further sharpen the wire.

Her father (I never did learn his name) had heard enough. He loaded up his shotgun and proceeded to her home. Ramkee was home with his father. They saw him approaching with the loaded weapon and Ramkee's dad decided he would try to diffuse the situation.

He met Marla's father in front of the gate.

"Where you going with the gun?"

"BOOM!!!"

And he was dead.

Ramkee seeing his father on the ground, realized his father-in-law was not in the talking mood. He scampered through the back door, jumped the fence and proceeded to sprint nonstop to the nearest police station two and a half miles away.

By the time the police arrived on the scene the flies were already buzzing around the corpse. Marla's father was at home awaiting the police. He would spend five years in jail guilty of manslaughter.

I would ask my father "How come they didn't hang him."

"There were mitigating circumstances" came the reply.

The next five years would be very difficult for Aunty Marla's family. People would shun them on the street, "They are the children of a murderer."

A few shopkeepers would even refuse to give them service. Some men would curse at the family as they walked past their house.

Years later, a few months before my fifth birthday, I went on a river lime with my aunt's younger brothers, my dad and some other men. My father explained that the older gentleman in the lime was Aunty Marla's father. He had recently been released from prison and they were taking him out that day to show him a good time. I remember him as a soft spoken, bespectacled, grey haired man.

About six months after our arrival the white family left. They were replaced by a black one with whom we got along quite well. They were the Gonsalves: Mike, Joyce and their three sons, Michael, David and Nicholas. Aunty Joyce and my mum soon became friends and were often at each other's home. The Gonsalves did not have a car so it was the norm for my mother and Joyce to do their shopping together on a Saturday. If my mother had to go out and we had no housekeeper on that day, Joyce would keep an eye on us let us come over to her house. Mike would sometimes take his kids to the nearby river and I would tag along.

I enjoyed my time with the Gonsalves boys. I had others to play with. Nicholas was my age, David two years older at eight and Michael nine. Aunty Joyce would sometimes babysit for my mother and for me it was fun as I would spend time with her children. On one occasion she took us to nearby Curepe to get a haircut. The barber used a buzzer for everyone and without fail we all cried when we saw the end result.

CHAPTER 6

The Transition

Prior to my parents' divorce, I had seen a great deal of Uncle Basdeo's family. Instead of spending money on a babysitter, my parents would send me to his house or Pa's. They would visit on weekends. I never did miss them too much as I was having fun with my cousins.

As boys, Uncle Basdeo and Daddy would accompany Pa on his trips to Guyana to race his horses. Pa made friends and one of them was Mohinder Jagan. Mr. Jagan was a well-known businessman with properties all over Georgetown. He had a huge four-bedroom house on Camps Street, a very upscale, residential area. He and Pa got along well. He had six children in and around the same age as my father and Uncle Basdeo. My uncle took a fancy to one of his daughters, Vashti. A slim, petite, pretty young woman, she was not short of suitors. Basdeo had a well-rounded, broad shouldered, slightly portly figure with a thick crop of black hair. However, he carried his extra weight well. He was loud, gregarious and had the infamous Darsan temper.

He did however, know how to conduct himself around a lady. With Vashti, he was polite and at all times gentlemanly. The respective fathers realized a sort of courtship was going on. It was done in a manner indicative of the times. They would be with each other's family, perhaps looking for an excuse to go to the veranda, away from the adults. There would be group plans to go to the cinema but they would sit apart from Vashti's siblings or simply go to the park to have their private moments.

Mr. Jagan was not adverse to the courtship. The Darsan family was one of the most respected Indian families in Trinidad. Mr. Darsan was a *neta* of the Indian community. [7] Vashti liked Basdeo. He came from a good family, she admired his strong, large physique. In playful moments he could pick her up like a child and twirl her around. He was at all times courteous and considerate of her feelings. The romance began in mid-1960 and by July of 1961 the wedding date was set for December 5. Nine months later my cousin Vinaya was born. Eleven months later his sister Vidia came into the world. Six months after my own birth the youngest of Basdeo's children Zeenat arrived.

They lived at the edge of Sangre Grande, their home nestled on a hill on the side of the Eastern Main Rd. Uncle Basdeo had his own farmland and we would amuse ourselves playing in the house, the front yard or in some of the flat grassland where the other labourers were.

Vinaya was my big cousin. I would follow him everywhere. He would tolerate me unless other boys his own age were around. Vidia was always kind and would find time for me. Zeenat and I would spend a lot of time together, however, we both had the infamous Darsan mouth and would have our fair share of falling outs. I would get angry with her if she did not want to share her toys.

"You are selfish!!

"We don't sell fish, we buy fish."

On one occasion late at night, the girls were bored for something to do. Vidia put on one of her formal dresses and started to spin in a circle. The lower part of the dress floated up in the air and stayed suspended in an umbrella like fashion. We all laughed and then Zeenat had her turn. Finally, I decided it was my turn. The girls were hysterical and called their

---

[7] *Neta*: Hindi word meaning leader.

mother to watch as I twirled with the dress ballooning up. Aunty Vashti had a good laugh as well. In no way was I gay, I was just a boy killing time with the girls. Lord knows how my father would have construed such behaviour had he been there.

Uncle Basdeo, a large, gregarious man, was known as sort of the black sheep of the family. He had lived most of his life well off as Pa had prospered. An intelligent man he had preferred to take the easy route in life rather than actually work and make any effort to better himself academically. As a boy both he and my father would steal some money from Pa's pants pocket as it hung on a hook. Whereas my father would take just enough not to be noticed. Basdeo would stuff his pockets to the brim, you could actually follow the trail of money on the floor to his bedroom.

In later years he would steal Pa's cheques, forge his name and make huge purchases or pay off his gambling debts. My grandfather would watch the cashed cheques in awe. This was *his* signature. He knew there was only one person who could access his cheques, have the indecency to steal from him and yet the ingenuity to forge his handwriting so well – Basdeo. He would berate him, even hit him. Uncle Basdeo would just stand silently and take the abuse.

"I don't know what to do. I just don't know," he would bemoan to my father.

"Let him make a jail," was the reply.

"You don't love your brother," said Pa, shaking his head in wonderment.

"Well then, let him keep stealing from you."

Many a night he would be out gambling or drinking. He would come with everyone already asleep. Yet, every morning he would be the first to rise. He would sit by himself at the dinner table playing Patience with a pack of cards. I would sometimes arise early and see him at the table. I would sit and look at him. He would give me a nod of the head and continue with his game. On some occasions he would show me a very serious exterior but it was just his way of having fun. He loved kids and would joke around with me even pretending to be angry when he wasn't. If he was teasing me, I would call him a "fatty bully," the ultimate insult for an overweight person in my opinion.

With my parents divorced, my sister and I were now in transition, me especially. Leila was still in diapers but it was I who would remember the change in our lives. Maids had become a greater part of our daily existence as my mother was alone.

My visits to Uncle Basdeo's house decreased dramatically; I could only assume because my mother looked upon them as my father's family or that she did not want to chance having to meet my father and Neelam there. The exception being my fifth birthday which my mum held at his house and invited all my cousins on her side of the family. Of course, my father knew about it but never bothered to come. It was a joyous day. I played games with the children and then a much bigger cousin was selected to cut the cake with me. She was pretty with long black hair, three quarters way down her back and much taller than me. She had to get on her knees. First, she gave me my slice. It was my first time performing this ritual and when I gave her a slice, I unfortunately used too much pressure and stabbed her tongue with the fork. She took it well, everyone laughed at my clumsiness and then we kissed each other.

Years later, my father heard me mentioning the event. He informed me that he and Neelam had been there a few hours before and that they knew we were coming so they made sure to leave. I was overwhelmed with disappointment. I don't think he noticed or even cared. As I got older, I would find out how truly indifferent and ignorant he was towards our feelings.

Pa loved his grandchildren. The fearsome, loud, character of Sangre Grande, was a doting, gentle giant with us. Sometimes, my mother would take me for a visit. She would stand before him like a little schoolgirl as he doled out money to her. He had no choice really. My father showed no interest in supporting his children financially and it was his father who stepped in to fill the void.

You would think up in the forests with not many people, no electricity and no TV, I would be bored. But once I was with my Pa I was never bored. We would sit together and chat, I would walk down the hill to visit the workers in their homes. If he had to go out, I accompanied him. He treated me practically as a friend rather than as an underaged individual.

However, he did spoil me a bit too much. If I didn't like something, I might decide to shout and curse. One day just for the fun of it, I started using expletives in front of my parents. There was no real reason, I was young and naughty. My parents had a firm yet defeated look in their eyes. I was surprised. I knew normally that would be a whipping. I looked at Pa, looked at them and I cursed some more out of curiosity to see what would happen. They continued looking straight ahead. Realizing I had some rare control over them, I let loose a torrent of curse words that would have put a construction worker to shame. Such behaviour would be deprogrammed once they got me home.

Those moments with Pa was a time of complete innocence. I could do no wrong and I was the centre of his attention.

In May of 1973, I had just finished spending the weekend with him. He with two of his nieces brought me home to Maracas Valley. They chatted with my mother. As he left my mother said, "Kiss Pa goodbye."

I dutifully, went up to him and kissed him on the cheek.

I would never see him again. Two weeks later, he was dead of a heart attack.

On June 10, 1973, Rampersad Darsan, got into his Ford Zodiak for the last time. He had some errands to run and invited Dad's cousin Padmini to join him. Padmini often spent time at the Estate. She would sometimes stay at the Curepe house and was quite fond of me, always willing to babysit.

On this day, Pa told Padmini she might as well come along rather than stay on the farm with not much to do. He had just bought a sack of flour and rice and decided that he would invite a friend to go for lunch. Not too far from the Grande bus station, he stiffened and clutched his chest.

"What happen Pa!" shouted Padmini.

"My heart."

He jumped out of the car. Holding his chest, he stumbled along the pavement: "I am dying. I am dying!!" he shouted at the pedestrians.

They just looked at him. No one offered any assistance. Perhaps they were simply in shock.

Padmini was distraught with helplessness. She had no idea how to drive a manual car. She guided Pa back to the vehicle. He somehow began making his way towards the Sangre Grande Hospital, the car veering to the left and right.

The sweat pouring down is face, he entered the hospital driveway with Padmini crying hysterically. He stumbled out of the Zodiak, leaning heavily on her. Together they made their half-way up the hospital steps, where he collapsed and died. Padmini screamed and the nurses came running. But it was too late.

My Pa. My beautiful Pa was gone.

The funeral of Rampersad Darsan took place six days later. I arrived with my mother at the Estate the night before. There were hundreds of people there. A makeshift tarp had been set up on the front lawn to accommodate the visitors. He had been the leader of the community for almost 25 years and the 'who's who' of the North-East as well as the Indo Trinidad community showed up to pay their respects.

As we entered the porch, Aunty Shanti stepped forward to greet us. It was probably the first time my mother and Neelam were in the same building and they made sure to avoid each other.

I entered the living room, to the far-right corner, there was a partial wall that blocked part of the dining room. Pa's coffin was located there.

Opposite the coffin at the other end of the room was my cousin Vidia, sobbing all alone on a sofa, a handkerchief to her eyes. Between Vidia and Pa, against the wall to Vidia's right were four Indian women, playing music and singing in Hindi.

My mother led me to the coffin and we both looked at Pa. Unlike the time that I saw her dead mother, I was unafraid. Perhaps because Pa's face was so familiar to me.

I spent the night leaning on my mother's lap, speaking with relatives and enjoying the chance to see my father again. Occasionally, I would run up to the coffin and look at Pa. At one point, I saw what seemed to be spit on his lips. I ran up to my mother: "Mummy, Mummy, Pa has spit on his lips." Aunty Shanti had actually been a first -year medical student in Winnipeg, however, not wishing to "overshadow" her husband who was studying Biochemistry, she switched her major to Spanish. Her father almost had a heart attack then. With her basic medical knowledge she explained to my mother, "It's not spit. That is froth coming up from his stomach."

She said it with calmly with a smile. Her demeanour would be much different the next day.

My mother and I left late that night and returned early the next day with Leila in tow. This would be our final goodbye to Pa. Hundreds were there. A variety of women were walking around serving snacks or beverages on trays. I knew Pa was dead. I understood what death meant. Perhaps being too young to truly understand what never seeing him again would feel like, I participated more like an observer rather than a bereaved.

At a certain point, the guests were told to leave the living room as some of the women had to "bathe" Pa. The washing (abhisegam) is a normal part of the Hindu religion as one prepares to take the body away from the house. Aunty Vashti and some Indian women closed the doors and began the ceremonial bath. Pa's head was positioned to face northwards. I was aware that his body was then bathed with a combination of milk, yogurt, honey and ghee, the big toes were then tied together. I found myself wondering if they were going to bathe all of him just certain parts. Taking him out of the coffin, performing such a ceremony and then putting him back seemed like a lot of work to me. I never did ask so I never knew.

About an hour later, Pa's coffin was brought out to the front yard. The Pundit began speaking in Hindi and the guests all gathered around the coffin. He mentioned that Pa seemed to be smiling. And it was true, there seemed to be a smile playing around his lips. It was then I heard Aunty Shanti crying: "Pa! Pa! she kept screaming as she buried her head into her husband's shoulder. He had his arms around her, patting her on the back. She continued shouting "Pa!" the ceremony being briefly interrupted as everyone looked at her.

I asked my mother "Why is Aunty Shanti crying?"

"Because Pa is leaving."

Just behind me Padmini wept silently, "He was such a nice man," she whispered to herself.

I was standing next to Aunty Vashti and her children. She said to us "Pray." I could not understand the logic of having to pray. Pa was already dead, what good would praying do for him or us now? However, she and all her children began to pray so I dutifully bowed my head and said the only prayer that would make sense to my five-year-old mind: "Dear God, please let Pa come back alive." I opened my eyes and Pa still seemed to be dead. I looked over at Vinaya and saw him still praying. I quickly closed my eyes and pretended to pray for another 10 seconds. If I had appeared to be the first one who stopped praying, maybe they would have thought that I had not prayed well enough.

At this point the hearse was brought forward, my father, Uncle Basdeo and some other men, gently loaded it in. Cars began to slowly make their way down the hill with Pa's body at the head of the procession.

Rampersad Darsan had lived in Caigual for 33 years. He had been one of the biggest landowners for 27 and a major figure in the Hindu and political community for approximately 25. It was the end of an era. The little boy from Penal who had left school at the age of 10 to help support his family by being a field hand, had left his mark. It was a classic rags to riches story. He had dined with Royalty, heads of government and millionaires but had never lost the common touch. He had arrived in Caigual as the common man's friend and died as such. A hard-working man, he had met his obligations and debts in life; sadly, not all who owed him debts had met theirs.

As the cars made their way out of Caigual and onto the Eastern Main Road, one car whizzed past us at a phenomenal speed. "That has to be Basdeo," said my father. As the oldest son, he had thought it his duty to be at the head of the procession behind the hearse.

We arrived at the local cemetery and Pa's coffin was lowered into the ground. The Pundit again said some words in Hindi. I stood next to my father, on the other side of the grave, Vinaya stood with his. The final act was for the mourners to throw stones on the coffin. Decades later, I could still remember this moment. I threw a big stone onto the coffin, looking for another to throw, my father gave one to me. It was smaller, as I dropped it, it knocked the bigger one off the coffin. A few more were thrown by the mourners and then we stepped back so the workers could bury him. I watched each shovel of dirt hit that coffin as it slowly began to disappear. It took less than 10 minutes and it was over. Pa was buried.

Another Divorce

In September of 1973, my mother went to someone's house in Barataria. I did not know the hosts but Aunty Vashti and the children were there. There were many people around and it seemed like a normal gathering. However, it was anything but normal.

After about an hour or so, Aunty Vashti and the children walked outside to the front gate. She was and her three children were in tears as they kissed everyone goodbye.

"Why is Aunty Vashti crying?" I asked my mother.

"Because she and the children are leaving Trinidad. They are going to Guyana."

Uncle Basdeo, like my father had decided to have an extra marital affair. His girlfriend's name was Kim, a petite, pretty, brown skinned Indian woman with dark brown, shoulder length hair. Aunty Vashti had suspected for a few months that her husband was playing around. She was a small, slender woman but she had a sharp mouth and a hot temper if stoked. She also was not soft. If she had to, she would stand up for herself and would not let any man physically intimidate her. During the previous Christmas, she and Basdeo had had many arguments about his late nights. He would try to brush her off. After all he was the man of the house. His father had done the same. Who was this woman to tell the bread earner what time to come home?

"You can't be coming home after midnight every night!!" she would scream.

"Shut your damn mouth. I will come home when I please. Who the hell do you think you're speaking to?"

"I will not shut my mouth you fat oaf. This is MY mouth. I am not your slave for you to take advantage of. Get your fat ass here at a decent hour!"

He ran towards her, right hand upraised. Despite his ten inch and 120-pound advantage over her, she refused to be cowed. Running towards the bedside table, she had a variety of medicine bottles. Bottle after bottle was hurled at Basdeo. He found himself like a heavyweight boxer, hands up in front of him and his head moving from side to side, as he tried to evade the projectiles coming from a variety of angles.

As she ran out of bottles, Basdeo tried to close the gap. But she jumped on the bed, leaped to the door, streaking through the living room, dining room and into the kitchen. Basdeo lumbered after her, the wooden floor and furniture shaking as his 200 plus pounds tried to catch up. Aunt Vashti now had dishes at her disposal, neatly arranged and draining next to the sink. Basdeo couldn't believe he now had to put up with plates and glasses coming his way. As they bounced off his bulky arms and shoulders and crashed to the floor, he thought to himself, Now I have to go and buy blasted dishes all over again.

He backed off. Both of them fuming at opposite ends of the huge wooden house. The matter was compounded when on Christmas Day he left the family to go "have a drink with the boys." Aunty Vashti suspected that it was not "boys," that he was interested in. They had some strong words. My three cousins became a bit teary eyed. They knew that their parents had arguments. They had witnessed some of the shouting and insults. But to have this on Christmas Day was a bit too much.

He picked up Zeenat, gave her a big kiss and hug: "Don't worry sugar plum, I'll be home before dark." Dark in Trinidad is usually about 6:00 pm.

He was home at 7:30 pm.

In early January, Kim decided she needed to speak to Basdeo urgently. She could not wait and was bold enough to go to his house. His home was located on the outskirts of town, up on a hill. The taxi let her off on the main road. She had to walk up about 80 metres of road and then another 80 metres of steps. Aunty Vashti was curious as to who this pretty, slim woman in her short, sexy mini skirt was and what she was doing coming up to her house unattended.

"Is Mr. Darsan here?" Kim asked boldly.

"And who are you?"

"Mr. Darsan is a family friend. He said he had some oranges for my father. He told us we should come and pick them up."

"BITCH!!!!" Shouted Aunty Vashti. She hurled herself off the top steps and ran towards Kim. "You not here for no oranges. You like other woman man!"

She began to punch and kick her. Kim fell as if made of tissue paper. She cried and screamed. "Aunty Vashti continued to kick and punch. "You want oranges, eh!! You want oranges!!"

Kim wailed and Aunty Vashti continued to beat her. Finally, out of breath, she pulled up Kim by her hair and hurled her towards the hillside steps.

Kim fled screaming and sobbing.

A few hours later, Basdeo came home in a rage. However, she was in an even bigger rage. She ran to the kitchen and grabbed a huge meat knife. "Try putting your hand on me. I will slit you open. Your whore is coming to my house!!? Your whore is coming to MY house!!?"

The children sat in the living room, observing and crying. Even Vinaya who usually tried to be tough sobbed helplessly.

Basdeo packed a bag and left. He walked right past the children without even looking at them. He didn't return home for a week. A few days later Aunty Vashti had her father buy her four tickets to Georgetown, Guyana.

Twenty days later, they were gone.

These were my closest cousins. I would not see them again for almost a decade.

Years later, upon reflection, I would wonder why my mother had not made an effort to explain the significance of that day. Had I not had the common sense to ask that question, it might have been years before I knew they had left the country for good.

My father and Uncle Basdeo, sadly, were the same in terms of their indifference. I later found out that Vinaya and his sisters did make a few visits during the seventies to see their father. Apparently, neither of our fathers thought it necessary that we should meet or some sort of family togetherness should be maintained.

As an emerging adult, I would discover that Rampersard Darsan's children did not seem to know much about the traditional nuclear family nor did they care. The conduct of parents in public and in front of their children can have an effect on them for better or worse. Sadly, the Darsan family's acute deviation from the norm would leave some of us with the latter.

CHAPTER 7

The Burning Bed and Much More

We lived for two years in Maracas Valley.

As the name suggests, it was a valley nestled in the hills of the TT's Northern range of hills, approximately ten miles from Port of Spain or "Town," as the locals called it.

In between some of the houses were thick, green, forested areas. And a hundred metres from our house in two different directions were small rivers.

I had never swum much in a river. I had not learnt how to swim and was afraid of the deep. However, Mike Gonsalves would take his boys swimming and they would invite me along. There was a shallow area and I enjoyed myself immensely.

We lived on a side road, more than a hundred metres long. On the right were three houses, we were the third. Just after our house, the road forked, at the end of the right fork was one house. If you took the left fork, it travelled along a river and at the end of the road, was a single, elderly white gentleman by the name of Jeremiah.

We had met Jeremiah on our first morning in the Valley. My mother had taken us for a walk to see the area and the river. Seeing Jeremiah at the end of the road and no one else around, she decided to turn back.

In his early sixties, his white hair was combed back. He wore big, black rimmed glasses.

Wearing nothing more than a pair of khaki shorts and a pair of slippers, he shouted out, "Don't run away. Come and say hello. I'm your neighbour."

He shook our hands. "My name is Jeremiah. I have lived here for 10 years."

After a polite chit chat, he invited us to the house for something to drink.

He opened the fridge and showed us a variety of options, including Coke and orange juice. It was at this point, he explained that his wife had died five years earlier. He had two daughters who lived abroad, whom he never saw. His voice began to break, the tears streamed down his face, plopped on to his round belly and began rolling down. My sister and I simply stared. My mother had the smallest of smiles on her face and listened politely.

On our way back to the house, she told us "I feel sorry for him. I think he's lonely."

As the years rolled by, slowly turning into decades, I never forgot his name for a simple reason. Jeremiah was a character from a Gothic TV series, Dark Shadows; a very popular American show in the 1960s and early seventies. He was a ghost with a bandaged, bloodied face, somewhat like a horrible looking Mummy. Both he and the show were quite scary to a five-year-old.

Occasionally Jeremiah would stop to talk to us as he walked past our house. One day he was nice enough to repair our black and white TV. As he walked away, I said "Bye bye Jeremiah." He turned around and shouted, I am 60 years old. I am not Jeremiah. I am MISTER Jeremiah to you!!"

"Really! My grandfather is 62."

I never did stop calling him Jeremiah.

The back yard of our house gently rolled up into a slight hill. Beyond the fence was a huge plot of land with two other houses attached. They had a front and back yard, as well as a valley that spread for an acre in front of the houses. There was no direct road from us to them. You had to go onto the main road and drive further up and make a left into their very long driveway.

On one occasion, my mother's fridge had broken down for a week, frustrated when Aunty Joyce confessed that there wasn't enough room in her freezer. She drove up the road to the houses behind us. She asked one of the neighbours for the favour of borrowing space in their freezer. The woman by the name of Katie Monroe, gladly obliged.

My mother would then every night before going home, stop at Katie's home and get some of her meat. She explained that Katie, was a nice woman who was helping us. She had two daughters and that on the following weekend, they would be having lunch with us.

The following weekend came and Aunty Katie arrived with her two children.

Katherine Monroe had been born Katherine Ganga in La Romaine, South Trinidad. Her father ran both a successful shop and hardware store. Katie was sent to York University, Toronto, in the late fifties to study Mass Communications. There she had met, a tall, handsome, white student by the name of Peter Monroe. They got married, immediately after graduation and set up house in Scarborough, the eastern part of Toronto. Two years later, with job prospects low in their chosen profession, they decided to try their luck in Trinidad. Peter was intrigued about the idea of living in the sunny tropics. Their first daughter Judy was born in 1965.

However, two years later, with no job offers from the island's lone TV station and Katie often impeded by the sexism of the time in terms of hiring a professional female, they opted to return to Canada, with its First World offerings albeit some damn cold Toronto winters.

Their second daughter Leanne was born in 1968. One year later, Katie caught Peter, between the legs of beautiful black, Jamaican, waitress. Katie was petite and Peter was tall. That evening, many dishes and knives were thrown in the direction of both Peter and his mistress.

He was kicked out of the house and three months later, Katie and her daughters were on their way to Trinidad. Peter had begged immensely prior to their departure. However, phone calls, letters and flowers had been of no avail.

As Aunty Katie and Mummy chatted, the girls, Leila and I played in the yard. It was a pleasant day. Over the next few months, we would see them occasionally. Judy was much more interested in chatting with Aunty Joyce's older sons, Michael and David. However, occasionally, we would all play on the street together. Sometimes the girls would be allowed to accompany Uncle Michael and the rest of us to go swimming in the nearby river.

Every one of the houses in our area was owned by one man, a local white by the name of Robert Bell. He had been a handy man for a French Creole, spinster who owned the properties. Upon her death 12 years earlier, she had left the collection of homes to him.

Mr. Bell found himself immediately boosted in life, financially. However, if you met him, you would not have known. Because he might have to fix something in one of the houses at any given moment, he wore a casual shirt, jeans and drove a red and white van. He usually had an assistant with him. This would behove us greatly in the near future.

Aunty Shanti moved in with us once again not to long after Pa's funeral. She and her husband Surujnath were on another break.

I had had a bad habit of playing with fire. I would light the end of my mother's bedsheet, look at the flame and quickly blow it out. I had been doing this for months. In hindsight, it was curious my mother never seemed to notice a bit of burnt bedsheet as she was a very meticulous person.

One day, as she and Aunty Shanti were eating lunch, I went upstairs and burnt the end of the sheet to whet my curiosity with fire. As I lit it and looked at the flame, I heard a noise outside. I looked out of the window and saw that it was a truck.

When I looked back, the sheet was on fire with a flame three times the normal size. I tried to blow on it with no effect. I went to the bathroom sink and filled a cup about halfway with some water. I tried dousing it on the now rising flame but again – to no avail.

At this point, I was crying with fear. The sheet was now properly on fire and you could smell the burnt material.

I had no choice to but to approach my mother. As I made my way downstairs, the tears streaming down my face, I heard her say to Aunty Shanti, "Do you smell something burning?"

Whilst a student in Winnipeg with Uncle Surujnath in 1969, there had been a fire in her apartment building. All the residents had been forced to rush out onto the street, whilst they waited for the fire trucks to arrive, one of their neighbours decided to go back in to get her cat. She was never seen again. Ever since then, Aunty Shanti had been very wary of fires.

My mother looked at my teary-eyed face: "What's wrong?"

"The bed is on fire," I cried.

"Oh my God!!!" screamed Mummy. "Shanti, come up stairs and help me!!"

"What!!!" shouted Aunty Shanti. "Fire!! Fire?? I see fire already!!!" bolting out of the house and leaving us behind.

As luck would have it, Mr. Bell was driving by with his assistant. My mother shouted at him. "Stop, stop!! Meh bed on fire. Mr. Bell help us!!"

With my aunt firmly planted outside, Mr. Bell and his assistant raced upstairs, followed by me and my mother. With about a third of the bed now on fire, they realized there was not time to waste. The two men hoisted the bed and threw it out of the window. I looked out and the image of the mattress floating downwards towards the yard with ashes rising and the flames burning as if in slow motion would stay with me forever.

Mr. Bell and the assistant raced downstairs and quickly stamped out the flames. The bed had been saved.

During my childhood I had received many a whipping. Beating children was quite normal during that era. Many of the beatings had been (in my opinion) overdone. Miraculously, that day, I did not receive a cut ass.

About six weeks later, Aunty Shanti and her husband had once again reconciled. My mother was going through her usual turnstile of maids.

One woman simply scared me because of her huge afro. I was not used to such a site. She did not meet Mummy's high standards and was dismissed in less than two months.

Then came Betty. A slim, tall, black woman of 19, she would outlast any of her predecessors or successors. She had one prerequisite to being hired. She was a Seventh Day Adventist and made it clear that on Saturday mornings she had to go to church, which my mother acceded to.

Around the same time of Betty's arrival, Mr. Bell once again came to the rescue.

This time it was a cat. This stray cat had a habit of climbing up the mango tree, crawling along the branch, jumping on to the first- floor roof and leaping into Leila's bedroom and into her crib. She would scream and cry and my mother would come running, all panicked. After a week of throwing the cat out, only to have it come back, my mother asked my father to help. He put it into the trunk of his car and dropped it off about two miles away. It was back in less than 24 hours.

As we didn't know when we would see our father again, she turned to Mr. Bell.

Seeing the cat, he picked it up and put it into his van.

"Don't worry Mrs. Darsan, I'll take care of it."

Five days went by and there was no cat. My mother was relieved.

A few days later, seeing Mr. Bell, she enquired "So Mr. Bell, what did you do with the cat?"

"I put it into a pillowcase, tied it and threw the case into a river."

"Oh my God! Mr. Bell," she moaned, "If I knew you were going to do that, I never would've let you take the cat!"

"Well Mrs. Darsan, the problem is solved."

For the next few days, our family mourned the poor cat.

CHAPTER 8

Time to Go to School

Whilst my parents were still married, I had started school at the age of four.

My mother was quite anxious that her children would have the opportunities she had missed out on. One of these was a private school. The idea being, instead of being in a class of 40, it would be around 20 and the child could get more individual attention, the facilities and resources would be better as well.

I started off at Mrs. David's Private School. The school focused on a Kindergarten level and Standard One. I began to learn the basics. Within one year I was an excellent reader with manageable math skills. For some reason, I had problems writing a 5 and would simply substitute it with an upside down 2. I could only imagine what my teachers thought of that.

Classes were taught in her huge garage, with about 15 students in total. I was quite proud of my reading ability and any book bought for school would be read and finished on the same day.

I would not even wait to get home, the moment the book was bought, I would begin reading in the backseat of the car.

"Jack is a boy. Jill is a girl. They go up the hill. They are playing. Jack has a bat and ball. Jill has a hoop. Jack's shirt is red. Jill's dress is yellow. Their dog is Rover."

I would read aloud in a somewhat mechanical voice. My parents would be silent in the front. I am sure that at some point it got on their nerves but they did not wish to stunt their son's initiative and zeal to learn.

After school, I would come home exhausted, collapse on the living room floor and go to sleep. They would have to pick me up and carry me to the bed.

Not too long after my parents' divorce, Mrs. David closed her school and started teaching at Holy Faith Primary school on Fredrick Street, in the heart of Port of Spain. My mother's office was on the same street, my father's was only a ten-minute walk away. Ironically, the house next door was where Aunty Shanti and Uncle Surujnath had lived for a few months. I had actually spent about six weeks of the previous school holiday there, unaware that my future school was just next door. Of course, it had been silent due to the holidays. By the time I had started at Holy Faith, Aunty Shanti and her husband had moved on to more serene and residential premises.

This was precisely the kind of environment my mother had wanted to avoid. It was a rough and tough place with 40 students per class. In just my first week, I got a good and proper cut ass.

I was sitting in another seat during lunch chatting with the students. A Syrian boy by the name of Michael Khouri explained: "This is my seat. Get out!"

"No. Wait 'til lunch is over. I am talking."

"Get out now!"

"No!"

He slapped me across the head. I got up for what would be my first – but not last – fight as a boy.

I had no idea what I was doing. I had never fought before and was no natural fighter.

Michael however, was.

I held him by the shoulders and pushed him. He spun me around, bit me hard three times on my back and started whaling on my head. I crumbled to the ground, crying.

One of the school prefects, a pretty red skin girl with two ponytails ran over and rescued me.

Parting us, she pulled me over to one side and explained "Don't fight. Ok?

For the next two years I spent at that school, she was always very sweet and looked out for me.

I never told my parents. Even then, I understood the unspoken code of not telling tales.

This code is what allowed Imran Younis, a student one year ahead, to take advantage of me. His mother was a secretary at the Ministry of Energy. As she knew my mother, sometimes she would walk me to the office with Imran if no one was available to pick me up.

One day, Imran decided he wanted to pick a fight with me. A skinny, Indian kid, with short black hair, he was easy to handle, despite the fact that I was no fighter myself.

Realizing that I could throw him around easily, Imran, acquired the assistance of his friend Jeff. He was taller than both of us and against the both of them I had no chance.

This went on every day for MONTHS. Imran would hit me or put me in a headlock whilst Jeff held me down or jumped on my back. I was never seriously hurt but it was irritating.

On a particular Saturday, my mother invited some friends over, including colleagues from the office. Imran came with his parents. It was the first time in ages I had him in front of me without Jeff. We went to my room to play and I beat the crap out of him. Slapping him, choking him and putting him in a headlock.

The following Monday, it was him and Jeff all over again.

I did not like school. Mrs. David was once again my teacher. However, the atmosphere was intense, I didn't like doing class work and there was the occasional bullying by the older students.

My mother was struggling after the divorce. She didn't have sufficient money to take care of two kids, my father was shameless in his lack of financial support and she would resort to borrowing money from friends, paying it back the following month, only to have to borrow it again at the end of the month.

She would battle an hour of rush hour traffic and drop me off to school, then Leila to the babysitter's and finally to work.

One day, as she let me out of the car, I dashed down the street, about thirty metres past the school and into someone's house. A middle-aged black man was in the living room, bent over a table, repairing it. I ducked down between a desk and a chair. He just looked at me and I looked back. A few seconds later my mother came running in.

"Did you see a little boy run in here?"

He nodded his head and pointed his chin in my direction.

My mother grabbed me, holding me by the arm, she hustled me down the road and up the school steps. Sadly, this struggling, single mother of two would have many more difficult days dropping off her son at Holy Faith.

In September of 1973, I was skipped a class. I went from Standard One to Standard Three. Four of us were sent there. I remember the teacher asking Mrs. David if she was sure about us. She assured her that she was.

I honestly had no idea why I had been skipped. I was unaware of any outstanding schoolwork on my part. After three weeks of being obviously clueless in Maths, I was sent one class back to Standard Two.

I felt a bit stupid at the time but it really wasn't my fault. During my promotion and then demotion, I did not remember at any time my parents being consulted.

Standard Two was memorable indeed.

There were approximately 80 students and two teachers to look after us. The older individual was Mrs. James, a slightly hefty black woman with permed, shoulder length, black hair. Ms. Chandler was a much younger, pretty mulatto woman.

I was not the best math student but I quickly became the number one reader in the class.

There were two rows of ten benches. Each bench had four students. I sat in the last bench. With me was a pretty Chinese girl, Lisa, a tall black student, about double the size of the other boys, Michael and a white girl, Petula. In hindsight, it was a cosmopolitan bench.

I quickly became enamoured with Lisa and stated to one and all, including her, that she was my girlfriend. There were never any romantic relations between us six-year-olds. However, she never denied or objected to the "relationship."

Michael was much bigger and tougher than the other boys so we all tried to be on his good side and his friend. He was completely clueless in any subject and many of us laughed at his ghastly inability but made sure to do so behind his back.

Sometimes students would be beaten with a ruler for getting too many wrong answers or for misbehaviour. I would try to beg my way out of the blows but usually without much success. We would be given anywhere from two to six blows on our hands depending on the gravity of our misdemeanour.

I hated the military like nature of the school. I lived for weekends. I would get up as early as 7 am and patiently wait for the national TV station to turn on at 9:00. Yet amazingly, I could never get up on weekdays. I would hear these horrible words coming from my mother's mouth: "Get up Sunil. School Sunil. School. Time for school." I would have to hear these dreaded words for 13 years and it irritated me every time.

I loved lunch time. I loved the end of the day. I adored weekends and the end of term holidays. I simply hated school.

What I did not know is that my mother was already making plans to remedy the situation. She had planned to enrol Leila in a nearby kindergarten. She was never satisfied with Holy Faith, she thought it too rough and wanted her children to be educated in a more "civilized environment."

Aunty Katie's children were going to a very respected school in Port of Spain, Morgan's Primary Preparatory school. It was considered one of the best in the country and was quite popular with diplomats; white collar professionals, foreigners and the local bourgeoisie. Many simply referred to it as "a white school."

Truth be told, any private school in Port of Spain had a higher percentage of whites than the government schools.

At Morgan's, the classes were smaller and students had access to resources such as a library, audio equipment not to mention greater personalized attention.

My mother had always wanted the best for her children. She had been denied opportunities as a child due to her impoverished state. She was adamant that the same would not happen to Leila and me.

Vijay Darsan, just laughed at her ambitions. "We must pay when government school free. Swimming lessons, ballet lessons?? Where you getting these ideas from?"

The concept of his children having opportunities and widening their horizons seemed to elude him. In reality, he would look for any excuse to avoid spending money on his children and their welfare. It had not embarrassed him when his own father had stepped forward to help our mother. He certainly wasn't going to be inconvenienced by something like school fees. Food and schoolbooks certainly were not free but he avoided those responsibilities as well.

There was a waiting list of two years but Aunty Katie stepped forward. She made up a story about Mummy being her cousin and that she was an extremely successful lawyer. Somehow, she managed to have us avoid the list. I came in and did some reading for the Principal, Ms.

Souness, a white Canadian. After having a short chat with me, I was assigned to a class and would start the following week.

My mother was proud and relieved. She had gotten her children into a school that was *nonpareil* in the country. It would be a struggle but this had been her life ever since returning from England.

A female professional in the 1960s often found it difficult to get a job as they would have to confront a fair degree of sexism. Her problems were compounded because of the Darsan name. Everyone knew who "Old man Darsan" was. Therefore, political bias would rare its head. Despite Pa's connections, she struggled to find work for almost a year until given a junior position at the Ministry of Energy.

Some of her friends whispered behind her back that it was a low paying job with limited advancement for a woman. But as my father explained to some, "She can't get a job."

Cintra Darsan, was a hardworking, ambitious woman. She had been that way ever since her childhood. Nothing she did was half measured, be it cleaning the house, studying or her career. She soon impressed her superiors with her work ethic and the quality of her reports. Not too impressed was the secretarial pool, who would have their reports sent back to retype certain errors.

After just a year, her presence at meetings with the Minister or the Prime Minister was considered the norm, due to her knowledge and value to the Ministry.

Her high level of excellence was matched only by her beauty. Short, slim and very beautiful with low cut hair just below the ears, she turned heads wherever she went. More than a few male colleagues were infatuated and many a foreign businessman found himself enamoured. On one occasion, a Saudi Sheik offer to "buy her." He put forth his offer to the Minister, who with a grin called her into the office. "Sheik Ahmed would like to buy you." The Sheik looked at her with a polite smile.

"What?"

"He wants to buy you," repeated the Minister, the smile growing wider.

"Oh, I'm sorry. I'm not for sale," she responded with a dazed grin and walked out. She was never quite sure if it had been a joke or not.

Aunt Katie and the girls left Maracas around July of 1974. My mother quickly made it clear to Mr. Bell that we would take her place. It was spacious and had a great view of the valley. There was another unit attached to ours. A man lived there with his daughter and mother. No wife was ever seen. They were a black family that minded their own business. One day while his daughter was playing with Leila and me, we disagreed on something. We began to fight and her grandmother immediately told her to come inside. She never played with us again.

Her father was prone to having a few men come over and drink on the weekends. They were a bit loud and my mother found it distasteful.

Making the move with us from the first house to the second was Genie. She was a white mongrel that had started coming around our house in late '73. She was adopted and was a wonderful watchdog. In mid '74 Genie disappeared for about a week. One morning as we were having breakfast and getting ready for school, she showed up.

I shouted out to my mother and everyone including Betty came running out. She would walk to the gate look at us and then come towards us and then repeat the actions.

My mother deduced: "She wants us to follow her."

So, we did.

She took us to a plot of bush opposite our house. About 15 feet inside was a litter of seven pups. Genie had been pregnant and given birth.

We were naturally in shock. But we had to battle rush hour traffic to Port of Spain, so my mother said: "we'll deal with this when we come back."

We returned home that afternoon to find Genie and her litter comfortably nestled at the back of our house. Some boxes had been placed around her to protect the pups from the elements. Uncle Michael and his wife had been decent enough to swipe away the grass with a cutlass and take the litter to our home.

Most of the pups were black in colour but one stood out. She was all white with a woolly coat. She was absolutely beautiful. We called her Cotton, short for cotton wool.

Genie and the entire litter moved over to the other house with us. Some months later, we gave away four of the litter and Genie, Cotton and two of the other pups remained with us.

Everyone loved Cotton and cooed over her. We were quite proud of her. One day she just disappeared. We were confused, she was too small to run away.

My mother then deduced that one of the many men liming next door probably stole her.

There was no proof but she was a very beautiful dog and someone had obviously stolen her.

A few weeks later the next-door neighbour asked my Mum for a ride into town as his car was not working. He sat in the back with Leila. I sat in my customary seat in the front.

As we sat silently in the rush hour traffic, Leila looked at him: "My Mummy said you and your friends stole our puppy." The car somehow became even more silent.

About a minute later he said to my mother, "I see a friend, I'll take a ride with him. Thank you. Bye."

After he had exited the car my mother could only shake her head. "Oh Leila … how could you?"

Three-year-old Leila had no idea what had just happened.

Our families never spoke again.

• • •

A few months later, unable to get rid of the other two pups, my mother dropped them off at the Port of Spain Dog Pound. What Leila and I did not know is that they were going to be put to sleep.

Sadly, towards the end of the summer holidays, it was Genie's turn to leave us. She had always had a bad habit of running after cars. One day she charged at a moving car, skidded under it and somehow avoided the back wheel, skating right past it on her back before it could roll over her.

The next day she was not so fortunate. Whilst we were on the main road with Betty waiting for a taxi to take us to our swimming class, Genie charged a taxi. The man never slowed down. The car hit her square in the face and flung her to the side of the road.

We ran over to her. She seemed to be unconscious with blood coming from her mouth. Betty shook her head: "We have to go to your swimming lessons. We'll check on her when we come back."

We returned two hours later to see Genie still on the side of the road, dead.

Leila and I had never suffered a loss like this and we were quite sad. One of Mr. Bell's employees who lived in the area and maintained the grass said he would get rid of the body.

I was never one of those people who needed to have animals around or felt the urge to pet them. However, Genie had become part of our family. We never had another pet again. My mother said dogs were a responsibility and that she would be the one doing most of the work. Somehow, she had made an exception for Genie. She had been a wonderful watchdog. Her death left a void that took us all a while to get over. For decades I would sometimes reminisce on the only pet we had ever had, Genie.

● ● ●

I had my interview with Morgan's after the school year had already started. Therefore, both Leila and I entered a bit late, around mid-October.

Mummy was usually in a rush every morning trying to get to work on time. However, realizing there might be some anxiety on our first day, she walked us to our classes. Mrs. Sloan was the teacher. I was in Class 2S. Leila was in Kindergarten.

Mrs. Sloan introduced me to the class and put me to sit next to Alicia, a plumpish, red skin girl. The boys wore chequered shirts with khaki shorts, the girls chequered dresses. The uniforms were in a variety of colours, pink, green and blue, etc.

It was a pleasant day and the work seemed easy. There were only 20 students in the class and the teacher did not have to shout in the very small classroom.

On our break I saw Leila in the yard and checked to see if she was ok. It was a very different environment for both of us and we were acclimatizing.

The classes were certainly different from what I had been accustomed to at Holy Faith. In addition to Math and English, we had story time. Mrs. Sloan would read wonderful books such as Cinderella, Sleeping Beauty, Snow White and the Seven Dwarves and many more. Even better she would sometimes play a record pertaining to one of the stories, with actors voicing the different characters. I loved story time.

We would also have to colour. Every student had a set of markers and a specific colouring book.

Morgan's may not have had a rough and tumble environment as my previous school but one still had the normal challenges of growing up with your peers.

One of them came in the person of Brian McCloud. A handsome, white boy with an already well chiselled physique at the age of seven. Simply put, he was an ass. He always seemed to want to harass people for no reason. For the next six years, I would have some altercations with him, the worst culminating in our final year.

However, in my first month Brian was unknown to me. One day with Mrs. Sloan temporarily out of the class, I happened to be standing in his way. He shoved me; I shoved back, only for him to step in with a very well executed combination. A left, right, left to the side of the face, then a straight right to the jaw, dropped me in a heap. I immediately began crying. Brian walked away as if he had expended just enough energy to flick a fly off his wrist.

This was even more humiliating than the beating Michael Khouri had given me the previous year. At least Michael had made a serious effort to beat me. Brian had defeated me effortlessly. As I say crying on the floor, the class watching, I realized one thing with great clarity.

I could not fight.

CHAPTER 9

The Babysitters

Parenthood is never easy.

A child is a 24-hour responsibility. Two parents cannot do it by themselves without support from others be they family or friends, etc.

For a single parent it's even more stressful and without support, it can be a frustrating and overwhelming experience.

In my father's absence, my mother was experiencing this first-hand. Not only did she have the full financial burden of two children to deal with, in addition, the basics such as getting them ready for bed, preparing them for school, cooking meals, cleaning, etc, was taking its toll. Her strict standards meant that maids did not always last very long. In addition, going out and having a social life was something she now had to think twice about.

With visits to Uncle Basdeo down to zero, four entities would step forward to help my mother with our upbringing. Pa, the Moonans, the Madray family and Aunty Thelma.

After Pa's death, she relied even more heavily on the other three.

The Moonans were a large family with a rum shop on Easter Main Rd. in San Juan.

They lived in a huge house behind and above the bar. They owned quite a bit of land throughout the East – West corridor of Trinidad.

Their oldest daughter, Armin, was a promising lawyer. She had met my parents at University in London. An intelligent, slim attractive woman, she had enjoyed the student social life with my parents before graduating and returning to T&T one year before them.

Upon their return to Trinidad, their friendship resumed with Aunty Armin. There were six siblings in the Moonan household, three of them adults but no grandchildren had yet been produced. They loved having me and Leila over. They would spoil us, feed us and make a general fuss over the two little "sweetie pies."

Aunty Armin would often invite my mother out and the family would gladly offer to babysit. If my mother was short of cash to pay the bills, she would lend it to her.

I was an extremely hyperactive child but they showed us both nothing but love and patience. My mother would never forget their kindness.

The Madrays were not much different in terms of their attitude to Mummy and the kids.

Originally from Guyana, Robin and Rhoda Madray had moved to Trinidad in 1959 with their three children, Sonia, John and Bobby. Pa had befriended Robin's father in Georgetown on one of his many trips. Robin and his family slowly settled into T&T life, however, in 1960, with things not going so well and Rhoda trying to stimulate a hair dressing business, he approached Pa for a loan.

They agreed on the sum of three hundred dollars. Robin signed the IOU and promised: "Uncle you will get your money back on time."

Perhaps Robin was confused as to what "on time," meant in Trinidad.

He was often late with his payments. If Pa called the house, he would be out or "you just miss him, he go come back in about two hours … Yes, yes, of course, he know about de money. He go call yuh back." Pa had no phone on the estate, so the calls from Robin to his Municipal office came after working hours when he had already left or so he was led to believe.

Pa had decided enough was enough and he would have to have a firm talk with Robin. My parents were home for a one-month holiday in the summer of 1962. Pa decided to take his son, the aspiring lawyer, to assist him in expediting the matter.

When Robin saw Pa and my father at the gate, his face dropped a bit. He knew what was coming.

After a few pleasantries, they got down to business.

"You know I have been patient in waiting for my money. You were very grateful when I gave you the loan. But you are always late. More than half is still owing. And apparently, although you knew how to contact me for a loan, I now have to run after you to get it back."

"Uncle," began Robin, staring Pa straight in his eyes, "the truth is I can't pay back that money unless I win the Lottery."

They both looked at each other for about ten seconds without saying a word.

Pa nodded his head, got up and walked out. My father followed him.

As they exited the gate, Robin, still rooted to his living room chair, Pa looked over at his son: "That son of a bitch. He owes me money. The least he could do is make an effort to pay me a little at a time. He telling me he can't pay unless he win the Lotto. You know if I was 10 years younger, I woulda hit him a lash in his ass. But I too old now, I cah make."

"I know," responded my father quietly.

Years later when I heard the story, I would wonder why my grandfather had not legally enforced the IOU. However, I would learn to understand that both Rampersad and Vijay Darsan were useless at dealing with people like Robin Madray. My father's legal background just made the situation even more embarrassing.

Despite the Madrays' shamelessness and apparent lack of appreciation to Pa, they showed great affection to my parents and the children.

After the divorce they would often babysit, my hyperactivity always well tolerated by all members of the family. If my mother went out with them, their children could be counted on to look after Leila and me.

At the time I was around five. Sonia was 19, John 17 and Bobby 14.

My mother went out with Robin and Rhoda during the Diwali celebrations of 1972. Diwali is the Hindu festival of light. Throughout the country, hundreds of diyas are lit around Hindu households. It's quite a beautiful sight to behold at night.

Leaving us with the Madray kids, my mother had gone out to celebrate the event.

John and Bobby were talking to two neighbours at the house opposite the street. As they chatted at the gateway, I walked over to join the conversation. A little, Indian girl, with two pig tails just past her shoulders walked out of the house, down the pathway and stood just about fifteen feet away observing us.

Bobby leaned over and whispered into my ear: "Why yuh doh go and give that girl a kiss."

Being much younger and trusting the older boys, I thought, why not.

I walked over and planted a kiss on her right cheek. I would never forget what happened next – with a blood curling scream, she ran all the way back into the house. I watched her run, the scream lasting the entire way, she disappeared into the front door and almost immediately her father stepped outside.

I felt as if I should panic but then I thought, why should I? I was with the big boys. If they had told me to kiss her, it had to be alright.

The very large, bespectacled father came down the driveway, looked at me and had a few words with John, Bobby and the others.

All I could hear was John say, "The little fellah get carried away for Diwali."

He looked at me and quietly walked back into his house.

Fortunately, neither of the Madray brothers ever played tricks like that on me again.

Aunty Thelma

In 1975 our family would move to Diego Martin, the deep North-West of the island. We would see much less of the Moonans and Madrays. However, Aunty Thelma (pronounced without the "h" by many Trinis) would be a constant in my life for the rest of the 70s and in Leila's case, well into the 80s.

Thelma Robinson had been born on Beaton St, Woodbrook, a neighbourhood, a mere two-minutes-drive from POS. Woodbrook in the 19th and early 20th century had been a sugar estate. The owner had lost his wife and only son in the late 1890s. He sold the land to a wealthy local Spanish family, who immediately parcelled it into lots and sold them to the burgeoning-coloured middle class that was emerging in POS.

Thelma's parents, both primary school teachers had bought and built a sturdy three- bedroom house. The Robinsons had five children, born between 1909 and 1918. Thelma was the oldest of the four girls and one boy.

Land in POS was not at a premium in the early 1900s. The majority of the Woodbrook homes were simple, yet comfortable and built on huge pieces of property, usually around five thousand square feet.

Looking at Thelma in the 1970s, she seemed to be an unremarkable, elderly, stout, black woman. However, that would be the furthest from the truth.

Old enough to remember World War I and a widow by the emergence of WWII, she had had a proper British education in the Primary and Secondary school system of T&T.

The Robinson children had grown up in an era where children were expected to know their place. You did not talk back to the adults and you had to know the social graces.

She was selected by the TT government in 1929, as one of ten teachers to go on a one-year course in London to further their pedagogy skills.

A year later she was engaged to a fellow teacher, Ian Clarke. He was also a Trini and had actually been working in London for the previous five years. They had met at the course. She remained in London but did return to TT in early 1931 to be married in her hometown of Woodbrook.

Ian was an extremely religious man and took up a missionary position in Africa. Naturally, Thelma accompanied him and together they taught in the British colonies there. The spent one year in Kenya, before moving to Nigeria.

They never had the luxury of being posted in the capital of either country but rather small towns where their services were in greater demand.

The Clarkes moved to a town just a few miles from the River Niger in August 1932. Ian taught Math, English and French. Thelma, Math and Geography.

Their plan had been to give three years of their lives to Africa, then return to London, where they would start a family.

They never got that far.

Three months into their Nigerian stay, Ian contracted Malaria. He died on Boxing Day, 1932.

A grieving widow, Thelma buried her husband in a cemetery overlooking the River Niger. She returned to her family in Trinidad, never remarrying. She would remain childless but would take care of over 50 children for over four decades.

She spent most of the 1930s teaching in Port of Spain. However, by 1939, with her parents deceased, she decided to rent out her front room and offer babysitting services. She was now living with her youngest sister, Anne. Thelma was stout, black with curly, black hair. Anne was white skinned, slim with straight, black hair. Such different siblings may have been a sight in Europe but in Trinidad this was pretty much par for the course.

They would spend the next fifty years babysitting generations of young children.

The name, Aunty Thelma, would become known throughout every street of Woodbrook. A respected elder of the community, there was no store or street where she was not recognized. The most boisterous of men if liming on the pavement, would immediately lower their tone if she approached: "Good day Aunty Thelma. Good evening Mrs. Clarke."

"So let me ask you something. You all have nothing better to do than just hang about on a street?"

"Well ... Mrs. Clarke, we just liming. You know how it is?"

"No! I don't know how it is. At your age, I was working. I didn't have time to knock about on the street. Well, just let me pass and don't block my way please."

"Yes Mrs. Clarke."

I first heard of Aunty Thelma in 1973. With no regular housekeeper, Leila would spend her days there until she started school the following year. My mother would walk me from Holy Faith to her office just a few minutes away and I would wait until she had finished work. We would then pick up Leila at Aunty Thelma's. She and her sister would always give me a pleasant smile and a wave. She seemed like a nice person. What I would soon find out is that this woman would become a thorn in my side for the rest of the seventies.

When Betty our housekeeper for the next two years, arrived around August of 1973, there was even less reason to see Aunty Thelma.

However, in late '74 both Leila and I were now students at Morgan's. The school was not near Mummy's office and it would be too inconvenient to have both of us there every afternoon. We had a chauffeur who would pick us up along with other children and drop us off at our destination. The others were dropped off at their home, for us it was Aunty Thelma's.

It only took a week for me to understand that spending the afternoons there would be no bed of roses. In the second week, I was eating some cake and some crumbs dropped into my lap. She immediately rushed over and started pulling my hair at the back of my head. "Are you a gorilla? Pick up those crumbs. Put your face over the plate!"

I could feel the tears rolling down my cheeks.

She would beat me if my grip on the knife and fork was wrong and on NO occasion were my elbows to be on the dinner table. "Keep your wings off the table."

She explained to me: "You need to know these things now so that you will not be embarrassed when you become an adult. Imagine how stupid you will look in society if you cannot eat properly and everybody else knows how to do it.

"When I was a young lady travelling in Africa, we were on a boat for five nights. A man came up to me and told me that he did not know how to eat socially. He was embarrassed to eat dinner with the others and could I please show him how. And this was *a white man* from Scotland. I told him to sit next to me and to just follow everything I did."

Every night the Scotsman sat next to young Thelma and dutifully followed her actions. By the fourth night he was a pro.

"Do you want to be like him? Stupid and embarrassed as an adult!?"

"No," I respectfully answered.

"No what???? Cat ... dog??"

"No Aunty Thelma."

I would brace for the possible lash as I answered.

I had been told to hold the utensils as one holds a pencil. Unfortunately for me, I did not hold the pencil as most people of the Western Hemisphere. My grip was between the thumb and index finger, much to the chagrin of my teachers and parents. No amount of coaxing could get me to hold it otherwise. I therefore, held them in this manner.

On one occasion, as I was eating a mid-afternoon meal, Aunty Thelma picked up a piece of wood about two feet long, ran across the kitchen and began hitting me on my back. I thought she had lost her mind.

"What happened?"

"Your grip on the knife and fork is wrong!"

It was the only grip I knew. But once she showed me the preferred method, I made sure never to err again, especially in her presence.

Many years later as an adult, her lessons would ring in my ears as I sat at a dinner table. On a few occasions, I would say "To hell with her. I'm a man now and will do as I damn well please!" I would rebelliously put my elbows on the table and relax. However, it would only take ten seconds for me to feel that I was doing something asinine and I would begrudgingly remove them.

Although we now had Betty at home. We were compelled to spend our weekday afternoons after school at Aunty Thelma's as she was in POS.

There would be many more lessons to come and many more beatings.

CHAPTER 10

Farewell to the Valley

My mother informed us in early 1975 that in a few months we would be leaving Maracas Valley and moving to Diego Martin in the North-West of the island.

We were comfortable in our surroundings and were not looking forward to it.

We enjoyed out last few months as best we could, wondering what to expect in the new place.

During that time, we received a lot of visits from Uncle Shirvan. He was originally from Sangre Grande like my parents. Both his and my father's parents had been the best of friends. Shirvan's father was a massive landowner in Sangre Grande. The family was as wealthy if not more so than Pa, however, you would never have known it from their lifestyle. They lived in a simple wooden, two-bedroom house. They had no living room furniture to speak of. They did have a long table with two benches that doubled for eating and a sort of sitting room. There was another long bench and a hammock in front of the house.

The only indication of wealth, was a Mercedes Benz, parked in the garage. Shirvan's father may have been a man of simple means but "he believed in having a nice, big, car," as my father put it.

His mother and Ma had been so close that after her death Shirvan's mother never drank alcohol again, as a sign of respect to her passing.

Uncle Shirvan had a sort of a shop about a mile up the main road. It served as a mini store/rum shop. I would visit him on my own and to my delight, always receive a free coke and some chocolates or sweets.

I noticed that for a month or more he was always around the house at night, chatting with my mother. She would let him do the talking, while she moved around the kitchen, a somewhat serious expression on her face. Years later, I would remember that look for a very good reason.

A few weeks after receiving the news of our impending move, I acquired first-hand experience of life in a Trinidad hospital. Relaxing at home on a weekday afternoon, I was jumping off a chair. At first, I would put one foot on the top of the backrest and jump. Then I decided to try two feet on the backrest. This would require a decent degree of acrobatic ability. Not surprisingly, I did not possess such ability. I immediately fell down, my left hand bearing the brunt of the fall as I placed it just under my chest.

I got up with a pain in my wrist and simply cried for a few minutes. It didn't hurt much until a few hours later as I tried to sleep. Finally, around 11 pm, I could take the pain no longer and woke my mother up. She realized it was serious as I moaned and cried.

Too sensitive to be touched, she concluded we would have to see a doctor. She drove down to Aunty Joyce's house and asked her to accompany us to the hospital. She didn't hesitate for a moment and in less than two minutes was dressed and in the car.

There was a private clinic about five miles from our house. We stopped there. A nurse examined me and concluded that it was probably broken. She told my mother she could pay or simply take me to the Port of Spain General Hospital. She opted for the latter.

As an adult I would wonder how the hell there was no public hospital closer to our house or did my mother just fail to think on that night?

We arrived at the hospital, filled out a form and waited. About twenty minutes later, I was given an X-ray. They informed us that I had fractured my wrist. I waited and some time later a doctor showed up and wrapped my hand in plaster of Paris. I was then taken up along with Mummy and Aunty Joyce to a children's ward on the fourth floor, the time was now 4:30 am. They chatted with the nurses and pointed to a bed. I lay down for a while. When I looked up, I could not see my mother. I walked to the front of the ward and looked around. At this point, I walked out into the corridor and began calling her "Mummy, Mummy." The more I called out, the more I cried. I looked at every corner and doorway, thinking she might be standing there. After all, she couldn't just have left me. I had now reached the end of the corridor and was still crying out for her, the tears streaming down my face. I looked at the elevator, wondering if I should enter it and continue looking for her downstairs. At that moment, a nurse realizing that I was missing, stepped out of the ward. "Ey boy. Come back here!"

I returned, afraid and sobbing. "Do you know where my mummy is?"

"She gone. But you will see her later."

"When?"

"I don't know, just later."

I simply could not believe that she had left me without saying a word. How could my mummy do that to me?

In reality, the nurse had told her to leave without saying goodbye.

"If you say goodbye, he will bawl and scream and not want you to go. So just leave and we will handle it."

As much as it hurt me then, they were right. I would have created a spectacle had she told me that she was leaving.

A few minutes later, a doctor came in and a young girl was given an injection. She screamed as they got the needle ready and screamed even more as they injected her. She continued crying after they left.

Oh my God!! I thought to myself. They are going to inject everybody before they go to sleep.

I cringed in the bed, curled up in a foetal position, waiting for the pain to come. Fortunately, no one else was injected that night or for the rest of my stay there.

I cried myself to sleep and the next morning was awakened for breakfast. The Ward consisted of two huge rooms with beds. The secondary room had a big table in the corner where the children ate their meals. At the very back were the washrooms.

After breakfast, I began speaking to the boy in the bed next to me. He was a black fellow, the same age as me. He had fallen down a flight of stairs. His name was Frank. He had arrived just two days before me.

There was not much to do, no TV, no games so he and I would chat. Some of the other children would walk by our beds and stop to talk as well.

Later that day my mother came by and chatted with me. She assured me that she would come every day after work.

The next day Aunty Hulsie came to see me. She worked at the Ministry with my mother and they had become the best of friends. I was surprised. But as the years rolled by, I would come to understand that she would always have an interest in Leila's and my welfare. She was well aware of how difficult life was for my mother as a single parent. We chatted for a while and then about twenty minutes later, I saw my father approaching. It was always a thrill to see him as he no longer lived with us. His visits were usually unannounced and much welcomed.

I immediately became animated. He had brought two comics for me, *Superman* and the *Two Gun Kid*. I didn't mean to be rude but I completely ignored Aunty Hulsie once he had arrived. After about five minutes she gave me a kiss goodbye and left.

I explained to him what had happened to my wrist. We had a great chat for about half an hour. We hugged and kissed each other and then he left. I was in fantastic spirits. My Daddy had visited me. For the first time I had comics to read. No one had ever given me a comic before.

Frank also had some comics so we exchanged with each other. He was a bit sad because his father also lived away from home and had not yet come to visit him.

My father had brought me some chocolates. The nurse had warned me not to eat the chocolate at night. "You will get a stomach-ache."

The lights went out at 8:30. By 8:45 I had already finished one of the chocolates. By 9:15 my stomach was in pain. I tried to put up with it but after 10 minutes it was unbearable.

"Nurse, my belly hurting."

"You ate the chocolates after I told you not to."

"Yes."

"Well why were you so stupid? Hold on."

She gave me a tablespoon of a sweet syrup to drink and in about five minutes the pain had subsided a bit.

During the day with not much to do, I would chat with the other children. We would discuss our injury or illness and our plans for the future. One boy had burns on the left side of his body. His sister had accidentally knocked over a pot of hot water on him in the kitchen. "When I get home, ah go spill some hot water on she!" And we all laughed.

There was an Indian boy on the far side of the room. He needed a wheelchair at all times. He would ask the nurses to bring his meals to him. However, they would insist that he go to the table like everyone else. He would struggle with the wheelchair.

"Can you help me please?"

"No do it yourself!" was the sharp retort.

I never could understand if they were trying to make him self-sufficient or it was unnecessary cruelty.

He would very slowly wheel himself to the table. I felt very sorry for him but simultaneously was quite glad for myself as I understood my situation could be much worse.

One night at around 9 pm, a black man showed up. He stood in front of Frank's bed and just looked at him. I stared at him and he explained: "I am his father."

"Oh! He was waiting for you to visit."

"Don't wake him up. Let him sleep."

He looked at him for a few minutes, placed a bag of comics on the bedstand and left.

The next morning Frank was crestfallen. He had waited so long to see his father.

"Well he said not to wake you," I explained.

It took him a few minutes to get over his disappointment. We then looked at his comics, feasting our eyes on the likes of *Archie*, *Richie Rich* and *Batman*.

My days at the Children's Ward were not that terrible. We were fed decent meals and we would amuse ourselves until the bedtime curfew. I was totally enjoying the comics that Frank and I had. I would spend hours reading just one comic.

A week later it was time to go. I said goodbye to the children and nurses. Frank said he would leave a few days later as well. We waved goodbye and I never saw him again.

The plaster of Paris was very hard indeed. It was like having concrete around your arm. None of the boys at school wanted to fight me because I would charge them with the arm. I had become more powerful albeit temporarily.

Five weeks later it was taken off and I slowly got the use of my arm again.

By May we were on the move. It was a sad farewell to the Browns. Aunt Joyce and my mother had become quite close. Not only would they often do their Saturday shopping together but it would be the norm for her to babysit and keep an eye on us if my mother had to go out.

As we left that day, everything being packed by men on a huge truck, they came to bid their final farewell, giving us all big hugs.

I would only see the boys one more time. Two years later, driving from the deep south of Trinidad, my mother made a stop just outside of San Fernando. She explained that Uncle Michael's family lived there and we were visiting. There was no Aunty Joyce. Uncle Michael informed us that she was now living in the USA and that they would follow in the future.

What I later found out was that she had actually gone to Canada and with friends, crossed the border illegally, pretending to be their housekeeper.

Cintra and I chatted and played with the boys while my mother conversed with Uncle Michael and his parents. An hour later it was time to go.

I felt a bit sad, knowing it might be a long time before I ever saw them again. Actually, it was never. A year later, Aunty Joyce sent for her family and they would live a long and prosperous life in New York.

I did however, see her twice during the next two decades, as she visited Trinidad. We would have wonderful chats about the old days and look at photos of the boys. Despite the infrequence with which I would see her, she would always remain my aunt.

CHAPTER 11

Welcome to the Gardens

Trinidad was first discovered by Christopher Columbus on his third voyage on July 31, 1498. At the time it was populated by a few hundred Indians comprising of the Amerindian and Carib tribes.

For the next three hundred years, the island would change hands between the Spanish, English, Dutch and the French. It was colonized for the final time by the British in 1797.

Trinidad had been extremely underpopulated for most of its first three centuries of colonization. By the late 1780s there were less than two thousand on the island. The Spanish government had granted land to the French inhabitants of the other islands to come to TT in the late eighteen century to augment the situation.

With the abolition of slavery by the British in the 1830s, the Africans were not going to work the sugar plantations unless properly compensated. This led to a massive Indian emigration to fill the void. The Indians were paid a pittance for five years and in return could have a paid passage back home or be given land in lieu of their voyage. This was how many Indians, even 150 years later were still landowners in the late 20th century. Almost one hundred and fifty thousand Indians would come to

Trinidad between 1845-1917. Thus, by the late 1800s, Trinidad was an ethnic melting pot of Europeans, Africans; East Indians; Chinese; native Indians, Syrians and a smattering of other ethnic groups. Not surprisingly there were interracial relations which led to the creation of a people as beautiful and exotic as you would expect.

As a child you do not know about racism unless it is taught to you or observed. I did not know it but during my early years while my parents were still married, my environment was basically Indian, the exception being my primary school. Once my parents were divorced, the ethnicity of my surroundings was greatly diversified, be it my mother's office or the neighbourhoods I would live in. Race was never an issue because no one ever made it as such. This does not mean that racism did not exist in Trinidad. It did. However, my environment for many years was devoid of it. It was the luxury of living in a multicultural setting as opposed to being the victim of ethnocentrism.

We arrived at Waterfall Gardens on May 1, 1975. The neighourhood had approximately 35 houses and was shaped in a U. We live on the left side of that U. Opposite our house was a huge plot of bush. With the exception of that plot, there were houses on both sides of the street. Further up the road at the end was a hillock. Outside of the Gardens was a main road, bordered by a river and beyond the river, the Northern Range.

If one continued to drive past the Gardens, you would see a semi-rural, lush area, with houses scattered here and there. After about two miles, the road became a steep hill and if one knew the path, you could take it to the famed Blue Basin Waterfall.

There were quite a few white families along with some blacks, brown skinned and a few Chinese. We were the only Indians. It would take years before that fact dawned on my infantile mind. As my mother would later put it, this was "the first house" for a lot of young couples. They were cheap and stuck up in the far North-West of the island "behind God's back."

Entrenched in the depth of the hills, we had no TV reception but somehow got a vague picture of Venezuelan TV as the country was located about seven miles from the nearby coast. We also had no phone, a sad norm for many people in Trinidad during the 1970s. We knew of people who had been waiting for six years or more for a phone in various parts of Trinidad, so we had no big hopes of solving that dilemma.

The Gardens would be where I spent the core of my childhood, achieving puberty, discovering girls, football and so much more.

The very next day, Cintra and I went out into the street. We were fascinated that the road was so empty so like the seven-year-old idiot that I was, I took off all my clothes in the middle of the road. Cintra, followed her brother.

A woman next door opened the kitchen door and we both bolted into the house leaving the clothes behind.

The woman was Maria Dos Santos, she was a Venezuelan married to a local. Within minutes she had come over to introduce herself to the family. Later that day she had us over for cake and drinks, introducing us to her husband Edward and their baby, James.

The Dos Santos family would become lifelong friends. Living in Trinidad, it was normal to become close to your neighbours, with the children constantly in each other's homes. Some of these neighbours over time would become like a second family. For the next six years in the Gardens, this is what Aunty Maria and her family became to us.

Later that day I saw a number of fair skinned children playing in front of our house. I recognized one boy on a bike. His name was Daniel Pereira, he had been in class with me at Holy Faith. He left not too long after me and was also attending a private school.

There were three white kids with him, Lara, Maria and William Watt. Lara was just a few months younger than me, Maria one year younger and "Billy" was around Leila's age.

For the next three years these four would be the core of my social group in the Gardens until another influx of children.

In every group there is always a bit of a silly character. Someone who is a bit wilder and different than the rest and this was Daniel. Always shouting or saying something silly. However, the incidents would be few until some years later.

On the other side of our house was a gentleman by the name of Paul Houghton. He came over in the first week to introduce himself. He was putting the final touches to his home and soon he and his fiancée, Babsie would be moving in.

Bob was a slim, red skin man, with curly black hair, a moustache and slightly balding. Babsie was a pretty, light skinned woman. She seemed pleasant enough. On some occasions she and Uncle Paul would come over and chat with mummy.

Within a few months, we no longer saw Babsie. My mother explained that she and Uncle Paul were no longer going to get married. Within two months of her departure, mummy and Uncle Paul had become a couple.

He started sleeping over. Leila and I had no problem with it. We were too innocent to understand the exact nature of the relationship but we enjoyed his company.

It was around this time that he rented out his home to an Indian couple, Ronnie and Tammy. Ronnie was an extremely tall man, talkative and a bit silly when he drank. Tammy was a nice, polite, slender woman. They would sometimes come over and socialize with Uncle Peter and mummy.

Ronnie was a handy fellow and started doing odd jobs for my mother. He would hang electric lamps, fix the doors and the windows. She would offer to pay. However, he always refused: "Nah man. We are neighbours and friends. I cah charge you."

November 11 arrived and it was my birthday. It was on a weekday so the neighbourhood children came over in the afternoon. I was eight years old. Amongst my presents were a pair of boxing gloves. I had become a huge Muhamad Ali fan and these were now my prized possessions. I cut the cake with Lara. We gave each other a quick kiss and then with my gloves on, we took a group photo.

The following Saturday, my father came to visit, armed with five comics for me and two for Leila. Although Leila and he shared the same birthday – November 3, he never actually visited for hers.

Like any visit of his, it was wonderful. He came armed with a few pounds of beef and other products. My mother was happy for these visits. It meant that she could rest while he did the cooking.

He would spend the rest of the day chatting with us or playing card games. We would be despondent when he had to leave.

Finally, at around 4:00 pm it was time for him to go. We gave him our hugs and kisses. He would promise us that he would come the following weekend but never did and we would spend all of that day looking at every car that turned the corner.

Ronnie was sitting in his porch. The day before he had been chatting with Leila and stroking her stomach. My mother felt uncomfortable with the way he was touching her and made it clear to him that she did not want him touching her in any way in the future.

As he saw my father leaving he shouted out "Mr. Darsan come here!!" He bellowed in a very authoritative manner as if speaking to a subordinate.

"I can't come. I'm on my way out."

"I said COME HERE!!"

"I have an appointment, I can't come. And you don't speak to me in that tone. I am not a child."

With that said, Daddy jumped into the car and left. Ronnie just sat on the floor of the porch looking downwards.

Within a few minutes he was walking into our living room.

"Mrs. Darsan, I want six hundred dollars for all the work I have done in this house. If I don't have it my twelve o'clock tonight, I will cut yuh ass!!

My mother looked up at him in shock.

"But you said that you would do it for free."

"I want six hundred dollars by twelve tonight or I am going to CUT YUH ASS!"

Betty stood silently at the edge of the living room, watching.

"Look you can't come into my house and talk to me like that."

At this point, he towered over her and pointed his finger into her face. "You better have my money by twelve or I will cut yuh ass!"

Leila and I just looked. It was a surreal experience as if we were watching TV.

My mother, her voice cracking a bit and on the verge of tears said to Betty, "Go call Drew, tell him I want to speak to him. Drew and Alice Carter lived behind our house. As you entered Cascade Gardens, theirs was one of the first houses in the neighbourhood. They had two cute children, a little girl a few years younger than Leila and a baby.

With no man in the house, my mother was petrified. Worse yet, we were in a semi desolate corner of Trinidad and no one in the neighbourhood had a telephone. So, she was unable to call the police if she had wanted.

Uncle Drew came over. First, he spoke to Mummy and then he walked next door.

"Ronnie, what's wrong?"

"I am going to cut her ass."

"What do you mean?"

"I want my money by 12 or I am going to cut her ass!!"

Ronnie walked inside and Uncle Drew followed him. We couldn't hear anymore but Leila and I were beginning to realize this situation was quite serious.

A few minutes later, Uncle Drew returned to our house and chatted with Mummy. She was visibly shaken. Even though I was a child, I could see she was trying to regain her composure but with great difficulty.

Within half an hour Uncle Paul arrived. He was quickly informed of the previous proceedings by my mother.

He and Uncle Drew went over to Ronnie's house and tried to reason with him.

But no matter what they said all we could hear from next door was "Ah go cut she ass!!"

Standing in front of Uncle Paul's car, both he and Uncle Drew were discussing the matter as Ronnie stared at them from his gate. At that point Uncle Paul said to him, "Alright Ronnie, I will give you the money."

"No! I want it from her or ah go cut she ass!!"

All the while, his wife Tammy, stood in the porch, silently watching. I felt sorry for her, she was a friendly, pleasant woman and this must have been embarrassing for her.

With the afternoon drawing to a close and the matter seeming far from being resolved, Uncle Paul and Mummy dropped us off at his house where he lived with his parents and went to report the matter to the police.

Around 8 that night, they both returned. The police had chatted with Ronnie. From what little Leila and I could hear, it seemed like everything was basically resolved.

It was a Sunday night. Usually by this time we would have done all our homework and been getting ready for bed. However, my mother needed to calm down before returning home.

Well after 9:30 we left Uncle Paul's home. At approximately ten o'clock we entered the Gardens and to our surprise there stood Uncle Drew and his family in front of their house. It was a bizarre sight at 10 pm, he with the baby in his arms, his wife next to him and their little girl holding her hand.

My mother immediately stopped the car. "What are you all doing standing in front of the house?"

"Ronnie is waiting for you at your house. He has a rope. He is sitting in your porch and he says he's going to beat you. Whatever you do, do not go home tonight," explained Uncle Drew.

My mother had always had a reputation as a crazy driver. Full grown men would scream whilst she was driving. Others would scatter across the road as if sighting the Four Horsemen of the Apocalypse.

Leila and I had grown up with such driving and were quite used to it. We would even be amused watching the scared adults.

However, on that night, even I became a bit scared. My mother raced down the narrow road, they tyres screeching as she turned corners. We did an eight- minute drive in four. As we arrived at Uncle Paul's house, she blew the horn frantically and he came running out.

Once she had explained the situation, he bundled us into his car and drove us to Santa Cruz, an area nestled in the Northern range of hills and about 20 minutes from POS. He was taking us to his sister's house. Gloria was a very attractive woman in her early forties. She had a dark brown complexion with shoulder length, brown hair.

She had met our mother once or twice before and once apprised of the situation was happy to give us refuge. This had now become a sort of adventure for both Leila and myself.

The next day we stayed at Aunty Gloria's house. Her young daughter of about 15 played board games with us. We were now missing a day of school. The adventure had taken a turn for the better.

I would never know quite how he did it but after making another report to the police with my mother, Uncle Paul had Ronnie, his wife and furniture ejected from the premises that very day.

We returned that night to a more sedate scene. Surprisingly, Uncle Paul did not accompany us. However, my mother made sure to stop at Uncle Drew's house first, to ensure that the coast was indeed clear.

A week later, my mother's closest friends came to visit her and offer moral support: the Mohammeds, the Khans and the Murrays.

Imran Mohammed, Hulsie Khan and Patricia Murray had all met my mother at the Ministry of Energy in 1971. She hit it off with all three very well and over the years they would become an extended part of our family.

Imran was a Petroleum Engineer who had graduated from the University of Texas on a Government Scholarship. An East Indian from the deep South of TT, his wife, was a slim, elegant, black woman, Janice. She herself, was a Cambridge graduate in Optometry. A very successful couple, they had recently moved from San Fernando to POS.

Hulsie Khan worked in the secretarial pool. My mother's high standards were infamous amongst the secretaries. They could not believe that Hulsie and my mother had become friendly.

"You talking to Mrs. Darsan? Really?"

Hulsie would just smile and say, "Once you get to know her, she's a very nice woman."

Her husband Javed was Chief of Sales for a white goods firm.

I first met Patricia Murray at the Ministry in 1972. Without a babysitter, my mother decided that I would spend the day with her at the office.

It was the first time I had done so and she took me around to introduce me to various colleagues. The last office was the library. It seemed to a very boring looking room, a sort of sterile environment with many shelves of brown and black books.

"This is Aunty Pat, the librarian," said my mother.

I looked up and saw this incredibly beautiful, slim, white woman with long, beautiful, curly, blond hair, halfway down her back. She had grey eyes with flecks of green.

She looked down at me, smiling.

Who is this beautiful woman? I asked myself.

We shook hands and she gave me a kiss and a hug.

After a few minutes of chit chat, my mother jokingly asked, "So you want to go with me or do you want to stay with Aunty Pat?"

"I want to stay with Aunty Pat," was the immediate response.

They both laughed incredulously: "Really!!?"

As I had given my decision, Aunty Pat quickly suggested that I sit at the desk next to her and draw something.

"What shall I draw?"

"Why don't you draw Aunty Pat. She's very beautiful," suggested Mummy.

So, I sat there looking at her and doing my best to create a portrait. She would look back and smile.

If anyone came into the library and queried as to the young man was, the response was "This is Mrs. Darsan's son, Sunil, my new boyfriend."

There would be some laughter and some kind of surprised response. I would allow myself a momentary distraction and then continue my drawing.

Pat's husband, Gerard, was a handsome fellow with blondish brown hair. Together they made a striking couple. Funny and talkative, he could be prone to outbursts of anger from time to time.

Uncle Javed and Gerard walked over to the fence and looked at where Ronnie had been living.

"So what kinda mad ass is this?" asked Uncle Gerard. "Just so he want to threaten and beat a woman. I guess this is what happens when you have no husband around."

They commiserated with my mother, doing their best to support her and uplift her spirits.

Aunty Pat held her hand, "Cintra, you don't worry girl. I am sorry this neighbourhood doesn't have a phone. We would've come running."

A week later, whilst in the supermarket, we happened to see the Minister of Energy, Mr. Dhanraj with his wife. He had heard Aunty Hulsie and Pat talking in the office.

The Minister was my one salvation at the Ministry when I had to wait there for my mother after school. At times I would wait until seven or eight pm, spending close to five hours, sitting or walking around waiting for my mother to finish work.

One day, whilst sitting in the reception area, the Minister waked up to me. I had no idea who he really was.

"What are you doing here?"

"I am waiting for my Mummy."

"Are you Mrs. Darsan's son?"

I nodded my head.

"Do you like magic?"

I nodded once again.

"Well come with me then."

I followed him into an adjacent reception room with an assistant. He opened a door and took me into his office. It was huge, with a sort of conference table at the front. His desk was at the very back.

"Sit down."

I then spent the next hour enthralled as he performed one trick after another. He would put one dollar in my pocket and take out five. Money would disappear from his hand and he would pull it out of my ear. He did a variety of card tricks.

I left that office convinced that there was no magic trick he couldn't do.

My mother was shocked when I told her where I had spent the previous hour.

"Oh my God. Please don't harass the Minister."

However, Mr. Dhanraj assured her that I was no bother and that he was the one who had offered the invitation. For the next few months I would go to the assistant, Mrs. Pinero.

"Mrs. Pinero, I am here to see Mr. Dhanraj."

"Of course Sunny, go on in."

"Mr. Dhanraj, I am here to see some magic."

"Alright boss. Come on down."

He never turned me away.

A few months later, Mrs. Pinero retired. The new assistant was a younger Indian woman.

"I am here to see Mr. Dhanraj."

"Mr. Dhanraj is *busy*," she said sternly."

After three such encounters. I stopped going to his office and waited to catch him in the corridors. Whilst everyone referred to him as Minister Dhanraj, to me he was always the "Magic Man."

Now it was *he* who had caught us in the aisle of the supermarket.

"I understand you had a problem with a neighbour."

"Yes, I did."

"I am sorry to hear that. My home is only a few miles from yours. Here is my number if you have similar problems again."

My mother didn't bother to explain that no one in the neighbourhood had a phone. She thanked him and accepted the slip of paper.

As a family we spent the next few weeks somewhat paranoid that Ronnie might return. However, the fact that he did not have a car and that our neighbourhood was off the beaten path, perhaps made it too difficult for him.

Slowly, life resumed to normal.

CHAPTER 12

Coffee Bean vs. Flour Child

Leila and I had now been at Morgan's Primary school for about a year. We were completely settled in and enjoying education at one of the best schools in the country.

Unfortunately for Leila life had taken a savage turn at the beginning of the new school year in September. She had been placed in Mrs. Bissessar's class. It was the norm in Trinidad to beat students in a school. But Mrs. Bissessar was like some kind of beast unleashed.

If you did not know the answer to a question, she would slap you, pull your hair and at times use a thick ruler to beat you on the palms of your hands. On one occasion she slapped a boy so hard that her ring left an imprint on his face. Even by local standards this was extreme. Years later, I would wonder how she ever kept her job.

I thanked the Gods that I had started Morgan's late and therefore never had the possibility of being in her class. Cintra was not that fortunate and every morning there was a battle to get her into the car to go to school. She would scream and cry, holding on to the porch furniture. My mother would have to physically detach her from the furniture and force her into the car.

"But you were never like this before. You were fine last year. What is the problem now?" This was practically a religious chant from her every morning.

I never thought to explain to Mummy why, although I obviously knew. After all, it was normal to beat the kids at school. It wasn't like Mrs. Bissessar was wrong by local standards.

As Cintra did her best to survive Mrs. Bissessar, I was in Mrs. Kerr's class. She was a beautiful, Caucasian woman who had four kids at Morgan's. I would remember her many years later due to key lessons that would stay with me throughout my adulthood.

In Trinidad, all primary school children were expected to know their twelve times table, basically how to multiply numbers in twos all the way up to twelves. Mrs. Kerr, would have us practice on a blackboard from zero to one hundred, sometimes counting in twos, threes, fives etc. It was the norm to reward students with Merits or Demerits for positive accomplishments or bad behaviour, respectively. A competition was set up and students were given a Merit (a star) for each table they knew and five stars to the first to know all 12 tables.

Every day we would line up and take a turn, usually doing one table a day. Somehow, I messed up perhaps the easiest table, the 11s, this set me back by one day. Alejandro, a student from Venezuela finished first and I came second, getting four Merits for my efforts.

We were taught how to use a Dictionary and I would never have a problem defining a word ever again. I simply starred in Mrs. Kerr's class, be it Vocabulary, Math, Reading, etc. However, as would be the norm in school life, I was hyperactive and talkative. It was quite common to put me outside during a class or to keep me inside during the lunch break.

It was during one of these lunch breaks that I experienced my first ever encounter with racism. The kids would all try to rush out at the same time in our zeal to get to the yard. I found myself bouncing shoulders with an older blonde, white student from the USA.

"Hey, watch where you're going you idiot!" he shouted at me.

"Watch where YOU'RE going fool!"

"Coffee Bean!"

I looked at him for a second, a bit confused. "Coffee Bean?" What did that have to do with anything? It took one more second for me to get it. Coffee was brown and so was I. Apparently, I was being insulted. I tried to come up with a witty response as quickly as I could. The best my eight-year-old mind could muster up was "Flour Child."

For the next year if he saw me, he would shout out "Coffee Bean," I would quickly come back with "Flour Child." Deep in my heart, I knew my response was lacking in originality but I had had zero experience in harassing people due to their race.

One day an old British teacher, Mrs. Root, heard us trading barbs in the school yard.

As soon as the break was over, she had his class and mine come together. We were quite curious as to why only we had had to congregate.

"I want to tell you all a story. One day a little girl had started her first day of school. She was quite excited. She made friends with another girl and they had a great time chatting and playing in the school yard. She came home and her mother and her friend were chatting in the kitchen. 'Mummy she said, I had a great day at school and I met this wonderful girl. We played all day. We chatted and shared our lunch. She's my friend. I really love her.'

" 'Oh,' said the mother's friend '… is she black or white?'

"'I don't remember' said the girl. 'I'll tell you tomorrow.'

"Class, what I am trying to say is that it really doesn't matter what race a person is. What *does* matter is the kind of person they are on the inside. So, I hope that you understand this and never judge people by the way they look.

"Ok. You can go back to class now."

We all looked at each other a bit confused and "Flour Child" and his classmates left.

Although I may have agreed with the moral of her story, I did continue to respond to the chant of "Coffee Bean," if I heard it for the rest of the school year.

CHAPTER 13

A Trinidad Christmas

Christmas was drawing upon us, Leila and I were trying to contain our excitement as we did every year and waiting impatiently for that all important day, December 25.

As usual we would wonder out aloud, how Santa was getting into our house. Trinidad had no chimneys. My mother would patiently explain that he had a magic key. We should not ask too many questions because he could hear us and he would get angry. Did we want him to bypass our house?

Leila and I would quickly stop asking our questions and discuss the matter in private. Whereas Santa usually dropped off his presents under a Christmas tree, our house was a little different. He would put most in a big red and white sock that looked like a boot and deposit it under our bed. Then a few others would be left under the tree.

There was always a change in the air once November came around, Christmas lights would go up in people's gardens, their homes and in stores. The Christmas songs would be heard blaring from people's record players, businesses and the radio. Most people had a green tree in their house but ours was white. We would help mummy set it up, hang the shining balls, the glittering streamers, electric lights and the Angel on the top. Leila and I would then immediately turn off all the lights and plug in the tree. We would marvel at the lights and colours.

Morgan's was having its usual Christmas play. That year the play was Scrooge. Flour Child was selected to be Ebenezer Scrooge. They younger kids usually had more minor roles and I played a vendor in the market. Years later I realized that all the starring roles in our plays usually went to very light skinned individuals. It didn't mean that they did not do a good job but in Trinidadian schools that was a frequency that was not always the norm. But then again, the demographics of Morgan's was not the norm for T&T. However, in those days having been influenced by the British and the Americans, we had been programmed to think that all major characters from the Bible were white. So, to many of us it may have actually seemed logical for whites or light skinned individuals to have the starring roles regarding the Bible or childhood stories.

The play was held just before the Christmas holidays. Mummy and Uncle Paul congratulated me on a job well done.

The neighbourhood children and I enjoyed our holidays playing and finding different ways to amuse ourselves. With the parents away for most of the day at work, it was as if we had the neighbourhood to ourselves and a greater form of independence.

On Christmas Eve, we all discussed the impending day to come. We talked about our list to Santa and what we might realistically get. That night we did not argue when told it was bedtime. After all, Santa was busy and he could not possibly come if we were still up. One did not want to make Santa Claus' job more difficult, there was always the possibility of no presents.

Once my eyes opened on Christmas Day, I would automatically swoop under the bed to see a huge red sock there. I would pull it out and marvel at what I had received. I couldn't believe Santa had been right there in the room with me. I would then go to the Christmas tree to see what other delights awaited me. Leila would hear me and quickly join in.

There would be the customary letter from Santa to both of us. That Christmas I received a football, a Hardy Boys book, some T-Shirts and a pair of jeans. Leila received a few board games, two dresses and a book.

To our delight our father showed up later, armed with the customary bag full of comics. He never bothered to wrap anything. He read our letter from Santa out aloud. He had an amused smile as he read. It would take me a few years to understand the source of the amusement.

Christmas day in TT is a day filled with presents, music and food. Ours was no different. My mother felt overwhelmed having to do all the cooking herself so it was a bit low key by Trini standards. There was baked chicken, beef, callaloo, rice, lentils, plantain, bajee (spinach cooked with spices) and salad. My father made sure to add a curry goat to the proceedings. Having a Christmas lunch with all of us at the table was a dream come true for me. Unlike Leila, I had remembered what it was like to be a whole family. I had prayed and wished that one day our parents would reunite. For that moment at the dinner table, I had a feeling of what other kids had, a family – together.

It may not have been reality but all of us sharing a moment like this was a rare jewel in my life. For a few minutes I would allow fantasy to take over reality and we were a family having our Christmas meal.

Inevitably, Daddy would have to leave. We would smother him with hugs and kisses. He would promise to visit us soon, which was never true. And then it was back to the real world – a family minus our father.

CHAPTER 14

The Undescended Testicle

As 1976 arrived, we were now fully into the seventies. The TT economy was thriving due to oil prices being high and Disco was the music of the era. Life was good if you were a Trini and the unspoken motto seemed to be "We are black and beautiful and can achieve anything."

As the school year progressed, it was announced by our family Doctor that I would have to have an operation. One of my testicles had not descended and although I had no idea what this meant, apparently it was serious. "He should still be able to have children," said the Doctor "but the sooner we move on this the better."

It was decided that the operation should take place over the summer holidays, giving me proper time to recuperate. I was a bit afraid as an operation seemed a frightening event.

I finished the school year starring in Mrs. Kerr's class. She was truly a good teacher and although she acknowledged my fine performance, she was not unhappy to know that someone else would be teaching me in September.

One week after the school holidays had started, I was sent to the Queen Elizabeth clinic for my procedure. My father amazingly even for something as serious as this had refused to pay for it. "You are sending him to a private clinic. For what? What's wrong with a public hospital? They're free and you just looking to waste money."

"Don't you understand the care is better and more specialised at a clinic?"

He sucked his teeth: "Steuupps! You are wasting money unnecessarily."

"Well then, I will pay for the clinic and you pay for just the procedure."

Without hesitating, he responded "I don't have the money."

"You have millions of dollars in farmland. You are a lawyer. Can't you sell some land, take a loan or something?"

"No, I can't."

"But this is your son!"

"I don't have the money. What do you want me to do?"

My mother was on the verge of tears. "You do nothing for your children. I do it all. All!! How can you just stand there while I assume the burden for *our* children?"

My father always seemed to be out of cash when the topic of child support came up. The fact that he didn't work for half the year (he preferred the term "semi-retired") living off his father's efforts never seemed to bother him. Despite his alleged financial woes, there always seemed to be money for the horses every weekend; drinking with friends, cricket matches and boxing cards.

I entered the clinic with some apprehension. The Doctor and injections had always terrified me since I was a child, now I had to handle an actual operation.

I was put into a room with an older white gentleman. Occasionally, his wife would visit and together with my mother we would have a chat. Realizing, how terrified I was, my mother coaxed the staff to allow her to sleep with me at night to help calm me.

Two days later, the time was nigh. I was not allowed to eat or drink for 24 hours prior to the operation. As my mother and I waited during the final hour, I was practically in tears due to the fear.

"Mummy, I scared."

"It will be alright," she said, squeezing my hand. "You will be asleep and you won't feel anything. Then you will wake up and everything will be Ok."

"But I so frighten."

She continued to hold my hand, assuring me that it would be painless and I had nothing to worry about.

Later, a nurse came and gave me an injection. It practically paralyzed my left butt and leg.

Finally, two nurses came in and I was transferred to another bed and wheeled away. I was all alone now. No mother around. I looked at these strange adults and kept thinking of the operation to come. As I was wheeled into the operating theatre, I saw four individuals all wearing masks, two men and two women.

As they got ready, I saw my doctor pull out the biggest needle I had ever seen in my life. It looked triple the size of a regular injection needle.

Is a horse, they going to inject? I asked myself.

As I saw the needle, I immediately whimpered: "I want my mummy."

"No. Your mother can't come into the Operating Theatre," said the Doctor.

I looked at this big needle and could only *imagine* the pain to come.

The Doctor looked at me, "I want you to count backwards from 100 to one.

As I started the counting, the needle touched my leg. I may have got as far as 97.

The next thing I knew, I was awake in my room. My mother was there smiling. The wife of the old man next to me, ran over to my bed and gave me a kiss and a hug.

"Yuh with us boy! Yuh with us!"

I was quite relieved to know that the operation had indeed not been that big a deal.

I convalesced for three days and then it was back home. As I had stitches in my crotch area, walking was a bit of an ordeal. The nurses wheeled me to the front door and told my mother they were not allowed to go any further.

"But he can't walk," she explained.

"Doh worry with he. He could do it."

"But can't you see he is struggling?" she said as I held her arm and shuffled very slowly towards the car.

"We are not allowed to wheel anybody beyond the door. And he alright. Don't worry, he could walk."

I was shocked at their heartlessness. But I had no choice. My mother and I – very slowly – made our way to the car. As she drove home, every bump seemed to hurt.

I was given VIP treatment for the next two weeks, all meals were served in bed. As I had been through an ordeal, many of my favourite meals were cooked; thus, callaloo and macaroni pie was served three times a week.

Six weeks later, it was back to the Clinic to have my stitches taken out. My mother was told to come at 10 am but at eleven we were still waiting. Finally, the nurses took me to a room behind reception.

With my luck a young Indian girl, a nursing student was brought to me so she could have proper experience. She was obviously in need of it. As she ripped each stitch out of me, I screamed. There were twelve in total. I screamed and cried. All my mother could do was squeeze my hand. It was obvious to my eight-year-old mind that this girl did not know what she was doing. I could not understand why they were letting her continue.

By the tenth stitch, I had run out of tears. My tear glands were empty. I continued to scream but had no tears left. I did not think such a thing was possible but on that day I learnt that it was.

117

I would never forget the pain.

Finally, with two stitches left, an older black woman who had been instructing, took pity on me and finished the job. She obviously knew what she was doing and I barely felt a thing.

With my stitches gone, I now had full mobility. I enjoyed the final two weeks of the summer holidays running, playing and awaiting the new school year.

CHAPTER 15

Goodbye Betty

As a reward for my suffering during the summer holidays, my mother took us to the Santa Flora beach camp. This was a private community of bungalows set up by the oil company Texaco for its employees.

It was a green, beautiful area built near the ocean. Approximately 20 acres of bungalows, its own private primary school, a beautiful social area with a pool, bar, tennis courts and added rooms for social events.

Leila and I loved it. We had never been abroad and this was like Disney Land for us. There was a twenty-five-metre pool and a children's pool next to it.

We had first gone there with the Murrays in 1974. Leila was still in diapers. I would spend hours in the children's pool doing my own version of swimming, away from the adults and completely content.

As my mother was well known in the Petroleum industry, she had connections which allowed us to stay at one of the bungalows free of charge. She would sometimes invite friends to come with us and we would all have a great time.

While other kids at Morgan's enjoyed trips to Europe or Disney World in Florida, this was it for Leila and me. Every year we would beg my mother to visit Santa Flora. The week swimming in the pool would the highlight of our year. In hindsight, it may have seemed a simplistic existence to any listener but to us it was Shangri La.

We returned to the Gardens with the new school year just around the corner.

Going to school in the morning was usually an ordeal. Whilst most schools started at 8 am, Morgan's started at 7. There was of course the rush hour traffic that one had to bear with. My mother would get up at 5:00 to do her customary yoga. Betty would wake us up at 5:30, ensure that we were dressed and fed by 6:00. The idea was we would then leave and be at school by 7:00 for the latest. However, Leila and I would find it hard to get up. I had no problem waking up bright eyed and bushy tailed on the weekend. But getting up for school was another matter altogether. We would usually leave a little after 6:00 with my mother screaming at us to get in the car, then screaming in the traffic all the way to school with other commuters looking at her, shaking their head and laughing.

Leila and I would try to sink in our seats so the people in the other cars would not actually see us whilst the shouting continued.

As a single parent, my mother simply could not do it all alone. Betty was an essential part of our life. Most housekeepers had never lasted long due to my mother's difficult standards. However, Betty was the outstanding exception. She did her work well. My mother had given her permission to beat us if we misbehaved and Betty had no problem complying.

However, upon our arrival into the Gardens the previous year, Betty had made friends with another housekeeper, Alicia. She and Alicia would lime and on some occasions, take us to the nearby community centre to look at the singing and limbo dancing.

My mother believed it was because of Alicia, Betty started to develop some bad habits.

Sometimes Betty would give her a little bit of backchat but what really irked my mother was Betty using her leotards to practice yoga.

She would put on my mother's yellow leotards, take her aerobics exercise book (in those days exercise videos or You Tube had not yet arrived) and have her own workout in the living room.

When we mentioned to my mother that Betty was using her leotards, there was a terse discussion.

"You crazy! You using MY leotards to exercise in. I don't want you sweating up in my clothes!"

"But is just exercise."

"That is not the damn point! You don't exercise in my clothes. You gone off or what? Don't do it!"

Betty's response was to exercise with the leotards half on. The top half was pulled down to her waist exposing her bear breasted self, doing her yoga in the middle of our living room.

My mother had to admonish her once again and finally she resorted to exercising in her dress. I was confused as to why she didn't have any shorts.

The straw that broke the camel's back was her referring to us as 'coolie."

We had been told not to use the term servant to describe any domestic, rather, "maid," was more acceptable.

One afternoon with my mother still at work, a salesman came to the house. He asked to speak to the lady of the house.

"My mother's not home."

"Well then may I speak to any adult that is here."

Betty was relaxing in my room, reading a book. "Tell him to come back when you mother is home."

"The maid said to come back when my mother is home," I told him.

Betty heard me and was not pleased: "Sunil, why couldn't you just say, 'Betty said to come back later.' You had to call me the maid. Dat is the problem with allyuh coolie, you always like to talk down to other people."

I told my mother what had happened and she immediately approached Betty.

"That is how you speak about me and my family!"

"I never said coolie," replied Betty.

I knew she had and was curious as to why she was denying it.

"My children don't use language like that. If Sunny said you did, then you did. You pretend to be so religious and then you lie like that."

Betty's response was swift: "Mrs. Darsan, I think you better find somebody else to work for you. I am giving you my notice."

Although I had never appreciated the beatings. Betty had been with us for almost two years and had become like part of the family. It would be strange not having her around. Two weeks later she left. We never saw her again.

CHAPTER 16

Nine Years Old and a Timex

Another school year had passed. I was now in Class Four with Mrs. Holt. She was perhaps only second to Mrs. Bissessar when it came to licks.[8]

Sixty years old, she had been a teacher since the 1930s. She had retired a few years before but had been coaxed back by our Canadian Principal, Ms. Souness. Mrs. Holt was adamant that her priority was the care of her grandson. She was told that he could come to Morgan's and bypass the waiting list of one year. That was all Mrs. Holt needed to hear. Conservatively dressed and always outside with a dark pair of shades, one might ponder if she was blind were it not for the absence of a cane.

She was a great teacher and some of my best academic performances were in her class. However, her beatings were spontaneous and could be severe. Imagine the Overseer of a plantation walking past the slaves and lashing them as he saw fit. She would walk down the aisle and lash away for any minor offence, perhaps your sums were wrong or you were not sitting up straight enough. The only time I or Brian McCloud ever cried from blows was in her class – both times for the same reason. We were

---

[8] Licks: Caribbean definition of a beating or corporal punishment.

doing our work and the unexpected blow of the ruler against our back took us by surprise. There was no opportunity to move and deflect the blow.

I was in class with my best friend Vinood Singh. He and I had met the previous year in Mrs. Kerr's class. We had not known each other well prior to that as we had been in different classes. I quickly took a liking to him and after a few months announced that he was my best friend. There was a white Guyanese at the time, Jason Mason, who was always coming around Vinood and me and in my mind interfering with our friendship. We had a few arguments here and there but continued to be around each other as Vinood was the common denominator. Jason was put in a different class so I now had more personal time with Vinood.

Another person I quickly became friends with was Varun Singh, a very thin fellow who had been living in England. He arrived with a thick British accent which he lost by the fourth month of school. His parents were Trini and his father had been a practicing Doctor in London. We learnt well and played well.

My ninth birthday was approaching. Daddy came to visit about a week before. He had promised me that as I was older, I would now be the owner of a watch. "You're just a little boy. I don't want to buy you anything expensive in case you don't know how to treat a watch properly."

The teas immediately began to flow down my face.

"Don't cry. I'll make sure it's a good watch," he assured me.

It was indeed a good watch, a Timex. I was enamoured with it. And my father was correct. I was not quite ready for an expensive one. I would throw it up and down on the bed just to watch it bounce off the mattress. I felt rather grown up wearing my Timex in public.

I had asked my mother for a birthday party.

"What?? A bunch of children running around here making noise. I can't handle that."

She allowed me to invite a handful of friends. Vinood and Varun would come from school and with about six of the neighbours' kids that was eight. She then invited about 20 of hers.

I was quite happy to have my two friends from Morgan's. My mother and her friends had a quite a bit of fun dancing their waltzes around the living room.

Then it was time to cut the cake. In the Caribbean, we have a tradition. When it's your birthday you select someone of the opposite sex to cut the cake with you and then give each other a kiss. I grew up thinking this was an international tradition until I started travelling.

My mother told me to select a girl. The only options were the Watt sisters. I had no interest in them and refused saying I would cut the cake alone. My mother then had the audacity to suggest I cut the cake with Leila. I thought she had lost her mind. Who cuts their birthday cake with their sister?

I cut the cake alone. For some reason, my mother then thought it would be a good idea to then have Varun cut MY cake with Leila. I protested at the stupidity of it but was ignored. I then had to look at them be cheered on by everyone else while the cameras flashed away.

I protested, screamed and cried. My mother threatened to beat me. About 10 minutes later, I had gotten over it and continued playing with my friends.

I had received a handful of toys and clothes from everyone. Uncle Robin and his wife had given me a T shirt with what they thought was a number nine on it. It turned to actually be a six.

By 8:00 pm everyone had gone home and it was time to get ready for bed and school the next day.

Another Christmas came and went. We spent that day visiting our family in Grande. As my mother had a huge number of siblings, cousins and friends, this was an all-day experience.

In general, I did not like visiting Grande as it took up so much time and cut into my play time at the Gardens. However, Christmas Day was

125

an exception. Everyone else was busy doing their family thing so it was only natural that we visit ours. All of our relatives were gracious and plied us with food and drink. Trinidad food is great and even more wonderful at Christmas time.

My mother would spend most of her time with Aunty Indira, her younger sister by two years. I enjoyed my time there as she had three children and we all got along with well, Robin, Richard and Natasha. Robin was five years older than me, Richard one year older and Natasha one year younger. Leila and I enjoyed chatting with them, they had a TV and both boys loved comics just like myself. In the days before satellite TV and the internet if there was one way to keep me quiet, it was to give me a stack of comics. I would sit down in a corner and just read, the outside world completely closed off. If it were up to me, we would have spent all day there. However, inevitably we would have to visit other family members and of course Mummy's favourite aunt, Aunty Val.

Sometimes Mummy would bring Aunty Indira and the kids along as she visited her other siblings. Indira's husband, Tony would just relax at home or visit the neighbours.

I always thought that Aunty Indira had a bit of a serious look on her face. She didn't seem to smile much. Uncle Tony on the other hand was quite gregarious. I later found out one of the reasons for her serious outlook. It turned out that her husband was a bit of a scamp. Always spending his money on gambling. There were times the family did not have enough money for food or clothes for the children due to his lackadaisical work habits and constant Poker games. When she had married him, her father-in-law, well aware as to what kind of son he had, gave them a lot of land in her name. It was his way of ensuring that both they and his grandchildren would have something to look forward to in the future.

On one occasion she had given Uncle Tony four thousand dollars. "This is for Robin's future so that one day he can buy some land. Go put it in the bank." He managed to lose all the money at a poker game in less than four hours.

She was furious and heartbroken at the same time. My mother could only shake her head. "You know the kind of man he is and that is what you go do? How could you trust him with so much money?"

Aunty Indira could only shake her head and look at the floor.

CHAPTER 17

"The Greatest"

During the school year, we continued to stay at Aunty Thelma's in the afternoons. We were on our best behaviour when around her but it didn't make much difference, she always found a reason to beat us, especially me.

There were three babies there besides Leila and me. One had Downs Syndrome and then there were Candy and Alicia. Candy was a light skinned Indian with jet black hair. Her mother had wanted to name her Cinderella but she was afraid the kids at school would tease her. Alicia was black and every bit as cute as Candy.

Both Candy and Alicia were approximately two and a half years old. I had known them for almost as long, as they had come as very young babies in 1975. I had watched them slowly grow up, getting bigger and bigger. Now they could walk and even talk. We had noticed over the last year that Candy was extremely temperamental. She would cry for hours and hours. She seemed quite fussy and perturbed. No one could understand what the problem was, she had no fever nor gripe.

In June of 1977 we discovered the problem. Her parents came to Aunty Thelma's with her. They had just been to the Doctor's. The diagnosis was that she had leukemia and would be dead by the age of 12.

It was the only time I ever saw Aunty Thelma cry. She and Candy's mother sat next to each other weeping, wiping their eyes with tissues. Her father just stood in front the window, silently looking straight ahead.

Leila and I stood in a corner, quietly observing the proceedings. It was surreal. I understood what they were saying. But my young mind could not grasp that little Candy would one day die whilst still a child. The only comfort was that she would be given a blood transfusion every six months which would alleviate her discomfort.

A few weeks later, Mummy called me whilst I was at Aunty Thelma's. "Uncle Paul will be coming for you at 4:00. He's taking you to the cinema."

The only thing better than going to the cinema was to go on a school night.

Uncle Paul was not the kind of man to joke around with time. If he said he was going to be there at 4:00, he was and not a minute later.

We were off to see the movie *the Greatest*, the life story of Muhammad Ali, the Heavyweight boxing Champion of the World. I was always amazed at the antics of Ali and after that movie my boyhood would never be the same again.

The film depicted the life of a young Cassius Clay who later became Muhammad Ali. His victory over Sonny Liston for the World title, losing it out of the ring because he refused to be drafted for the Vietnam war and his amazing comeback over George Foreman to regain the Championship. His fight for civil rights and a mouth the likes no one had never heard before left me enamoured. This to me was the ultimate fighting warrior. That was it. I was going to grow up to be the Heavyweight Champion of the World!

As we made our way home, I recounted the movie, throwing punches in the air a la Ali. Uncle Paul just smiled. As we arrived in the driveway, my mother came out into the porch to meet us. I ran out of the car, straight past her and into my room.

I stood in front of the mirror and began throwing combinations. Mummy followed me into the room and looked at me. "Mummy!" I shouted, "I'm going to grow up to be the Heavyweight Champion of the world and I'm going to call myself the Greatest!!"

I continued to throw punches in front of the mirror, oblivious to everything else. She just smiled and left me to my newfound ambition.

"I have never seen a child so excited by a movie," said Uncle Paul with a smile and a shake of the head.

CHAPTER 18

Intelligent and Inquisitive

During the summer of '77 Leila and I became quite excited. My mother had announced that during the Christmas holidays with both of us older and Leila finally seven, we could visit our father on the holidays.

She had not wanted a young child to be in that bush without her and if I had gone by myself Leila would've been too hurt.

We spent the summer holidays playing and reading a lot of books as the Gardens had no TV reception. Daniel, the Watts, Leila and I would play, ride our bikes or simply find ways to amuse ourselves. My mother would buy a lot of books during the school year and put them in a box. As the summer holidays started, we would then have a supply to keep us occupied. That summer I became acquainted with the classics such as *Kidnapped, Robins Crusoe* and *Little Women*. They were supplemented by any amounts of comics I could cajole my mother to purchase for me: *Batman, Superman, Spider-Man, Plastic Man, Richie Rich* and *Big Lotta* amongst others.

Another aspect of that summer was Daniel and I constantly butting heads over our rivalry for the affections of Ana Manning. Ana was a beautiful blond, blue eyed girl who lived on the main road just outside our neighbourhood. Her father was a black Trini, who whilst working in

London in the late fifties had met her mother, a local white Brit. They lived with Ana and her older sister in the Blue Basin area.

I was enamoured with her blond hair, tanned white skin and blue eyes. A few months after meeting her, I announced to the kids and to her that she was my girlfriend but nothing official ever took place.

A few months after the "announcement," Lara Watt had her ninth birthday, she was just two months younger than me. She had a party and I was selected to cut the cake with her. Ana attended the party. The next day I was surprised to see her at Lara's house quite early. She had slept over, the Watts had made a trip to the supermarket, leaving her alone with their dad, Uncle Michael.

As he mowed the lawn, she invited me inside to see a huge tent that Lara and her sister had in her room. The tent was being used as a doll house. Ana and I entered, we started kissing and it felt good. We then decided that we would take off our clothes but not our underwear. As we kissed and I felt her soft, wet tongue against mine, I suddenly experienced a huge erection in my crotch area.

I was aghast. What the hell was this?

I tried to lie on it so she wouldn't notice. Poor innocent little nine-year-old, I had no idea that it was a perfectly normal reaction to being aroused and that obviously the operation had been a success.

Whilst we enjoyed our semi naked romance in the tent, Lara's father continued to mow the lawn, unaware to the goings on in his house.

Fast forward eighteen months later and this boldfaced Daniel Pereira, stepped up and said *he* was Ana's boyfriend. I was unamused at his temerity.

He was a nuisance to say the least. He would try to sit next to her or invite her into his house and not invite me. We would sometimes ask her to choose who she wished to be with. There were times she would choose one over the other. It was my first introduction to the whimsical ways of women and having to compete for their affection.

● ● ●

That September I started school once again feeling just a little bit older. I was now in Class V.

As we sat around looking at each other and getting reacquainted, in strode a tall, slim, black woman with a puffed out Afro and dark shades.

I had never truly realized how many white teachers we had or brown skinned ones until that moment. She simply stood out due to the colour of her skin and the size of her Afro. Years later, I would wonder if this was some kind of affirmative action on the part of Morgan's.

Her name was Diana O'Sullivan. Our first meeting was rather inauspicious. I was sort of stuck between my desk and chair. As the class stood up to greet her, I found myself pushing the desk forward and the chair backward to give myself space to rise.

Both desk and chair made a grating sound on the floor. She looked at me, "It's alright, we know you are here."

"Excuse me?"

"I said it's alright. We know you are here. You don't have to make so much noise."

As the weeks progressed, we got to know her and found out that although she could be serious, she was a good teacher who wasn't opposed to a good laugh with her students.

My hyper and talkative ways did not seem to faze her as it had done other teachers.

If in her opinion I had misbehaved too much, she would say to me with a very serious face, "Sunil, you will spend the break with me."

This was supposed to be a punishment. But it turned out great for me, she had wonderful lunches which she shared with me, rice, callaloo, macaroni pie and sweet bread.

"This is punishment?" I asked myself.

Later at a PTA meeting, she explained to my mother. "I want to crack up at some of the comments he makes. But I give him my serious face and inform him his breaks will be spent with me."

At that age I was what Trinis would describe as *lickrish*.[9] As my father had put it, "You don't eat to live. You live to eat." I would slyly get myself into trouble especially on Mondays and patiently wait for Ms. O'Sullivan to offer me part of her sumptuous lunch. She would chat to me about my family, hobbies and other matters of interest.

One day, the class laughed at me as I had once again been informed that I would be detained at break time.

"Allyuh so schupid!" I shouted. When allyuh outside playing, I does be inside with Ms. O'Sullivan eating Macaroni pie and callaloo!"

"Oh no Miss. That is not true, ent?"

"Yes, it is," she responded with a hint of a smile.

The students collectively frowned and gave me a *cut-eye*.[10]

As the months passed by, it was obvious that Ms. O'Sullivan had taken a great liking to me. Even if I was not in trouble, she would have a student fetch me to share her lunch with me, especially callaloo or roti.

I could never quite understand why she liked me so. I knew I was considered talkative and ill behaved.

My mother was also surprised that any teacher could overlook my behaviour.

"Don't you find him too talkative and hyperactive?" she asked.

"But of course! Of course he is! This is to be expected with a child as intelligent and inquisitive as he is."

My mother was left speechless. Her hobby seemed to be telling people stories about my bad behaviour. If any teacher complained, she would simply agree and then start complaining more than they did. I had often been praised for my academics by teachers but Ms. O'Sullivan had actually found a positive in my overly outgoing personality.

---

[9] Lickrish: gluttonous or greedy.
[10] Cut-eye: to give someone an angry or disapproving look.

CHAPTER 19

Anything but a Father

December quickly came and Leila and I had our long-anticipated visit to Caigual and Reading Hall.

We were saddened by our father's indifference to Neelam's harassment of us. However, he would find the time to chat with us, play games and take us out on his errands and for visits to friends. There was enough joy in these activities for there to be a temporary healing.

We left Caigual, anxious for another visit and missing Daddy immensely.

I would cry, telling my mother that I wanted to live with my father. She would patiently explain to me that as a young boy it was better to live with my mother. However, as a young adult I could decide for myself where I wanted to live.

In just a few years, she would make an acute U-Turn on that decision.

I enjoyed Ms. O'Sullivan's class. She was a good teacher who encouraged me. I didn't realize it but I was benefitting from exactly what my mother had hoped for in sending us to Morgan's, more individual attention from the teacher and a less rough and tough environment of a government school.

I was older now and considered a tough kid amongst my peers but I still couldn't handle Brian McCloud.

Despite my toughness and that of Brian's there were two people in my class that neither of us could outfight, Camila Charles and Alicia Martin. Yes, they were girls but they simply didn't fight like one.

Camila was a slim, pretty redhead with freckles. A nice girl who never bothered anyone. But if the odd boy harassed her, he was annihilated in seconds with a flurry of punches and that included Brian McCloud, which was impressive. One year, during a class Christmas party, Brian though it would be funny to put ice down the back of her dress. She ran after him, hit him two punches to the face, spun him around, punched his back four times and then poured ice down his back. He slinked off in tears.

No boy wanted to admit it but we were all wary of having a confrontation with her. However, as she was not a troublemaker and I never really bothered girls she and I got alone fine.

Alicia Martin was a stocky mulatto (referred to as red skin by the locals) girl. She was friendly and outgoing and like Camila, only fought if bothered. She was thick and tough like a pint-sized heavyweight boxer. On one occasion as a joke, she picked up me and another boy by our shirt collars and our feet were actually raised off the ground. If we had been unsure of her strength before, we were in doubt no longer.

As my school life flourished, my relationship with Leila suffered an inverse reaction. Due to my father's and her teasing and making me self-conscious of loving my sister, I was determined to make sure that never happened again.

I would not tolerate her in my presence and would shout or hit her if she took too long to go. I had never before raised my voice or hand to her.

Leila always found it more difficult to make friends in the neighbourhood as the girls were a few years older or younger than her.

One day as a number of us limed at the side of our house, Leanne got fed up with her.

"You're always saying stupid things. I hate you coming around me and I am sick of you." As she said this, she punched Leila four times on the arm.

Leila began to cry. I felt sorry for her but this would be a prime lesson for both her and my father to learn to never tease me about loving my sister as if it were a bad thing.

I laughed, "hit her again."

Leanne punched her a few more times in the arm. As Leila, cried, I laughed: "It good for you."

The maid hearing the commotion, ran around the house. "Come with me Leila." She looked at me and the kids disparagingly.

"Sunil, how could you do such a thing? You let people hit your sister and laugh about it?" she said later scolding me.

"I don't care about her," I shouted. "I don't like her and I don't want her around me!"

"But she is your sister."

"I DON'T CARE!!"

We had spent just one holiday with our father and his lack of intellect and parenting skills had left and irrevocable effect on our relationship.

I always felt sorry about that incident and the memory would plague me as an adult.

We had simply become victims of a father who was anything but a father.

CHAPTER 20

Breaking Biche

During the course of 1978, the demographics of the neighbourhood would change dramatically.

For almost three years, it had been the Watts, Daniel Pereira, myself and Leila as the principal children in the neighbourhood in terms of who to play with. The babies or the tots didn't count.

Martin Pinto and his sister Sarah arrived in January. Martin was three years older than me, big, fat and strongly built. Sarah was a year younger than her brother and quite pretty with her long, fair, brown hair. Martin was a very brown Chinese looking fellow, his sister was quite fair. As their mother was Chinese, I assumed that Sarah looked like her dad. I had to assume as their parents were divorced and his father was never seen visiting.

Martin was another person to interact with and he had video games at his house. It was a very basic version of tennis, with the sound "ping, ping," coming from the TV screen. This was the technology of the time and we enjoyed it.

Although I didn't realize it during my childhood, I was a bit portly. Not really fat but I had a stomach. I was uncoordinated in terms of sports and was quite slow. It was the norm for me during Sports Day at school to be in the last three, struggling with two other fat guys not to come last. To my credit I never did.

If I was a bit fat, I got even fatter after a visit to my father's estate. He believed in seeing his children eat. Leila ate like a bird and for some reason didn't seem to like meat. In later years she would become a vegan.

My mother now used every holiday to get rid of us. Understandably she needed a break from bringing up two children on her own. What she did not know is how we were treated. Sunita was allowed to harass us with impunity. I in particular, was slapped, bitten or hit sometimes even while I was sleeping, waking up to see Neelam giggling, standing over the bed.

It was amusing for her to see us harassed. But if I were to hit Sunita. She saw no mirth in it: "That is my child! Don't hit my child!!"

Sometimes she would find reasons to harass me on her own: standing in front of me while I tried to watch TV, putting her head over my shoulder while I read a book and reading the pages out aloud just to disturb me or standing behind me while I played cards and telling everyone what I had.

I could not understand how an adult could harass children like this. My father would laugh and do nothing. If I cursed at Neelam, I was instantly beaten. I usually needed a 24-hour recuperation period after one of his beatings. I understood that Neelam was a bitter, nasty woman but I could not understand how my father could condone such behaviour. We were his children. How could our Daddy who had been so kind at our house laugh while people teased and hurt us?

Just before the Easter holidays began, my mother decided that it was time I started doing serious preparation for the Common Entrance exam that I would be writing the following year. These exams also known as 11-plus determined what high school you would go to.

TT followed the British system of education. You wrote Eleven-Plus to go to high school and O Levels to get to form VI. You had two years of Form VI. These were basically the equivalent of the first two years of university. If you passed your A Levels in Form VI, you were then allowed to go to university.

These exams defined you as an individual. If you failed any of them, you were classified as a failure with a limited future. So, failing at an early stage such as Common Entrance could have a devastating effect on an entire family as they agonized over their child's future.

I was one year behind in school for the exam but a lot of children throughout the country were in this situation. My mother sent me for private lessons with Mr. Louis Moore. A renowned teacher at a government school on Maraval Rd.

We started in March. I remember my first day there. This school was called

Newton's and was famous for turning out first choice students.

You had four choices of high schools and if you couldn't get into any of them, you were assigned to a government school of lesser prestige. There were 80 students beginning their lessons at 4 pm. I arrived half an hour early and I could hear the sound of someone getting blows, the strap bouncing off their hand. I was already terrified.

The English was never a problem but being a year behind in Arithmetic did have an effect on me. I was never much good in that subject and being asked to do work I had not yet confronted just compounded the problem.

I would quiver as I saw student after student being beaten for getting their sums wrong. The class was really two classes separated by just a space. Each section holding forty students. On the right was his regular class from Newton's. On the left, were the non-Newton's students myself and other boys and girls from around the city. His regulars seemed quite eager to impress Mr. Moore. They would press their middle finger against their thumb and slap them with the index finger making a loud clicking sound. Forty students doing it simultaneously was quite loud. This was supposed to tell the teacher they were over-brimming with eagerness to give the answer.

I simply could not get used to the constant blows being given to students in our class and the others as well. You would try to do your work and hear the slapping of the leather strap as someone got beaten, wondering when you would be next.

Licks was occasionally given in Morgan's but this place was like some kind of Nazi Camp. I went home at night dreading the next day and having to face Mr. Moore. I would dive into my bed praying for the morning to never come.

During the summer holidays, we actually had to attend lessons three times a week. I couldn't believe that even during the school holidays I could not escape this man. Students were usually beaten with a piece of leather a foot and a half long and about three quarters of an inch wide. On one occasion as I gave in my homework on his desk. I saw the leather strap broken in half. He used a belt that day, the next day, the belt was broken lying on his desk. I felt sorry for the boys of Newton's and had a massive newfound appreciation for Morgan's.

Towards the end of the school summer holidays, the Carters left Waterfall Gardens and migrated to Canada. A few weeks before their departure the Lara family arrived. They had three kids, Shane, Anastasia and Solange. Shane was 13, Anastasia 12 and Solange 10.

With the departure of the Carters, the Douglas family took over their home. The Douglases had two sons, Richard and Gary. Gary was my age and Richard the same age as Shane. Their parents Peter and Jane were a good-looking couple. Peter, a local white, had been a top goalkeeper and 400 metre runner for Queen's Royal College (QRC). Jane was a beautiful, fit, red skin Barbadian woman. She had met Peter in Barbados during a tour by QRC. They had had a brief but torrid romance and somehow kept it going despite him getting a Track scholarship to Long Island University and she migrating to London with her family. Despite being the same age

141

as my mother, she was fit and lightning fast, capable of beating every teenager in the neighbourhood.

At this point the dynamics of the neighbourhood completely changed. The Douglas boys were athletic. They would invite me and the other kids in the neighbourhood to play. Now there were as much as six of us playing cricket or football. Anastasia was a tomboy and she would join in.

I had never played much football. The Douglases were skilled. I just ran around trying to kick the ball and was amazed at how easily Richard could glide by all of us. Martin never seemed to actually play a sport. He would just watch us or play videogames, cards or a boardgame.

The new school year started with a brand-new location. Morgan's had bought a prime piece of real estate in West Moorings, a very well to do neighbourhood. Unlike the previous building, this one was in pristine condition, made of solid concrete and actually had two yards, an inner one and a field at the back of the school.

There would be two class VIs, the Common Entrance one and the other that did not have to write the exams. Naturally, I was in the CE class. Mrs. Holt, my Class IV teacher was in charge of the other one and I thanked God I would not have to put up with her and her blows again.

Our homeroom teacher was a petite young white woman by the name of Jillian Witherspoon. With Shoulder length brown hair and a rather longish nose, she was well mannered and pretty.

Jason Mason, who I had sort of despised ever since Class 3, was sitting in the aisle next to me. My best friend Vinood was in the back of the class. Jason and I started talking to each other in class and then the conversations would continue during the breaks. By the end of the month, we were friends, always chatting and I no longer felt any animosity towards him.

Jason was one of the best artists in the school. He had drawing pad, where he would draw and colour a number of Superheroes, e.g., Superman, Spider-Man, the Human Torch and many others. I admired his skill. I had none and my drawing would make him laugh as I would draw too many muscles. He would show me the basics, how to make the V shape of the chest and stomach, basic biceps, triceps and arms and even muscles for the stomach. All of a sudden, my drawings looked less ridiculous.

He informed us that he would be leaving Trinidad in December as his family would be moving to New York. As the months passed by, we played a lot and became even closer.

One of our classmates had a birthday part in early December. About fifteen of us, sat on the floor of his living room, watching a Davy Crockett film from a projector. We ate chips and hot dogs, drank a lot of Coke and had a great time.

When Jason's mother came to pick him up. I walked downstairs with him, realizing my friend, perhaps my best friend was leaving and I would probably never see him again. As the car drove off, he stuck his head out and shouted, "Goodbye Sunil!!!" We stared at each other until they turned a corner.

I never saw him again.

This was a serious school year, we would be writing CE in about seven months and our collective futures were on the line. Lessons with Mr. Moore were in full swing. I continued to be in fear and felt ridiculed as students would laugh at me because of my poor Math skills.

During that year I had begun to have nightmares. I would see sums in front of me. They were easy but they kept piling up. One problem would become two, four, five. I would become overwhelmed. "2, 12, 22, 124!!! I can't do it!! I can't do it!!" My mother would run into the room and wake me up.

"I can't do it Mummy!! I can't. It's too much!! Ninety-six, 2 228, 165, 5x6, 12x9, 125x8!!!"

"It's Ok. It's just a nightmare. It's alright."

She would take me to her room. I would hug her tightly, screaming numbers for an hour. "I love you Mummy!! I love you!!"

"It's alright Sunny. I love you too."

By early October, enough was enough. I just couldn't handle the stress of Mr. Moore and his lessons. I would get up every morning with dread, knowing that after school, I would have to face him. I thus, had my first experience with *breaking biche*[11].

I had never done this before. But I simply didn't know what else to do. Instead of walking towards Maraval Rd., I would make a right turn about a hundred metres after Aunty Thelma's street. I would slowly make a U-turn and go into a completely opposite direction. The first time, I had no idea where I was going. I stopped just outside a cemetery about two hundred metres from the Trinidad Electricity company. At first, I would sit under a huge tree on the pavement and just watch the people and cars. However, one day, knowing I had a few hours to kill, I decided to take a walk in the cemetery. I was fascinated watching the tombstones of people who had died in the early 1900s or even the nineteenth century. I wondered who they were, what their life had been like, had they had any children? I thought of my own life, how I was still in the early stages and these people had lived all of theirs and moved on and now there I was standing above their skeleton.

I relaxed by the cemetery for the next three months. However, during the Christmas holidays, Mr. Moore decided to continue the lessons. My mother dropped me off directly in front of the school and I had no choice but to enter. I found myself wondering how I was going to dodge him and what in the world would happen to me if I couldn't?

I tried to sit as far in the back as I could and in the middle of the bench, hoping to get lost in the crowd.

"For those of you who were not here last week, I have some handouts."

Knowing I had to face the music sooner or later, I decided to grab the bull by the horns. I got up and walked towards him along with a few others. He looked at me, eyes wide open.

---

[11] *To break biche* – to miss school without a legitimate reason.

"Darsan!!??"

"Sir, I wasn't here last week."

"Boy! I haven't seen you for *three months*!!"

"Three months Sir?"

The class burst out in a guffaw of laughter.

I continued to watch him with passive innocence.

"Tell your mother I want to speak with her when she comes to pick you up."

"Yes Sir."

Uncle Paul was the one who came to pick me up. He and Mr. Moore had actually known each other in the past having socialized in the same circles.

"Paul!! I haven't seen this boy for three months. Please tell his mother. I don't know what is going on."

Uncle Paul just looked at me.

As we drove away in the car, he looked at me, "Ok, tell me what happened."

I explained that I had not gone for three months. And with additional probing from him. I explained what I had actually done and how I had spent my time.

My mother was informed when we got home. She looked at me in a resigned manner, "Go to your room."

An hour later, she called me into the living room. I was firstly informed that there would be no TV for two weeks nor was I allowed to go out and play during that time. In addition, I would be checked on every day after lessons to ensure I had attended and this would be verified with Mr. Moore.

"But I don't like going to him for lessons. He beats."

"I have told him not to beat you. Don't worry."

Despite her assurances, I was still petrified of the man. I simply never felt at ease in his classes.

CHAPTER 21

A More Tolerable Caigual and Common Entrance

We began 1979 with anticipation. Common Entrance was at hand and the future of my Secondary education would be determined in the next few months.

I continued to go to Mr. Moore's classes, starring in English but having only moderate success in Arithmetic.

My social life in the Gardens was flourishing. With the influx of a variety of families, there were now around twelve kids to play with. The Douglas brothers were at the backbone of a lot of the activities. They were always eager to play a sport and with a handful of other boys, the street in front of our house became the place to do it. There was actually a huge lot of bush exactly opposite our house with grass about three feet high. One day the neighbours became fed up and with the kids about ten of us using cutlasses chopped it away. Amazingly we now had about 1200 square feet of land to plan on. That grass would never grow high again as we beat it down constantly playing football. Cricket was reserved for the firmer surface of the road.

On the day of the CE exam, I was up bright and early. I arrived at a school called Mucurapo Jr. Secondary, a lightly regarded high school in terms of academics. And with about a thousand other students began the exam. I will never understand why but being a bit mentally exhausted as I began the final part, I simply chose whatever option I felt like (as it was a multiple-choice exam). I finished before everyone else and the Examiner looked at me curiously as to how I could have finished so soon.

A few months later the school year was finished and the summer holidays began. Thirty days later, the results were printed in the newspaper. I did not get any of my four choices but instead Woodbrook Secondary, considered a good institution outside of the regular four choices. I wondered what could've been had I not messed about in the final section. I did not tell my parents as I knew they would get angry with me. Years later when I reflected on how hard my mother had worked to provide for us with no help from my father, I simply was too ashamed to tell her. I kept it to myself and simply marvelled at my foolishness.

In Trinidad we have no summer, jut the Sunny and Rainy Season. I am guessing because my school had a strong North American influence, we used that term for the July-August holidays.

Usually about a month or so into the summer holidays my mother did the customary getting rid of us AKA "sending them to their father." However, we were informed that in July, we would have a holiday in Tobago for a week. Leila and I were over the moon. We had never travelled on a plane before and after hearing constant stories from the other kids at Morgan's, NOW, this was our chance to actually travel. My imagination ran wild with what the experience would be like being in the air.

A few weeks later we were on the plane. Mummy made sure that both Leila and I got window seats so we could maximize the experience. They passed out donuts and coke. When they offered seconds I refused as I had been warned for years by my mother about my greedy ways and how to properly behave in public. However, knowing her son, she turned around and assured me it was ok to have a second one.

Leila and I loved Tobago. We stayed at an apartment at the Tobago Resort. We had our own kitchen and there was a pool for the guests. Mrs. Pineiro's older daughter, Celia, joined us. We had a great time, visiting the beach and Nylon Pool, a shallow area in the middle of the sea. The glass bottom boats were amazing, allowing you to see the sea life swimming under the ocean's surface. Everything was going great until Celia introduced us to a parent from the little primary school she ran from home. The woman, Janice, was a local white woman with two kids, Dannie about two years old and Jane, the same age as Leila.

Jane had a crush on me and followed me everywhere. Her mother thought I was too loud and I made it clear to her, "It's none of your business how loud I am."

She then decided I was also rude and told Jane to stay away from me. Jane ignored her. Janice then decided to tag along everywhere we went. She actually spent a night with us at the hotel. We were watching a ghost movie. She decided she didn't want her children to watch such a show and asked my mother to turn it off.

I was aghast. "So what the hell I supposed to do now! She don't want her children to watch it so I have to not watch it too!"

In my mind I was thinking, Take yuh damn children and leave!

Nevertheless, my mother complied with Janice and there was no TV for the next hour.

The next night was a big night in Tobago, local boy Claude Noel, a boxer, was challenging for the World Lightweight Title. Fighting against a Venezuelan for the title in Puerto Rico, all of TT tuned in. It was entertaining until he got knocked out in the thirteenth round.

After a week in Tobago it was off to our father's. Leila and I had no interest anymore in spending more than two weeks watching thick green bush, chicken shit in the yard and sometimes on the porch, no TV and putting up with the harassment of Neelam, Sunita and my father, being beaten if I spoke rudely to defend myself and constantly allowing Sunita to hit me without any punishment. I would occasionally have enough and curse out at Neelam or hit Sunita but I would be beaten thoroughly by my father.

We were picked up at Aunty Indira's house. With him was a young Indian fellow, he kept looking at me with a pleasant smile.

"This is Ryan," explained my father.

"So, I hear you fail the Common Entrance. Well that doesn't surprise me because I know you are stupid."

This would have been a horrible thing for any parent to say to a child but at this point I was getting quite used to Vijay Darsan and his idiocy.

I explained that I was actually one class behind and therefore was not quite ready for the exam.

"Yeah, but I know you schupid so it doh matter," he continued with a grin.

Ryan was a handsome, slender fellow with medium length black hair and a moustache. He was from Guyana and was a guest at Daddy's house. He kept looking at me with a fond smile and I took a liking to him right away.

He was Vinaya's cousin from Georgetown. His father was Aunty Vashti's brother. He had come to T&T to live. And whilst he was looking for a house and a job, my father would put him up.

He was 21 and a business graduate from Seneca College, Toronto. His father ran a very successful bakery in Georgetown. It was assumed that Ryan the eldest of three children would help manage the family business. His parents had been divorced about five years earlier. His father had picked up with a young, pretty, prostitute in Georgetown and eventually left his wife, marrying the woman and settling down with her. Ryan's mother decided that with the Guyanese economy in a free fall, the family would move to Trinidad. He considered it his duty to help his mother settle in as his two younger siblings were still in school.

My days in Caigual were now a little less boring. Ryan would chat with me about his life in Guyana and Canada even about girls. Late at night, he would play cards with the family or we would just talk the night away. It was amazing how this one extra person could make a difference in a place that had become some sort of glorified prison for Leila and me.

We still had to put up with Neelam's teasing and of course Sunita getting away with harassing me. Because I was less submissive than Leila, Neelam enjoyed trying to get a reaction out of me. If she saw Leila look sad or cry, it was enough for her. As usual my father laughed and did nothing. I could not understand how any woman could be so classless and stupid with children. It was as if she were a stupid child herself.

Due to Ryan's presence, the month in Caigual went along more quickly and pleasantly than normal. My father would usually take me out with him and as an added bonus, he, his friends, Ryan and I would go to the races every Saturday. We were even able to cajole him to spend some money and take the family to the cinema.

On one occasion, we went to a boxing card at Sparrow's Hideaway in Petite Valley, just a few minutes' drive away from where we lived in Diego Martin. The main event was TT's Eddie Marcelle vs Mark Harris of Guyana. Marcelle was a top ten contender and looking for a crack at the Commonwealth Crown. He easily beat Harris and everyone walked out excitedly discussing his chances for the Commonwealth Title.

Thanks to Ryan, Caigual was tolerable. But I was happy at the end of August to be back in civilization: electricity, friends, kids to play with and no more bush and mosquitoes.

CHAPTER 22

No More of Aunty Thelma!

September of 1979 marked an important moment in my adolescence. I was on the verge of my twelfth birthday. Due to the increased activities in the neighbourhood, I was no longer the pudgy kid of years gone by.

Constant eating and sports had left me naturally broad shouldered and well-muscled. I was bigger than most boys my age and they were not eager to start a fight with me.

However, as a young boy growing up, there are always older boys and there will always be a few stupid ones who want to push you around.

Within the next twelve months, I would have massive altercations with Richard, big, fat, Martin and the Lee Sing brothers.

Richard would occasionally want to bully the younger boys as he did his brother. It would be something mild like pushing them into a pool or throwing the odd stone at them. But if you retaliated, he would want to fight or get angry. I guess in his mind you should take it but not have the gall to retaliate. He was careful however, never to exhibit this ignorance with the few boys bigger than him.

David Spade lived just outside of the neighbourhood. He was the same age as Richard and they were in the same year at QRC. Although

David was a naturally muscled individual, he was mild mannered, respectful and never tried to push anyone around.

On one Saturday in early October, David and his older brother Dean, decided we would go to Carenage for a swim along with Richard and Gary.

I felt cool, like an adult. We were making a lime on our own and not needing a parent to drive us. We arrived at the beach and were having a great time until Richard decided to be Richard.

He picked up some sand from the ocean floor and threw it at me. I decided to do the same. Apparently, it was ok for him to do it to others but not vice versa. He waited until I had turned around slapped me twice across the back of the head. As I turned to confront him, he then threw the muddy sand into my face. Some of it got into my eyes and I was temporarily blinded.

I was prone to a temper in my youth but I needed someone to push me for it to emerge. And I had been pushed.

I ran after him but David kept holding me back. I picked up what few stones I could find but he managed to stay out of range. I kept trying to get around David but he was big and strong and managed to hold me back. The more he withheld me, the angrier I got.

"I am going to fuck yuh mudda cunt up!! You fucking bitch, you want to hit me!! I will FUCK your ass up!!"

Dean had had enough and decided it was time to leave. They put Richard in the front seat and David in the back with me to restrain me. After about 10 minutes of me continuously trying to get to the front seat and cursing my head off, Dean decided he couldn't drive like that and told David to put me out.

It was at least seven miles to home. I was too angry to care and I started to walk.

Approximately half an hour later and two miles into my journey, all of a sudden, Mummy and Uncle Paul pulled up alongside me in his car.

"Get in," said Uncle Paul quietly.

"So what happened?" asked my mother.

I explained the situation. Amazingly, neither of them had much to say about it or scolded me.

I went home and as I exited the car, the neighbours just stared at me, having already been told about what had transpired.

Richard and I did not speak for about two weeks. And I made it plain to his brother, "If he tries any shit with me, I will FUCK him up!"

About two weeks later, we were all in a group. Richard mentioned he had some new Superman comics.

"Really," I said looking at him.

"Yeah, you want to see them?"

"Sure."

We went over to his house and just like that the feud was over.

Within two weeks I would have my final altercation with the tyrannical Aunty Thelma. For years I had been in fear of her, being beaten for trivial matters. For some reason, no amount of complaints to my mother made a difference. I couldn't figure out if she was intimidated by her or just so desperate for a babysitter that she allowed the beatings to happen.

The year before I had been playing with a boy at her brother's house behind hers. He was about three years older than me and apparently delivered newspapers to their home. We played with some toys and had some fun, something I didn't have a lot of around Aunty Thelma. Later that afternoon at Thelma's, she called me to the back of the house. To my surprise, my mother grabbed me to hold me down and Thelma raised a belt to beat me. I immediately began screaming, asking what I had done wrong.

They explained that some ornaments were missing from her brother's house and the paperboy and I had stolen it. After a full minute of begging and assuring them that I had done no such thing and didn't know what they were talking about, they relented. I expected that kind of behaviour from Aunty Thelma but was confused as to how my mother could be so stupid just to believe what others had said about me without at least speaking to me.

In 1979 I was at my wit's end as to how to avoid this woman's wrath. Anything could be considered worthy of a beating and the wrong response would be construed as rudeness. I decided to just sit in a corner and be quiet. If spoken to, I would respond in a quiet, passive manner. I would thus, give her minimum reason to have a problem with me. After a few months, amazingly, she complained to my mother that I was too quiet. She would be the only person during my childhood to make that complaint. It seemed I could not do anything quite right in her eyes.

Matters came to a head in late September of 1979. I was sitting on the front steps when she came out in her usual abrasive manner.

"Boy, don't walk throughout my house in you dirty shoes. Look at my blasted floor."

I looked and the floor was indeed dirty. However, I knew that amount of dirt was not from my shoes.

"I didn't do that."

"Don't tell me you didn't do it. Look at the blasted floor. Take off your shoes. And don't be rude."

I snapped.

"I told you I didn't walk through the house in no dirty shoes!!" literally bawling at her.

She jumped, perhaps realizing that physically, I could no longer be pushed around.

"Sunny, do not shout at me like that!"

"YOU don't shout at me like that! You always shouting and getting on for no reason!"

With that, I walked out of the front gate. She came out onto the street. "Get back here!"

"Hull yuh ass!! You always want to beat people for no reason. Hull yuh ass!"

Some of the neighbours stood on the pavement looking on curiously.

To the casual observer, I had overreacted. But after years of being bullied and abused. I had had enough. I no longer allowed my mother to beat me and I had had enough of constantly being in fear of this old woman.

A year before the same thing had happened. My mother had made me apologise. However, on this occasion, I would have none of it. "I am not going back. I am fed up of her always wanting to shout at me or beat me. Hull she ass!!"

Realizing she could not force me to return, she simply gave me money for taxi fare to go home in the afternoons. I would take the taxi to the last stop and walk the last mile and a half home.

A week later she told my mother, "It's ok. Bring him back. I doing it for you because I know you need help with the children."

"Hulls she ass! I responded. "She want to help you? She want your damn money!"

The Aunty Thelma era was over.

CHAPTER 23

Handling the Bullies

I started my final year in Morgan's on September 7. I did feel a bit special. After all those years of having older kids around, now WE were the older kids and of course school prefects.

Mrs. Skeene my Arithmetic teacher had a serious appearance and was not averse to beating. However, she seemed for some reason to have a soft spot for me. She had been my teacher in Class VI. Although sometimes stern, she could have a light side as well and would even joke around with me. I assumed I had misjudged her but she always seemed to have a special liking for me. I couldn't figure out why as most teachers seemed to quickly get fed up with my behaviour.

She was now with us again in Class 7 but we had a new English teacher, Mrs. Scott who had replaced Mrs. Root.

Mrs. Root was not an easy teacher to replace. She was magnificent in reading books and you swore you were actually there in the story. Our favourite was *the Black* about an Arabian racehorse and a young American boy.

In time, Mrs. Scott would get fed up with me like so many others before her. On the other hand, Mrs. Skeene's fondness for me never waned.

However, I soon discovered that the key to surviving a class with Mrs. Skeene was to do her homework. She didn't joke about such matters and if it was not done, that was an automatic 10 blows on the hand with a ruler. She was an equal opportunity beater and the girls got the same amounts of blows as the boys. Not wanting to be beaten, I always made sure her homework was done. I never could understand why my classmates knowing the consequences would frequently not do theirs.

As the first term progressed life was good except for one glitch, Mrs. Scott simply could not handle my mouth and somewhat hyper ways. She decided she had had enough and made it clear to the principal that if I did not leave the class, she would simply leave the school. Mrs. Skeene on the other hand, explained that I was absolutely no problem for her. I didn't know it but I was on the verge of expulsion. Mrs. Skeene suggested that as Mrs. Scott was my homeroom teacher why not move me over to the other Class 7 next door, her class. Mrs. Scott would still teach me English but see much less of me.

The problem was somewhat reduced, however, Mrs. Scott still had the occasional anxious moment with me.

One problem about growing up is that there will always be a few older boys who like pushing you around simply because it's easy to do so. As someone with a strong spirit, I would do my best to fight back. In addition to Richard Douglas, there was Martin Pinto.

Martin had been reasonably friendly with me when he first came to the neighbourhood but in the previous year with a few older boys around he paid less attention to me. I was fine with that but what I could not tolerate was if we had a disagreement, he would assume it was ok to slap me behind the head or throw a stone at me.

It was difficult to fight back, he was about four inches taller than me and outweighed me by about 60 pound. I was about 5'2", 120 lbs, not small for a 12-year-old but simply not big enough to handle this bullying pig.

One day as I flew a homemade kite in front of Richard's house, Martin began laughing at how crude it was.

"Look at that shit kite! Who make it, your mother?

"Nah. Your mudda make it last night after I leave she bed."

Everyone began to laugh.

He walked over, threw me to the ground and ran off with my kite throwing it in a drain.

Furious, I knew he had a book about fishes in Richard's porch. I ran over to it and started ripping pages out of it.

"Laugh now, yuh fat fuck!!"

He may not have found it funny but the other boys just chuckled and looked at him.

He walked over and with his left hand twisted my shirt. With his right he picked up some dirt from under a plant and started putting it on my head and inside my shirt. I became furious. I did my best to attack him, screaming, I surged forward and tried to hit him. He just laughed and put out his big, meaty, left hand against my head and kept me away. I did my best, screaming in rage and trying to reach at him but to no avail.

Aunty Jane heard me screaming, ran outside and immediately parted us. She took me inside and gave me some sorrel to drink, all the time saying, "Calm down, Sunny, drink…drink, just calm down." Sorrel never tasted so good.

She then went outside, "Martin, come here! What the hell you doing with Sunny?"

Martin explained what had happened.

"And why did he need to rip up your magazine?"

Once she had gotten both our versions, she looked at him, "But who are you to mash up his kite?"

"But he talked about meh mudda."

"But nobody attacked you or touched you! How is it you don't harass the other boys in the neighbourhood like that. Who are you to put your hands on people or destroy their property!"

Her eyes narrowed and her Bajan accent became more pronounced, "If you ever try that shit with my children, I would hit you a good lash in yuh ass!"

"Yes Aunty Jane."

The other boys just looked on. I had calmed down at this point and walked home.

A week later, some of the boys came over to my house. As he walked in with them, I said, "Get out! I don't want you in this house!"

He looked at me and laughed, they had entered through the kitchen door so he picked up a pot from the stove and said, "Why don't we see what we can mash up in this house."

I grabbed it from him and shouted, "Get out! Yuh fat fuck!!"

The all laughed and followed him out of the house. I walked to the street with them but Martin turned to me and said, "Go somewhere else."

"Fuck you! This is the road."

He slapped me across the head. I was furious but knowing that there was no way I could handle him, I ran inside the house and grabbed a meat knife. My mother who had just entered the kitchen grabbed my hand, realizing something was wrong. We wrestled with the knife for about half a minute.

"What's wrong?"

Once I had explained, she walked outside and confronted Martin. Aunty Jane also happened to be passing by.

They both spoke to him. He explained that he was only joking with the pot.

"Does my son go into your home and make such jokes?" asked my mother, giving him a quizzical look.

"Well, it was just a joke."

"How come you don't make those jokes with other people in their home?" countered Aunty Jane.

"You know who to play the ass with. You don't do this shit with the older boys but it's easy to 'joke' with someone half your size. You want to come and make that kind of joke in my house Martin?"

"No Aunty Jane," he said apologetically.

And with that everyone dispersed and went on their way.

CHAPTER 24

A Hypocrite and a Disappointment

As Christmas approached, we were once again sent off to our father's. It was now a nightmarish experience for both Cintra and me.

I in particular, was fed up with the way both Neelam and Sunita constantly harassed us with my father's smiling approval. I was 12 years old and I no longer loved my father.

He was a hypocrite and a disappointment to two children who had adored him.

He was content to laze around, sell his father's land to augment his social life and gambling and would make the occasional appearance in court.

The beautiful manor like house was now in great disrepair, with every visit we would see more and more holes in the floor, more rotten wood. A house that had once been the marvel of all of Sangre Grande was now a rotting, crumbling, mess.

These visits were a sufferance that we just did our best to get through.

Ryan was no longer there. His mother and two younger siblings had come over from Guyana and they now lived in Sangre Grande.

Although I missed his company, there was a bonus in him living in the town. I could spend time at their house and of course they had a TV and electricity.

Despite having a fine home to live in, his mother had decided to come to TT to look for a better way of life as Guyana's economy was crumbling under their dictator, President Forbes Burnham.

Aunty Farina, and her two other children, Gary and Zara were inviting and friendly to me right away. I enjoyed liming with Gary and playing cricket with him and the other neighbours. I would spend half the holiday with them, enjoying the social atmosphere and of course access to a TV.

My father didn't mind as it meant less complaining and fighting amongst the children in his own house.

The previous summer, I had been saved by Aunty Shanti. Aware of Neelam's pettiness towards us and my father's nonchalance, she was tired of seeing me harassed. She offered to take me to her home in Tunapuna for a few days. I was happy to get out of the bush and be anywhere with electricity.

She had a colour TV and would take us out from time to time. As a teacher she was on holidays herself and we would watch TV late into the night. There was a great miniseries on called Roots – the true story of an African slave brought to the USA and his descendants. The crowning moment was when she took us to the cinema to see *International Velvet*, starring Tatum O'Neal, Christopher Plummer and Anthony Hopkins.

• • •

At the time, I had met her tennis instructor, Keith Singh, the former Junior Champion of Trinidad and ranked number two in the country. At 22, he was eight years younger than her and to my surprise, they were married a few months later. She was now busy with married life and although I did not see her on that visit, I now had Ryan's family to spend time with.

After spending a few days with them, my father told me I had to return to Caigual.

They had not seen me for a few days and as I ate at the huge kitchen table by the window, he and Cintra sat with me.

He started his shit as usual but this time it was directed at Leila, "Finally, my favourite child is home. East son, eat. My favourite child."

He glanced at Leila with a sly smile, as her face became sad, he continued to repeat himself, the more he spoke, the sadder she looked, eventually, the tears began to roll down her face. Seeing her cry, he laughed, "Don't worry, he's eating scraps from last night," and walked off. It took her a while to compose herself and stop crying.

Despite our differences, my heart broke for her. The site of her face slowly crumbling until it dissolved into tears would stay with me for the rest of my life.

I would never be able to understand how any man could do that to his child.

Things would only get worse.

CHAPTER 25

"The Ganges River" and the Lee Sing Family

Nineteen eighty was the dawn of a new decade. I was a few months away from my teens and entering secondary school. The last stages of my childhood were being left behind and other than having to wear short pants to go to school, I felt like a young man.

The girls were getting bigger as well, extremely noticeable were Anastasia and Judy, well formed, nice legs and abundant cleavage. Yes, the other girls were attractive as well but as their breasts were far from well formed, I paid them scant attention.

Anastasia and Judy were contrasting individuals. Ana as she was called had a naturally tanned complexion, shoulder length, slightly wavy brown hair, piercing brown eyes and was quite pretty. She loved to play football and cricket and actually had a bit of skill in both sports. She was as tough as she was pretty and could handle herself in a fight with any boy. She was indeed a tomboy.

Judy, like Anastasia was medium height and attractive but that was where the comparison ended. She didn't really play sports and had an air about her when she spoke as if she thought she was already an adult. Her father and younger sister were both Canadians. And we had to constantly hear how Canada was better than TT. It was common for the girls at the time to walk around in very short shorts. However, hers always seemed to be a more vulgar than the others. It was compounded by her sitting on her wall, legs cocked up in front of her, watching us play cricket on the street. Ample leg, thigh and partial butt was advertised to us with Richard in particular seemingly distracted. When bowling the ball, he would pause just before delivery, glance at her and then deliver. She had had a haughty way of speaking to the other kids which sort of alienated her from many with the exception of some horny boys. One day as she posed on the wall watching us play cricket, one of the boys hit the ball in her direction. She had no time to jump off the wall and just held her head grimacing in anticipation of the impact. The ball seemed to get stuck deep between her thighs and just disappeared.

Me in my usual mouthy manner shouted, "Oh guuud, like that ball disappear in the Ganges River!"

After that day, many a boy in the neighbourhood would cheekily refer to her as (the) Ganges behind her back. I was the only one who would sometimes say it to her face.

In late '79, I had an immensely athletic look due to constant sport with the boys in the neighbourhood. I still ate like a horse but burnt it off just as quickly, leaving me broad shouldered and much bigger than those of my age. With a full moustache, no one thought I was in primarily school and most people assumed I was 16 or 17.

I may have had some size but there will always be older, bigger boys. Those who are willing to throw their weight around with the smaller ones.

I had had my altercations with Richard and Martin but there were more to come.

The Lee Sing family had moved in up the road in early 1980. They were half black and half Chinese. Their father, a Chinese immigrant, had died some years earlier. Their mother was a fair skinned black woman with soft brown hair and a slight beard. The boys in the neighbourhood could never understand why she didn't attempt to shave.

The three boys were Chao, Apo and Yip Lee. Chao was a relatively cool fellow about 23. He seemed to be some kind of mechanic and there was usually a car or two under repair in front of their house. Apo was around 16 and younger by two years was Yip Lee. They had a sister, we guessed was around 15. She rarely left the house and at times you might see her in the porch. My mother always thought the house looked scruffy, with the grass uncut and old cars parked in front. She didn't come out and say it but intimated that they seemed to be of a lower class.

I never had a problem with Chao, he was down to earth and unlike some bigger boys never tried to force his personality or bully the younger ones. Whenever Richard got too mouthy or would try to cheat and not take his out in cricket, Chao would put him in his place. Chao was much bigger than he was so he never dared challenge him.

His two younger brothers, however, were wild and crude. They would tell us that their father had been trained by Shaolin Monks in China before coming to Trinidad. Obvious nonsense but to youngsters, a believable story.

In those days it was normal for people to make cassettes, this could be done by taping off the radio or actual records. Apo offered to make a cassette for me. Without asking my mother's permission, I took a blank cassette from her room. I figured it was for a good cause and the music would be enjoyed by the family. He listened and wrote down a list of the songs I wanted, including songs from groups such as the Bee Gees, the *Grease* soundtrack with John Travolta and Olivia Newton John as well as Dian Ross amongst others.

A week later, I asked him for the cassette only for him to put me off. Two weeks became a month, then six weeks. Finally, he would just dismiss me and say, "I don't know."

Realizing he had never had any intentions of making a cassette, I asked him back for my cassette. "I am not giving it to you. What can you do about it?"

As he was bigger, I just shouted at him telling him what a thief he was. He shrugged it off and walked away. From that day on, I made sure that he never entered our house again. Perhaps I also suffered from not having an older male in the house like most of the kids did or he surely would have been dealt with.

An example of how to have handled them was Mr. Pouchette, who lived at the very end of the road, two houses away from the Lee Sings. The Pouchette children, Michael and Silvia had gone to school with us. They had stopped around 1975, the year of their parents' divorce. But for the next two years, Leila and I would continue to see them when they visited their father until they eventually left for New York with their mother in 1977. I would always say hello to Mr. Pouchette as I knew his children.

His driveway was very long and extended all the way to the end of the road two houses away from the Lee Sing family. The driveway to his house commenced obliquely opposite the Lee Sing's. He seemed to be having a regular problem with them as they would move his dustbin. One day he was arguing with them about the problem and they were brushing him off while the neighbours looked on.

"You young and fresh," he said sternly.

"Well you old and stale," responded Apo.

"If you and your brothers think yuh bad, I could bring some boys and straighten yuh out!"

The argument went to and fro but at no point did Apo try to play Bad John for Mr. Pouchette because he was a full-grown man.

CHAPTER 26

Shit in the Water Tank

The commencement of 1980 meant that life would become a bit more intense for all students doing their Common Entrance Exams that would dictate who would get into the best high schools.

The exams would be in mid-June but all students were being drilled at school and those who could afford it would take private lessons.

I was taught by a retired schoolteacher who lived not far from the Queen's Park Savannah in POS. She really just gave me exercises to do and then corrected them and showed me my mistakes. She had about seven children of various ages. The work was no different from what I did in Morgan's and therefore, was not that stressful. No one beat or threatened me so really, I had no issue with her.

With the Easter Holidays in March, it was a chance for a small respite from all the schoolwork. However, life would not be a bowl of cherries for those two weeks.

It was normal for us to sometimes play a game of All Fours, a popular card game in TT. During the Easter vacation, whilst most of the parents were away at work, a group of us were playing in our porch.

In the midst of the game, Yip Lee casually put his foot up on the small table we were using.

"Who do you think you are to have your stink foot up on that table?"

"I am yuh muddah man. Dad."

"Who?"

"Dad!"

I leaned over, "Who?"

"Dad."

I slapped him across the head.

"Who?"

"Dad."

I slapped him across the head again.

He was asked the question four times and received four blows across the head on each occasion when giving the same response.

He ran out onto the street and threw a few stone on our roof. I ran after him. But as he reached his porch, I stopped realizing he had a dog and brothers.

I in turn threw a few stone on his roof. He tried to retaliate by throwing stones at me but I would duck behind one of their cars and he kept hitting the car instead. The boys who had followed the altercation up the street, laughed at how he was doing more damage to his family's car than me. I found myself wondering if he was somewhat mentally challenged.

I returned home and the boys and I laughed at how stupid he seemed to be.

If I thought he and his brother were low class, I was about to find out exactly how low they really were.

The next morning as we attempted to get ready for school, we could not use the water as it came out of the pipe. It was a dusty brown colour.

We went over to the Dos Santos' house and quickly washed up there. At work that day my mother called up a plumber to come over and sort out the problem.

A polite black gentleman came over that afternoon, he climbed up to the top of the tank and after a few minutes, he jumped down and looked at us very solemnly.

"Madam," he said, "somebody do you a real duttines."

"What happen?"

"You eh go believe this but somebody went and put shit in your water tank."

"Shit!!" responded my mother, her eyes filled with disbelief.

"Yes."

The moment he said it, I knew it was Chao. Although I was angry, I needed a moment to get over the shock. I just couldn't believe that he was that backward.

The next day he and Apo were laughing. From a distance, they shouted "Ey boy, how yuh water tank? How yuh water tank making out?"

I couldn't believe they were stupid enough to reveal themselves like that. However, I realized that even if I were to retaliate, for example, stone their house at night. Then it would continue. I had to sleep eventually and they had me outnumbered. If my father had been there, especially with the characters he knew, perhaps it could have been handled better. But he wasn't so it was better to let sleeping dogs lie as my family was outgunned.

CHAPTER 27

Big Boy School and Noticing Laura

The Common Entrance Exam would be written in the first week of May. We had been well prepped by our teachers at Morgan's and with my private lessons (which I now did not need) I was ready. I was still a bit nervous as only the top five percent would get their first choice. I had never seen myself as an academic despite doing well during the last few years.

I knew that my mother was anxious. These exams dictated people's future in TT. She wanted the best for her children and I could never understand why I was not as academically gifted as she was.

On the day of the exam, there was no dilly dallying. Leila and I were ready. My mother tested me on my twelve times table and some spelling whilst she drove in the traffic. My school would write the exam again at Mucurapo Junior Secondary. It was just about two hundred metres away from my First Choice, Holy Father's College. I paced myself well, checking each answer as I finished it. Most of the Math problems I had seen in practice and English had never been a problem for me. I made sure not to be foolish in the final section as I had been the previous year.

Finished, I then checked everything again. When that was finished, I breathed and relaxed for ten seconds, then again rechecked.

With the exam done, my classmates, most of whom I had known for almost half of my short life looked at each other and smiled. It was over.

I expected to do well but I just did not see myself being in the country's top five percent. We would see in about six weeks.

The next few weeks were quite relaxing. We just did reviews and played games with our teachers. Two weeks before graduation, there would be back-to-back parties for the class. Alicia Martin would throw a graduation/farewell party at her house. Aneil Sarwan, would have his birthday party one week later. Aneil had lived in London prior to coming to TT. His mother was British and his father from India. Despite his mother's heritage and all her children being fair, they were given Indian names. It looked like a great way to finish our last year of primary school.

A few days before Alicia's party we were informed of the CE results. We were all given an envelope and told to open it.

Sunil Darsan, we are pleased to inform you that you have passed for Holy Father's College, First Choice.

I didn't bother to read the rest. I just smiled and put it away. The boys around me enquired and once informed, they all shook my hand. Then all of us started to check with the others to see who would go where.

I was relieved. All those years leading up to the CE, the speeches from my mother, the anxious look on her face. I was on my way – big boy school.

When she got home that day, I waited for her to switch off the engine, then calmly told her, expecting to get some kind of shocked, pleased reaction. She already knew. Mrs. Skeene had phoned her at the office.

"Very well done Sunny," she put her arms around me and gave me a kiss.

Alicia's party was great. Her mother, Mrs. Martinez, had always liked me. When she chatted with me, she would speak as if we were on the same level. She seemed quite pleasant. We had a great time dancing and laughing. The Disco era was ending, however, two very popular soundtracks at the time, were from the movie *Grease* starring John Travolta and another Travolta movie, *Saturday Night Fever*. Some of the boys had the Travolta hairstyle from *Grease* and copied his moves as we danced away.

Then came the slow music. I had never actually danced slowly with a girl before. It looked easy enough but I wasn't quite sure I could do it. Kathy Ayoung was someone I had had a crush on for most of the school year. Skipped a level because she was so bright, she was a very sweet, pretty girl, partly of Chinese descent. Laura Kanhai, a Jamaican girl who had also been skipped some years before to join us was also there. Laura asked me repeatedly to dance and I kept refusing.

"Because you want to dance with Kathy?"

I was shocked. How did she know?

She asked three times and every time I refused, she would say the same thing. Alicia's older brother and his friends danced to the music while we watched.

• • •

The following week Aneil had his party. We met at the Country Club in Maraval. We had a great time swimming and later on hamburgers and drinks were provided for everyone.

A few hours later, we were driven to his home in Petite Valley, a beautiful, two storey-house. Mrs. Sarwan popped in a video and we all found a spot in the living room to watch. I sat on the floor with Laura behind me on a big poof cushion. A few minutes later, she tapped me on the shoulder, "Sunil, move a bit so I can see the screen."

173

Trying to move to the side, she said, "Wait, move back. Ok, lie down."

I did and assumed all was well. Thirty minutes later, I got up to receive a drink and realized that I had been lying in her lap. She obviously did not mind. I found myself thinking that was rather bold of her. I quickly gulped my drink and resumed my position. I must say, I did enjoy the rest of the movie.

Eventually, the parents came to pick up their children and only Laura and I were left. Aneil invited us to his room. At some point Laura knocked over a lamp.

Aneil shouted, "Oh my God!! I love that lamp."

Laura began to laugh convulsively, "I'm sorry. I'm so sorry."

As she laughed, I looked at her. And for the first time, I saw her in a romantic light. She was a pretty girl and I finally noticed her after three years of school together. She was half black and Indian. And what I saw in front of me was an attractive Dougla[12] girl, slim with long black hair who had caught my attention.

We chatted a bit more and then were informed that her mother had arrived. Mrs. Kanhai sat down to chat with Mrs. Sarwan. After about five minutes and realizing that she may not be going soon, she walked over to me, whispering, "Let's go back to Aneil's room."

In a nanosecond, I thought of the romantic possibilities that could take place and assumed that was why she was asking me.

Before, I could properly complete the thought, her mother overhearing her, shouted, "Oh no. Stay right there!"

And my moment was gone.

A few minutes later she left and a half an hour later, finally my mother arrived.

That night would be the first of many in which Laura dominated my thoughts.

---

[12] *Dougla*: a person of African and East Indian descent.

The final two weeks prior to the summer holidays entailed two horrific bicycle accidents for two of the kids in the neighbourhood, Daniel Pereira and myself.

Daniel's accident took place the day after Alicia's party. With a bunch of kids liming in the Dos Santos' garage next door, Daniel showed up on his bike. Clowning around, he decided to ride the bike in circles without using his hands for control. It was something that kids did, referring to it as "riding no hands." Daniel obviously wasn't too adept at it. He fell face forward with his two upper front teeth taking the brunt of the fall. The children quickly rushed him home, leaving behind his bike and a huge pool of blood on the ground. Richard looked at the blood closely, leaned forward and picked up the two teeth and duly delivered them to Daniel's parents.

Mine would occur on the penultimate day of school. It was a Thursday and the kids were waiting for their parents to pick them up. Some who lived in the neighbourhood came over to lime with us and at around 2:30 there were only a handful of us there. I took my time as I knew I would take a taxi later. Gerry, a white kid who lived in the area came over to chat with us. He had a Free Spirit ten speed bike. My mother had bought me one the year before when she visited Los Angeles on business.

I asked Gerry to take a spin. I had a way of turning corners on the very side of the wheel in a very Daredevil like manner. I rode around the roundabout in front of the school at top speed. Then I turned the bike around, went in the opposite direction, turned back and aimed for the roundabout pedalling as fast as I could. At the last moment I swung the bike sharply to the right intending to avoid the huge green circle, inadvertently, my left hand slipped and dropped on the brake. The front brakes snapped off, the bike went upside down and I skated across the road on my back – still in the riding position. My shirt ripped right off. After skating about 15 feet, the bike and I then did three quick 360 side flips on the road – all the time I was still attached to it in the riding position. As the bike came to a stop, I looked at the road, I could see blood dripping on it coming from just above my right eye.

Mrs. Scott in addition to being the English teacher had also been a nurse in Canada. She lived a few hundred metres away.

"Sunil, call Mrs. Scott," said the children.

"No. I have to go home," I said as I walked to the school pipe to wash off the blood.

I was in shock and not quite aware of how serious the situation was.

The students ignored me and ran to her house while I washed the blood off. It just kept coming and coming. As she approached the school, she saw the blood on the road, "Sunil, let me help you. Do you know I followed your blood on the ground, that's how I knew where you were."

All the wounds were on my right side. She put bandages on my shoulder, just below my elbow and on my knee. It would take decades for those scars to fade but they would stay with me for always.

The next day was the final day. We had a farewell speech with the principal. The parents were invited and we all chatted afterwards. I was a little sad but quite excited. I was no longer a little boy. I was just a few months shy of my thirteenth birthday and about to enter one of the most prestigious high schools in the country.

CHAPTER 28

Revenge Accomplished

My mother attempted to send us off to Caigual right off the bat once the school holidays had started. But I had decided that I would do my best to avoid that place. If my father was there to pick us up there was not much I could do. But if she were attempting to drive us to Sangre Grande, I would simply refuse and run away from the house. I would delay the inevitable by a week, two if I was lucky then somehow, she would get me to leave or ask my father to pick me up. Leila would also benefit as she would not take her without me as well.

In July, every time she packed my bags and put them in the car, I would just run and hide for a few hours. It lasted two weeks until my father was sent for. The good news was that in early August we would go to Barbados with Mummy. She was being sent there on business and decided that seeing most of the trip was already paid for, she would take us as well.

Caigual was the usual bore it had become. I made sure to avail myself to Daddy's library. Aunty Farina was happy to let me sleep over and lime with her children. Ryan and his siblings were always nice to me and I would hang around with their friends from the street. Normally, as a town boy, it might have been a bit of a boring existence in Sangre Grande for me but as the other option was Caigual, I shut my mouth and was grateful for what I had.

The two weeks went by pleasantly enough and then it was back home and off to Barbados. Leila and I were over the moon. We had never actually left TT before. Going to Tobago required a plane but it was not really considered out of the country.

Barbados was fun. It was small and flat. Not seemingly as developed as Port of Spain, however, Bridgetown seemed organized and the people were polite and friendly. I was surprised to hear TT Calypso on the radio every day. Mrs. Scott and her children had come to stay there as well. We were all staying at the Rockley Resort. A beautiful establishment that had apartments sprawled all over the property. In addition to pools for each block of apartments, they also had a supermarket on the property.

We played with Mrs. Scott's children and often swam with them in the pool. Surprisingly, Uncle Basdeo called us. He and Aunty Kim were also in Barbados on holiday. Hearing from Daddy that we would be there, he made sure to contact Mummy and arrange a meeting. On one occasion, we met in the centre of Bridgetown. The ladies went shopping and Uncle Bas and I went "for a walk."

In true Uncle Bas style, he asked around for a local betting shop. He bought a burger and a coke for each of us and the proceeded to make his bets.

The next day he took us all to the local races. My father would usually give me 20 dollars TT to bet with at home but my mother insisted that I only have ten Barbados dollars. We had great fun despite me not winning most of my bets. Leila, bet on a few horses which seemed skinny and neglected. "I feel sorry for them. Nobody else is betting on them."

That night, Uncle Bas invited us to their hotel, we had dinner and watched some limbo dancing. He and Aunty Kim left shortly after and it was back to having fun at the Resort.

We were informed that a storm was heading our way, Hurricane Allen.

That very day the hotel staff came around and put tape in an X pattern on the glass doors of our balcony. They then threw all the poolside furniture into the pool.

Allen came and it was exciting for an hour or two as we looked through the glass door at the trees swaying in the wind. We chatted, read a book and tried to find a way to pass the time. By the next morning, the hurricane was over. The guests were walking around and talking to each other but our mother wouldn't let us go outside.

"WHAT is the problem?" I asked in exasperation.

"Stay in."

"But why? Everybody else is outside. Look. It's fine, the wind is gone."

However, with no logical reason, we were made to stay in for the rest of the day. Finally, at around 4 pm, we were allowed to go out and socialize.

A few days later, Mummy arranged for us to go horseback riding while she worked. We were thrilled, we had never ridden a horse before.

A Trini living in Barbados arrived. An elderly man with a van. He explained that he had owned racehorses in TT but now lived in Barbados with his wife. We picked up one more person, a pretty, blue eyed blonde. Her name was Joyce. She was Swedish but lived in New York City.

She was quite friendly. She chatted away with a beautiful smile and explained that she rode horses regularly in the park in New York City. We made it quite clear that it was our first time and we were wondering what to expect.

We arrived at the farm surrounded by a thick green forest. Joyce was given a huge brown horse, I a medium sized white and Leila a smaller white one. I found it rather easy to handle my horse despite my inexperience. Our guide held an extra rein to assist Leila in case of problems. At one point we had to climb a rough, muddy hill about thirty feet high. Joyce looked back at us in concern. However, I handled it fine despite some trepidation. We finished off at the beach. My horse was quite anxious to run. At one point I pretended to have problems holding him back and enjoyed the sprint along the beach until the guide shouted at me "Reign him in. Reign him in."

It was a great day. We enjoyed another nice chat with Joyce on the way back. Her smile and blue eyes would stay with me for the rest of my holiday.

Upon our return to TT, we were shocked to discover that someone had entered the house and stolen our cassette recorder. It was a nice radio, otherwise known as a boom box in those days. My mother had bought it on a business trip to New York earlier that year. There was no sign of a break in and strangely enough the thief had made no effort to steal anything else. The police were called and they too were amused at the culprit's lack of ambition.

"Mrs. Darsan," said one of the officers, "this is obviously a child. Only a child would do something so trivial. Does anyone else have access to your house?"

My mother assured them that such was not the case. In frustration she blamed me for the theft.

"You caused this. You always wanted to play the recorder in front of your friends. All the neighbours knew we had a recorder. It is because of you it got stolen!"

I was left to fee that somehow, this had become *my* fault.

Once back, there was no escape. We had to go to Caigual. I spent time with Aunty Farina's family to help mitigate the matter. However, I had no choice but to put up with the teasing from Neelam and Sunita. Being someone who always spoke up and stood up for himself when bothered, it was quite hard for me which probably led to my temper tantrums at home. However, I was able to find one way to get back at them.

For the first few years I had known her, I had assumed that Neelam did not like children other than her own because of the nasty, petty way she treated us. I had never met anyone quite like this but I had resigned myself to handling it as best as I could because my father seemed to be amused by her behaviour.

However, I slowly realized that she was actually nice – to other people's children. She was as sweet and kind to her nephews, nieces and any other child she met. Her pettiness seemed reserved only for Leila and me.

Sunita had started Primary school the previous year. She was not doing very well. In fact, she was doing terribly. She had a limited ability in terms of basic Math and even spelling. In comparison to a similarly aged student at Morgan's, she was atrocious. It was one of the few times my father would vent his frustration and shout at her as she was unable to do basic sums. Amazingly, he would not bat an eyelid if she cursed or behaved in a vulgar manner. Unused to a harsh word from him, the shouting and verbal abuse would bring her to tears. I would stand behind him and give her a broad smile enjoying this rare moment of discipline.

Neelam and Daddy had always been proud of her loud, vulgar ways. They saw their child behaving like an adult, others just saw a little girl who was crude in an unfettered fashion.

They were not used to her being ridiculed. I would point out her limitations as much as I could and laugh. I would also make sure I did it in a room full of people so it would have greater impact. They were obviously uncomfortable but knew I was speaking the truth. There was certainly no smile on their faces in terms of Sunita's discomfort or public humiliation.

One other opportunity I discovered to help vent my anger towards them was when leaving if my father wasn't around. He sometimes could not be bothered to do the long drive to the Gardens. He would hire a taxi and have the person drive us home. We would wait at Aunty Farina's if he had to work. Neelam and Sunita would be there as well.

This was my chance. I was on the way home. I wouldn't see my father for months. Therefore, I could say whatever I wanted and there would be no beatings.

As we chatted in the living room, Neelam looked at me. "Your mother must be vex you coming back. She probably can't wait for Christmas to come to get rid of you again." She gave me that broad, insolent smile as if waiting for a reaction. So, I gave it to her.

"Why don't you shut yuh ass, yuh semi-illiterate bitch!!"

As she opened her mouth to retort, I shouted "SHUT UP!!! You are semi-illiterate. You have no education. Shut yuh damn mouth!!

"This is why yuh mudder doh love you and gets rid of you!"

Aunty Farina looked at her in shock, "What's wrong with you. You are a big woman. Why you speaking to him like that!"

I decided to max this rare opportunity of unmitigated payback. "Look at yuh stupid child! She's a damn fool. She can't learn anything in school. You know where she got it from!"

I then turned to Sunita and pointed at her mother, "Look! That is your future. A dumb bitch, spreading yuh legs in public. Just skinning up, gossiping and never working. You will be a dumb, useless bitch like your mother!"

Neelam sprang towards me to hit me, Aunty Farina and Gary immediately jumped in front of her and held her back.

I picked up a knife from the dining table. "Try it bitch!! I will fuck you with this!" brandishing the knife. "I pray for the day when you put your hands on me. I will fucking KILL you in front of her!" I pointed towards Sunita.

Neelam looked at me in shocked silence. She obviously was not used to being spoken to like this.

Zara looked at me in wide eyed amazement. She clearly was not used to a scene like this.

"You stay away from my child. You understand me!"

"Fuck you! When yuh child slapping me while I sleep, you giggle. When she leaves bite marks on my skin you say nothing. But it's different when YOUR child getting bothered, eh! Fuck you. I will beat her cunt if she comes around me. Your child is a stupid, dumb, bitch, just like her mother!!"

The whole room looked at me in shock. If Ryan's family was unaware of the dysfunction in our family, they knew about it now.

As the car arrived. We grabbed our bags, I bid the family farewell and gave Neelam a sly grin.

"I will tell your father!" she screamed.

"Tell him I said to send you back to school, you stupid bitch!!"

As I was about to enter the car, she started shouting some more. I bent over and shook my ass at her. Some men passing on the street laughed. We all looked at her and laughed some more as she pointed her finger and continued remonstrating in the porch.

We sped away, me waving from the car window at her and smiling.

Revenge accomplished.

CHAPTER 29

Meeting Hogg and a Big Thief

Throughout the summer I had thought about Laura incessantly. Whilst staying at Caigual, I had even had a few dreams about her. I had liked girls before but none had ever really had such an effect on me.

During the last weekend of the summer we went to my favourite beach in TT, Maracas. Whilst the neighbours and their kids chatted, I took a walk along the beach. I would walk to one end and then back. On the way back, I looked to my left and saw Laura standing waist high in the water. She waved and called out to me. I waved and continued walking. I was trying to play it cool. What I would later realize is that I was quite friendly with girls but when I was attracted to someone, I could be rather shy. It would be ages before I saw her again and it would not be what I had hoped for.

Despite my obsession with Laura the new school year was starting. Getting into a prestige high school in Trinidad was a big deal. It was a sign of intellect and status. We were given an orientation one week before and sent to our respective classrooms.

On the first day my mother exhibited her driving skills by somehow driving past the school three consecutive times. Despite my screaming and shouting and that of my sister, she seemed unable to ascertain that the 30 metres of wall she was driving by was the actual school despite having driven past it on many occasions before. An inauspicious start to say the least.

I started the day socializing in front of our classes with my classmates waiting for the bell. Once it rang, we began making our way to class only to realize the rest of the school was going in another direction. We followed them into the hall where the principal, Clyde Pinero, was waiting to address the assembly. He was a man of legendary status at Holy Father's and throughout the country in terms of education.

The Pinero family was well known in Port of Spain. Three of the boys had become priests, the eldest being the Archbishop. The two girls were nuns and Clyde happened to be the only sibling who escaped the priesthood but only just. He had acquired a degree in Theology from London University in 1952. On hiatus before doing his Master's in Business Management in Ireland, he met his future wife Janet in Trinidad and made a sharp left turn away from the Priesthood.

He was a former national footballer, hockey player and a top cricketer and tennis player, which endeared him to the Holy Father's boys even more.

We would find out that he was a no-nonsense kind of man, willing to distribute the strap in generous quantities.

He welcomed us to HF encouraging us to work hard and do well, reminding us that the football season was upon us and that the school's First Eleven needed our support at matches.

Our class was made up of 20 benches attached to a desk, two students to a bench. These benches went back to 1945 when HF first opened its doors. On the top corner of each desk was a hole. This is where the former students would put their small jar of ink for their fountain pens. None of us in 1980 were using an inkwell but a few of the boys actually had fountain pens. I sat in the back in the middle aisle. Next to me was a white boy, Carl Ball. A handsome fellow with dark blond hair.

He spoke with a stutter which was more pronounced if he had to answer questions in class or read.

On my third day whilst walking in the inner yard which stretched in front of our class, I saw a group of Form Ones running around a slightly portly white fellow, he had his hair combed straight, hanging over his forehead. He looked a bit nerdy and the boys circled him, shouting, "Hogg! Hogg! Hogg!" all of them having a hearty laugh.

I immediately intervened, "Allyuh leave the boy alone!"

"His name is Hogg!!" they shouted, laughing.

"His name is not Hogg! Leave him alone!"

He walked up to me with a calm smile, "My name is Arnold Victor Hogg, with two Gs."

"Your name is Hogg?"

Still smiling, he repeated "My name is Arnold Victor Hogg."

"Your parents name is Hogg?"

"My name is Arnold Victor Hogg," all the while smiling.

I looked at the boys, looked at him and smiled, "Ok."

I walked off and the boys continued their chant of "Hogg!" enjoying the *picong*[13].

Hogg and I would interact only occasionally during the next five years, playing football on the field and sharing a few classes in Form V. He was a nice, pleasant fellow whom no one ever had a problem with. Sadly, just thirty years after first meeting him, he would die of a heart attack , the father of two.

My name would not have been Sunil Darsan if I did not get into some kind of trouble and the next day was the day.

It was normal to ask a friend already in the line of the canteen to buy something for you so you did not have to wait too long. I asked Ball to get me a Coke and a beef Pattie, a Form I from another class decided that I would not get served in front of him.

"Nah, you eh getting served before me. I waiting before you."

---

[13] *Picong* – to mock someone in a friendly manner.

"I asking my friend and he is in the line so hull yuh ass."

He grabbed me and we both tussled with each other, our shirt buttons falling to the floor. There was an uproar from the other boys and within a seconds a tall red skin Prefect parted us. He wasn't just a Prefect, he was the Head Prefect.

"I don't want to take you to the Dean in the first week of school but you are fighting so let's go."

The Dean was a Pakistani by the name of Mr. Zaheer Ali. A man I would come to know only too well during the next two years. It was the Dean's responsibility to handle the Report Cards and discipline for various forms. Mr. Ali was in charge of From I and II. He was a short, bald, powerfully built individual.

"It's the first week. I really don't want to beat you but it's my Head Prefect who has sent you. Not a good start gentlemen."

He pulled out a leather strap of about 16 inches in length and half an inch in thickness. "Put out your hands." This was the standard issue throughout HF.

We both received four and were sent on our way. Thus, we acquired some degree of infamy, the first boys to get beaten early in the school year.

HF did not have the intimate, relaxed environment of Morgan's. You could feel the imminent discipline hanging in the air. Almost like a military style environment. This was what a government school was like in TT. And it was a helluva shock for the North Americans who migrated to Trinidad and had to adapt.

I did reasonably well in the first month and I was quite proud to walk in public with my grey shirt and long khaki pants indicating which school I attended. But then the novelty of being a Holy Father's Boy wore off and I just never bothered to study. I was however, always good in English as that required no effort on my part.

There were two teachers who caught our attention, both for different reasons, Janet Elias and Bridgette Fernandez.

Ms. Elias was a very beautiful woman of Syrian descent, 25, she had long, thick, black hair that went halfway down her back. She possessed a beautiful smile and a wonderfully, ample bosom. The moment she entered the class and said good morning, you knew this was a sweet woman. I was immediately smitten. What I didn't know is that so were approximately 900 other students.

She taught French and Spanish and would be our Spanish teacher for the next year. She had a habit of sometimes wanting to sit in an empty seat towards the back of the class while she spoke or observed the us. I would coax Ball to go sit elsewhere. The empty seat next to me was prime real estate for observing the class as it was dead in the middle and right up against the wall.

The people in charge of discipline at HF were the Deans, the Principal and the Vice Principal. Our class was quite talkative and at times this stressed Ms. Elias. She was a good woman and did not want to send a student to the Dean for what would be a certified beating. However, despite her pleas, the class kept on being hyper.

It hurt me to see the stress and frustration on her face as she scolded them.

I took it upon myself to handle the matter. I was bigger than most boys my age and not afraid to get serious if I had to.

As she finished the class one day, again saddened by their behaviour, I stood at the front and commanded their attention.

"Listen. Ms. Elias is a nice woman. We are really lucky to have her. You guys know what the other teachers are like so come on. Try to behave in her class and talk less."

They laughed like it was a joke.

"Well let me put it this way, you upset Ms. Elias again and I will upset you."

The laughter stopped.

Ms. Fernandez was a completely different character. A slim, beautiful black woman, she had copper toned skin and slightly, curly, black hair that was just above her shoulders. Teachers sat on a podium that was about an inch above the ground. On the first day, she walked in with a skirt about an inch above the knee and a long slit up the right side. She sat on her chair and just spread her legs wide. We pubescent youths just looked at each other. My seat at the back provided an optimum view and I was never so glad to have such a seat. The boys groaned and moaned as one. She looked around at them with a broad smile, well aware of what she was doing and the reaction it had incurred.

She would cross her legs occasionally, giving full view of her thigh via the slit. As I was unable to get a proper vantage point, I would make an excuse to throw something in the dustbin, taking my time to go and return, soaking in her nice, smooth, legs.

Whilst giving us homework a few days later, she bent down, exposing beautiful, round, brown, breasts, her nipples barely covered by the bra.

As she gave the homework, the boys moaned collectively. She looked up, "Do you want more?"

"YES! YES! More! More!"

So naturally, more homework was given.

Michael Bacchus was a boy I had become quite close to after the first month of school. Ironically, we had had a fight in the second week. Our French teacher was absent and we were all having a good time chatting and relaxing. I had walked over to speak to some boys and upon my return to my seat, Bacchus was sitting there having his own chat.

"Get up."

"Wait. I am not finished speaking."

"Get up now."

"But what wrong with this coolie? Wait boy!"

I was not in the waiting mood and hit him a slap across the back of his head.

He was tall dougla as tall as I was. He sprang to his feet and we both put each other in a headlock. Stumbling back and forth, we knocked over a few desks with neither of us really winning or doing any real damage.

Some of the boys lied and shouted that a teacher was coming and we immediately stopped. That encounter behind us, we started speaking in one of the study halls and immediately hit it off, chatting about the boys in the class and ex-girlfriends. By the second month, we were regular liming partners.

At some point in October, he came offering forms for the *Blue World*. It was a popular TV show for kids that also gave you the option of having pen pals from around the world.

The fact that it was connected to the Blue World, immediately caught our attention. He gave everyone a form to fill out and collected three dollars per person. He got approximately ninety dollars. As the months rolled by and 1980 became 1981, I would remember about the pen pals.

"What happened with the Blue World? I eh get no pen pal yet."

"It coming man. Doh worry. It go come."

Every time I asked this question, I would get the same answer. It was only about six months later, the truth slowly dawned upon me.

"Wait nah. Every time, I ask you, it coming. Is six months now. We eh getting no pen pal. You steal dat money."

He gave me a smirk. "Nah, it coming."

With the passing of every week, I became more direct. "You bitch. You stole that money. You took the classes' money and just keep it."

At this point he didn't even attempt to deny it, he just walked away.

I had certain principles and one of them was that I did not steal from my friends. Apparently, Bacchus was a very different kind of person.

Sadly, it would not be the only time that he would scheme and steal from us.

CHAPTER 30

The Alcoholics

During the previous two years, I had had two up close experiences with alcoholism. The first was Mummy's boyfriend, Uncle Paul, the other was our neighbour, Uncle Peter.

I noticed in early 1978 that we were not seeing Uncle Paul as much as we had. Mummy explained that he was ill. Occasionally we would visit him on the way home from school. He lived with parents and he would be in his bedroom.

A few weeks later whilst visiting him, Mummy said we would go to nearby St. James to get some food. She drove us with Uncle Paul in the front seat. She walked into a chicken and chips place to get some food and within seconds Uncle Paul was out of the car.

He walked a few metres down the pavement and looked at a rum shop, then he walked in.

When my mother came back to the car, she gave us a quick look "Where is Paul?"

We explained that he had walked into the rum shop and pointed.

She dropped the food into the car and walked briskly to where we had pointed. I quickly hopped out of the car and followed her. She ran into the shop, grabbed him and started screaming.

"I am getting food and this what you are doing?"

Pulling him, she shouted "We are going home!"

He meekly followed, "Ok, Ok. Calm down."

She was anything but calm. She was never a good driver but that night, enraged and trying to get home, she scared us all as she drove way too fast and almost hit a few cars.

"Oh my God!" screamed Uncle Paul. "Take it easy. You go crash the car."

"Shut up! Shut your mouth and don't speak to me!"

She dropped him at his house and screamed at him to get out. He tried repeatedly to calm her down.

"Close my door and get out!"

Leila and I knew something was wrong but we weren't quite sure what it was.

It would be another month before we saw him. He came to visit us on the weekend and on this occasion, he was driving so I assumed he was better.

After about half an hour, he explained that he was going over to Judy's house next door to say hello to her mother and her boyfriend, Uncle Matthew.

Matthew was a tall, muscular, broad chested, handsome, black man who certainly did not look his 45 years. He had lived with Judy's mother for two years before moving out. However, despite his departure, he would often visit and sleep over. The older boys in the neighbourhood cheekily called him "Matt the rat," referring to his ongoing sexual relationship with Judy's mother without any apparent commitment.

Uncle Paul was gone for approximately half an hour and then returned. My mother gave him an egg sandwich. But as he ate, I could not help but notice that something was wrong. The more he ate, the slower he ate, the slower he ate, the sleepier he seemed to become. Eventually, he just stopped eating, the food falling out of his mouth onto his chest, his head hanging to the left, his eyes closed.

Still a naive boy, I found it strange that he had fallen asleep whilst eating. My mother however, was more aware of the situation.

Looking at him, she shouted "Oh Jesus Christ!"

She ran next door and confronted Aunty Kathy and Matt. "The man is drunk. Did you give him a drink!!??"

Both she and Uncle Matt looked at her with a somewhat blank and fearful expression. "Well, he asked and we didn't know what to say," explained Matt.

"Well damn it! I don't want no drunk in my house! Matt please help me to take him home!"

Uncle Matt ran over to the house. "Paul! Paul! Wake up nah man!"

Uncle Paul continued to sleep. After a few more shakes, Uncle Matt gave up and together he and Mummy walked a drunken and half-awake Paul to his car.

Uncle Matt drove him home in Uncle Paul's car and Mummy followed in hers to bring him back.

We never saw much of him again. A few months later he came over but my mother refused to acknowledge him.

I really didn't care if she had a boyfriend or not. But there were times I found myself missing his company a bit. It was only natural that in a house where I was the only male, it was nice to have another one to bond with. He would joke around with me and even back me up on occasion.

One such time was when I had a fight with Daniel at Aunty Maria's house. She was having a birthday party for one of her sons. Daniel threw a glass of water at me and I ran after him. Just as I started to hit him, his mother came and broke it up. As she spoke to us, he kept pulling at my shirt and pushing me. Uncle Paul observed what was going on. He later explained to me "He knew you had stopped fighting because his mother was there and that's why he tried to take advantage of you. The next time he does that, hit him."

Another incident which I never forgot had to with Aunty Thelma. I had been given a document from the school. It was to be given to our parents. Not wishing to lose it, I asked her to keep it for me. "Boy! I don't have time for your schupidness!"

I put it next to the telephone assuming that was an easy place to remember and that it would be safe. By the time my mother arrived a few hours later, it had disappeared.

I asked both Aunty Thelma and her sister if they had seen it. They had no idea what I was talking about. There was then a big discussion in front of some of the parents regarding my "carelessness."

I reminded Aunty Thelma about her response when I had asked her to look after it.

"But you didn't tell me what it was!"

"Every time I answer you, you tell me I am rude. I didn't want to upset you."

The conversation went back and forth. My mother observed with not much to say. When it came to Aunty Thelma and the way I was treated, she seemed to be some kind of well-trained pet, unable to question or admonish her.

Uncle Paul upon hearing the story later that day from my mother, retorted "But the boy eh do nothing wrong. If he ask her to hold it for him and she say she eh want nutten to do with his schupidness, how it is his fault?"

He seemed to be the only one who understood this.

I had always admired and envied the Douglas family. In them I saw the kind of family I would have liked to have had in a different world. The parents were friendly, warm people. Aunty Jane was one of the coolest mums you would ever meet. She had a great sense of humour, was athletic and artistic. There seemed to be a close, loving bond amongst the parents and the children. However, all families have their demons.

They had moved to the Gardens in late 1978. Approximately a year later, as I walked into their house, I saw their father in the porch, rolling around on the floor in just his underwear. He was screaming the worst possible profanities. We simply were not used to seeing the parents in the neighbourhood behave this way.

I looked at Gary. "What's wrong with your father?"

"I don't know," he responded with an almost bored expression.

"But he's rolling around in his underwear cursing. What happened?"

"I don't know." And with that he turned his back.

Richard grabbed a football, "Let's go play some ball." It was a very good attempt to get us out of the house and it worked.

For the next few weeks, he was in a semi coherent state. He would occasionally visit the neighbours under the pretext of a visit but really hoping to get a drink. However, they were well aware of the situation and refused.

I didn't realize how bad things were until about a week later. Informing the family that he was going to take a walk and get some exercise, he walked out of the neighbourhood.

Approximately half an hour later, he returned. As he came through the open gate, Gary could a hear a sort of sloshing sound…*gloog, gloog, gloog* … it was coming from his father's crotch.

He looked at his father's pants as he walked past and him and realizing that this was not normal, informed his mother.

She immediately went to the bedroom, put her hand down his shorts and pulled out a small bottle of Vat 19 rum.

She walked to the kitchen with her husband right behind her. Turning on the water in the sink, she poured the rum away.

"OH GOD!!" shouted Uncle Peter. "Doh do dat nah man! Doh do dat nah!"

She had a vexed expression and refused to look at him. Turning off the faucet, she threw the now empty bottle into the garbage.

When the boys heard what had happened we could not help but laugh at his gallant yet failed attempt.

One of the positives about being around an alcoholic is that it gives you a very stark idea of the disease and the manner in which it hurts not just the addict but those close them.

I saw how it inconvenienced his family. They would joke about it sometimes and what they had to put up with but you knew deep down inside that it was a heavy burden for them.

Aunty Jane got a job as a secretary at Morgan's in early 1980 and left around three months later, dissatisfied with her salary. She later joined the TT Sentinel, a daily newspaper and worked her way up the ladder, three years later becoming the Head of Human Resources.

Uncle Peter would continue his battle with the bottle for almost another two years. He would have some good periods and you would think this time he would be better. Only to see him some time later walking around the house in a daze.

Ironically, for the first year at the Gardens, I had never seen him drunk, even when drinking with the adults. But when it happened, it was obvious that it was a problem that controlled him instead of the other way around.

Finally, in late '81 he joined Alcoholics Anonymous and a few months later was in the work force again.

However, for the rest of my years I would remember how this nice, outgoing man, a former star athlete, had lost so much because of alcohol. Because of this no matter how much I drank as an adult and how drunk I would occasionally become, I would always make sure to take a break. I knew that if I did it and refused offers to drink from others, I would not have such a problem creep up on me as it had with Uncle Peter.

CHAPTER 31

The Porn and the Thief

By January of 1981, I was firmly entrenched as a Holy Father's student.

Being in Form I, I had to contend with a bunch of older, bigger boys, trying to feel special by bullying me or others in my year. I would occasionally stand up for myself. But realizing I was outgunned by people who knew they were physically superior to me and were only too happy to take advantage of it, I learned to look the other way.

One person who made the acclimatization easier was Larry Richards. Despite their surname, his family was Indo Guyanese and had migrated to TT three years earlier. They had come to the Gardens in 1979 so by the time I entered HF, I had known him pretty well.

Larry was considered a success story at HF. Having come from Guyana in the middle of the school year, he was put in Mucurapo Jr. Secondary. However, he wrote the 14 plus and with outstanding results, he was given a spot at HF. The year before my arrival, he had passed his O Levels and was now in Form VI. Seeing that less than forty percent of the Form Vs were good enough to make it to Form VI, this was an accomplishment, even more so for someone who had come from a Junior Secondary school.

Larry was a down to earth fellow who never tried to make himself look special around the younger ones, very much unlike Richard. So not surprisingly the two of them would have a clash from time to time.

Larry would give us advice on how to fit in and how to avoid trouble. It was nice to see him not only in the Gardens but at school as well. However, Larry, like the rest of us, had his problems.

One day, two of his classmates came to visit after school. They parked their car in his driveway and went for a walk through the neighbourhood. I tagged along as well. We showed them the nearby river and they marvelled at how natural and beautiful the scenery was.

As we slowly made our way past my house towards his home at the end of the street, his father was waiting.

Mr. Richards was quite drunk and he started shouting the moment he saw Larry. "Where the hell have you been boy! I looking for yuh scunt and cah find it nowhere."

"Who de hell is these two?" pointing at his classmates. "Tell dem to get dey scunt out of my house. And if they faddah have a problem with it, I go kick up he ass!!"

Larry, opened the gate, telling them "I sorry. I sorry."

He tried to walk them to the car at the head of the driveway but Mr. Williams shouted "Get yuh rass in dis house boy!!"

"I sorry. I sorry," he said with his head bowed.

I walked home feeling sorry for him. He was a good guy who had done nothing wrong but his drunk father had just completely embarrassed him for no reason.

We didn't know it but he would have many other episodes with his father which we would not hear about. Finally, about a year later, missing school because of problems at home, he would just eventually drop out of Upper VI abandoning one of the finest high schools in the country and any possible opportunity for a university education.

To his credit, I met him about 30 years later, I saw him on the streets of POS, balding and with a bit of a belly, the most successful insurance agent in the country and holder of an MBA from the University of the West Indies via night school. He had simply refused to be held back.

One of the joys of being at home during the holidays was not only having the neighbourhood to ourselves whilst the parents worked but accessing their pornographic collection.

Daniel's parents had a fine set of magazines which we occasionally saw but the Gray family had an even better one. Jean Gray was a kid who lived at the corner, a few houses before mine but on the other side of the street. His parents were also from Sangre Grande. Porn magazines were illegal in Trinidad but Mr. Gray when travelling would enhance his collection. And it was quite impressive. There were approximately 20 magazines in a closet in the same room as Jean. We had first been introduced to them the previous year during a nationwide teachers' strike. At one point we had had no school for a week and with the parents away at work, Jean brought us in and introduced us to a collection that left us breathless.

On every occasion that we were at Jean's house, it was surreal as we sat on the floor, not a sound to be heard, looking at the photos and passing the mags on as soon as we were finished with one. As a maturing 13-year-old, this was the closest I would get to a naked woman for quite some time.

Of course there is always a character who has to spoil it for everyone else and one of those individuals in our neighbourhood was Shane, He was always a bit wilder and more stupid than the others when there was no reason to be.

One of the jokes he liked to play on us was to shout, "Jean's father is here!!" We would panic and run out of the room only to find out that it was a lie. He had done it many times and every time we would check rather than have it be true.

On this day after about a half an hour of deep investigation of the magazines, Shane did his usual "Jean's father is here!"

Not a soul moved. We had been through this too many times before to be bothered with him.

But there was a little voice in my head telling me to check. I looked out and couldn't believe that I was seeing Mr. Gray exit his car. He had come home for lunch which he usually never did.

"Oh Jesus Christ!!" I shouted, running back into the room. "Jean's faddah here!!" As one we all threw the magazines at Jean and fled the room. For just a moment Jean looked like a boxer at the wrong end of a combination as about six odd magazines bounced off his face almost simultaneously.

Priding myself on being a good liar especially in times of strife, I thought I would stop Mr. Gray in the garage and ask about the score in the match that the West Indies was playing. It would give Jean some valuable, extra time to put back the magazines. However, when I saw him, I just sort of froze. "… Hi," I said meekly. Everyone else did the same. He just looked at us, nodded his head and responded.

Some of the other boys were liming on the street, they just started to laugh. We had walked out of the house, all very silent and just looking around. As one guy put it, "Allyuh look like you just come out of jail and was looking around like it was the first time you had seen sunlight!!"

They all had a good laugh but it was no laughing matter for Jean; he found himself scrambling to pick up about twenty magazines that were on the floor and return them to the cupboard. Not surprisingly he was caught and was given a good talking to by his parents.

For the rest of the term, if there was a teachers' strike, students had the option to stay home or go to school and have a study hall. Jean was given no choice, he was sent to school every time. He made sure to let us know how inconvenient it was. No amount of cajoling could ever persuade him to show us the magazines again.

For years I blamed Shane for this. "If he wasn't always lying and full of shit, we would have believed him and reacted faster. That fool spoil it for everybody!!"

Shane was a character that I would have problems with throughout my time in the Falls. He would look for trouble when there was none to be had. He also had other lowly ways that in time, I would slowly discover.

Back in 1979 he had asked me to borrow a key from our house to see if it would open his front door as he had come home before his family and didn't have a key. This was not an unusual request. The houses in the neighbourhood had been built by the same constructions company and it was possible that a key in one house could open a door in another.

I lent him our front door key which happened to work. The next day I asked him for it. "You'll get it later, it's at home."

This went on for a month until I realized he had no intentions of returning the key. I decided not to argue as we had a backup. But it was just the beginning and he would be problematic for the rest of my years in that neighbourhood.

At the beginning of Form I, I was now physically bigger and some of the older boys were not that imposing anymore. Shane was quite short for his age. So even though he was older than me by two years, he was about an inch and a half shorter.

He would always be looking for a fight. If we were playing cricket, he would want to throw the ball at me or throw my bat hard, down on the ground for no good reason.

He would take my bike without asking and go out of the neighbourhood with it. If I told him not to, he would wait until my back was turned and take off with it. I would run after him screaming to stop but he would just go on and come back whenever he pleased. He would always find a way to harass me. I sometimes wondered why me so much and I figured it was because the other boys were bigger. But he never really went after the smaller ones like he did with me. Perhaps it was because they had a father who was around to look out for them.

The tension was building and it was only natural that it would come to a boil.

At the beginning of the summer holidays, the boys were playing raising. We were playing at the corner from my house which happened to be in front of Shane's. This was a game where we tried to keep the football up in the air passing it around without it touching the ground. Six of us were in a circle. Occasionally the ball would touch the ground and we would start again. At one point for no good reason he just banged the ball off my body at close range.

"What the ass wrong with you!!!" I shouted.

"You want to do something about it??"

I immediately grabbed him and put him in a headlock.

"Yuh bitch!! You want to fight. I go teach you how to fight!!"

All the boys started shouting as I applied pressure to his head. He tried to punch me in my kidney but he had no leverage or power and I really felt nothing.

After about twenty odd seconds, we were parted. Richard immediately tried to shake my hand. Apparently impressed with my performance.

"I am fighting and you want to shake my hand??" I shouted at him. Unimpressed with someone who seemed to want to encourage a fight rather than stop it.

My mother had heard the shouting and from the porch could see the commotion. She arrived just as it was over. She looked at Shane's father, a schoolteacher at one of the Secondary schools, who had been standing on the corner with Jean's father. Both of them had looked on with no apparent reaction.

"You see these boys fighting and you just stand there watching?" she said to Shane's dad.

"Well, boys will be boys," was his nonchalant response.

"But you are the adult here. You are just going to watch and make no effort to stop it?"

"Well, it's not a big deal." He turned his head and looked away.

Realizing she would get nowhere with him, she walked off.

A few months later, I saw him running around the neighbourhood with a Jolly Roger's T-shirt. The Jolly Roger was a ship in Barbados that threw parties for the tourists. You could buy a T-shirt as a souvenir. I thought nothing of Shane wearing it as anybody could perhaps give it to you as a present. However, my mother was more aware than me.

Upon seeing him playing on the street, she called me over, "Sunil, where did Shane get that T-shirt from?"

"I don't know."

She went to the clothesline in the back yard where she had hung it up the night before, not seeing it, she then checked my bedroom just to be safe. However, as she knew it had been on the clothesline, she was already sure of what had happened.

She made it clear to me, people in Trinidad can't get a T-shirt like that unless they go to Barbados. "That boy took it from my line."

I couldn't believe that he could be that bold and low.

She approached him, "Shane, come here. Where did you get that T-shirt?"

"My friend went to Barbados and brought it back for me."

Seeing Mr. Lara in the porch, she called out to him. Explaining the situation to him, he looked at Shane. "Where did you get that T-shirt from?"

"Daddy, my friend Errol from Woodbrook went Barbados and buy it for me."

Mr. Lara, immediately hit him a slap on the side of the head. "Take it off!!""

Eyes, glaring, he shouted, "Shane are you an ass or an elbow? How the hell you could go and steal clothes from people line?"

He tried to protest but Mr. Lara knew his son and was aware that he had no friend who had brought him anything from Barbados.

He was made to take it off right there in the middle of the street.

The boys on the corner started to laugh. I watched my mother return home with the clothing and was amazed that anybody – especially a neighbour of mine could be so classless and crooked.

Richard and David just looked at him.

"Boy!!" Richard shouted, "You have to be stupid!! You steal a man shirt. From Barbados to boot. And then try to put it on the same day you steal it like nobody would know!!!"

All the kids guffawed looking at him incredulously.

Shane had always had a reputation as a liar and a person who could not be trusted, this was just another nail in his coffin.

It would take me about fifteen odd years as a mature adult to one day realize that it was he who had stolen our recorder from the house during our trip to Barbados.

It was like jigsaw pieces clicking together and then a light bulb flashing in my head. He was a thief, he took our key and would not return it. He stole my clothes from the backyard. The police had made it clear that the person had not broken in and was obviously a child.

As a young boy and not accustomed to being surrounded by low class thieves I was too naïve to understand then. When the realization dawned upon me years later in the mid-nineties, I could only shake my head. Not being someone who stole from the neighbours and lied, I could not conceive that other children in the neighbourhood could be that lacking in class and shame.

I did not know it but in time to come I would quickly come to terms with other characters like Shane and my naivete would quickly dissipate.

CHAPTER 32

Farewell to Laura and a Slimmer, Better Version of Me

During the summer holidays of 1980 and for the first few months of Form I, I had found myself consumed with thoughts of Laura Kanhai. However, the closer we got to the end of the year, the more time I began spending with Anastasia.

Any young boy would have been smitten with her. She was beautiful and had a well-proportioned figure. She was friendly and never and treated others with disrespect. However, she was a tomboy who could handle herself and would not let anyone push her around.

From time to time, we would have personal chats. Sometimes if we all went to the Falls together, she and I would hang back on the return and allow the others to walk ahead of us while we spoke.

Uncle Imran and Aunty Janice were still close to my mother and so was their daughter Noor. Between late 1980 and early '81, she seemed interested in spending time with us at the house. She even went to the Falls with Leila and me. I assumed she just enjoyed spending time with us, despite the fact that she was two years older than me.

Around March of '81, she invited me to a Form IV party in Federation Park. This was quite a well to do neighbourhood and I was quite impressed that although I was in Form I, I had made the grade for a fete with much older kids. She told me that Richard was invited as well.

I didn't realize it at the time. But the effort to spend extra time at our house and the invitation for me was just a ploy to get closer to Richard to whom she had taken a liking.

My mother – as was the norm when I had a party to go to – agreed to drop us off and pick us up at 2:00 am, the cut off time for the event.

We arrived at 8:30 – the customary half hour late – as no one ever showed up exactly on time in TT. There were about 20 people hanging around on the front lawn and the porch. Richard and I got some drinks and took up a position in front of a hedged that lined one of the windows. There was a concrete formation around it and some people were using it to sit on.

About half an hour later, I saw a group of white kids arrive and sit in front of the hedge mere feet from us. Because of the dim light it took me a while to realize that Laura was in the group.

I realized that if it were her, then she should have been able to see me as there was no crowd around me. She seemed quite close to one of the boys, a blond fellow who had his arm around her.

I mentioned it to Richard and he made sure to look her over. A few minutes later, she was sitting on the blond guy's lap.

I looked at Richard, "She sitting on his lap?"

Richard laughed, "It look like she have a man."

My thirteen-year-old mind was trying to compute what I was seeing. "Well … maybe it's just her cousin?" I responded, trying to grope for any explanation other than what seemed to be the obvious.

After a while, I turned away and tried to mind my business. However, I noticed that instead of eating the sandwiches that had been provided for us, they guy was breaking them up and throwing some my way. I looked at him quizzically and tried to take a step away and not get involved in a tussle. He was older and bigger than me. Plus, he had friends around and I would be obviously outnumbered.

But he kept throwing the bread and the amounts just got bigger. One of his friends, admonished him. "Hey, you looking for a fight for no reason! The man didn't do you nutten."

But he continued, I gave him a hard glare. He smiled and there was Laura sitting on his lap, looking back at me with a broad smile. I couldn't understand how she was going along with this. She must have recognized me.

He found a bunch of more sandwiches and a minute later there was a vast amount of broken bread thrown at my head. I picked them up and threw them back. He immediately jumped up and grabbed my shirt.

"You looking for a cut ass boy! Why you throwing bread at me?"

"Yuh ass started it!" I shouted, doing my best to grab his shirt as well.

Thankfully, some other boys saw what was happening and made sure it was broken up. He wasn't going to argue with three guys bigger than him so he went back to his seat.

I moved a few feet away from them to lighten the tension. Before doing so I glanced one more time in their direction and saw Laura looking back at me with that stupid smile.

I was trying to understand why this fool had singled me out. I could only think that Laura must have mentioned me. I wondered if he was jealous of me. But what was there to be jealous about?

Noor showed up a little later and we did not mention the incident to her. We chatted with her and her friends and even danced in the cleared out living room.

Surprisingly, it was Richard's father who showed up to collect us with my mother in tow. Uncle Peter was on his latest alcohol recovery and seemed pretty much like the outgoing fellow we had first met years ago.

"So how was the fete? All yuh pick up any girls?"

We just smiled and mumbled a reply.

For the next few days I allowed the shock of what had happened at the party to settle in and accepted that for some reason Laura had been a part of the harassment I had endured. She certainly didn't seem sorry about it. I chalked it up to stupidity and being influenced by someone older.

My pride kicked in. I decided that any friendship or interest I had had in her was now gone. I did not tolerate that kind of treatment from people and no true friend of mine would ever do that to me.

The following month Morgan's was having their annual Sports Day. Leila of course was still a student there and I was anxious to go not just to see my old stomping grounds but I also hoped to see some of my ex-classmates.

Sure enough, a few of them did show up. Some had younger siblings and others showed up in the hopes of reconnecting. One person I was happy to see was Gordon Paul. We had been friends ever since my first year at Morgan's. We had practically grown up together and he was like an unofficial brother. The Paul children were renowned for their sprinting ability. His bigger brother Barry had never lost. Gordon always came second to an Indian fellow by the name of Martin Lalsingh. Martin never lost a race in primary or secondary school. Gordon's younger sister, Bettie was in Leila's class and she too was undefeated.

Gordon was a slim black fellow, with a short Afro that seemed to be parted to the side. A broad grin on his face, we were always pals and seeing him reminded me of the gentler, more fun times of Morgan's.

We and some of the other boys walked around, chatted, watched the races and of course any young girls that were noticeable.

Then came time for the Old Boys' Race. The distance was 100 metres. Thank God Martin Lalsingh was not there. There was Gordon, four older boys including Barry and another three from our year.

Lara Watt shouted at me, "Sunny!! No chance." And shook her head.

208

I was already nervous and I just nodded in agreement. I had never been much of a runner at Morgan's. Although I had slimmed down and gotten a bit faster every boy in that race had been faster than me during our primary school days.

The starter, realizing that we all seemed nervous, gave us a moment, "Alright gentlemen, calm down. Breathe, take it easy."

We did our best to calm down.

"On your marks!!"

We got down on one knee, our fingertips on the ground before us as we had seen in the Olympics.

"Get set!!"

We raised our knees – fingertips still on the ground, every fibre in our bodies tense bracing for the next words.

"Go!!!"

And we were off.

We were all in one line except for that damn Barry who was already about five feet ahead. At the halfway mark we were still in one line, however, Barry just kept widening the gap.

At the 75-metre mark, Gordon had started to pull ahead.

As Barry hit the finish line, he was so far ahead, that he had time to turn around and look at Gordon who was in second place, "I WON!!!" he shouted.

About three feet behind Gordon were the seven of us all in one line, I leaned forward with all my might, just as I had seen them do on TV. We then all slowed down and crashed into the fence thirty feet beyond, I turned around to see a bespectacled white man running towards me with a number three sign in his hand.

I think my ex-classmates were more in shock at my placing than who had won. I had beaten boys two and four years older than me.

They called us up on the podium and pinned a ribbon on our chest. I had a yellow number three ribbon. All the students cheered and for the first time in my life I knew what it was like to stand on the podium. After all those years of fighting it out with the fat boys to avoid last, I was now one of the elite. And it felt good.

I tried to look cool as if placing was no big deal. But I was beaming with pride inside.

Some of the girls from my old class came running up to me.

"Sunny. You?? I can't believe it. What happened since you left Morgan's?"

I just smiled. I was as surprised as them. But during the last two years, constant football, running and swimming at the Gardens had obviously had a positive effect on me.

CHAPTER 33

The Art of Jock and a Woman Not All Together There

Not too long after Morgan's Sports Day my mother was off on yet another business trip. She knew I would no longer stay at Aunty Thelma's and of course my father was too far away.

A few weeks before she had met a woman called Pepe, a middle-aged individual with coal black, long hair with flecks of grey at the roots. She seemed in her mid-forties.

Pepe was from Jakarta. She had been the housekeeper for an old English woman just outside the neighbourhood. She had been let go and my mother had decided to have her be our live-in maid.

The boys and I had no idea where Jakarta was. Uncle Peter asked on our behalf and we were informed that it was the capital of Indonesia.

We found ourselves wondering how the hell she had gotten from Jakarta to our country. Despite being a housekeeper, she was quite a talkative woman and would speak to the neighbours as if she were their friends.

When my mother left for the USA, we were left under Pepe's care for approximately two weeks. For most of the school year I had been coming home from school with Jean's family as he too went to Holy Father's. for the next two weeks, I would go both ways with them.

I took advantage of my mother's absence by staying late out on the street. Sometimes the boys who lived up the main road would come in and lime well into the night with Tomas.

Tomas was in his early forties. Every day around 4:00 pm, he would be sitting on the roller in the small lot opposite our house which the boys used to play football on. He was always spruce looking, hair well combed, a nice T shirt, shorts and athletic shoes, smoking and just looking around. Shane had taken to liming and smoking with him at night and the fellows from the Community Centre's area had followed suit.

My mother was not impressed with a full-grown man liming with boys at all hours of the day and night. I would chat with him during the day and maybe exchange a few more in the evening. However, my mother wasn't around now and I had decided to chat with Tomas and anyone else that would be on the street at night.

Pepe was a bit angry and thought I should be in bed by 7:30 pm. I ignored her.

Tomas seemed pure Trini, however, I noticed that his parents had a thick accent. I later found out that they were from Venezuela and had come with Tomas and his siblings to TT in the late forties. According to him, he had been a decent footballer in his youth, Vice-Captaining Midvale, which was once a top football team from Port of Spain.

He did not seem to work and I was curious as to what kind of living he made. He had two brothers who ran their own business and he would occasionally "help them out."

I would lime with him under the streetlamp as we discussed any topic of interest. Strangely for a few nights, it was just him and I as the other members of his group were not around.

The fathers would sometimes have a chat with him. But as they actually had full time jobs, he usually spent his time with the other youths.

One night as we chatted well after 8:00 pm, we were talking about the young girls in the neighbourhood. "I too old," he laughed. "But this is your time Sunny. You eh have your eye on one of these girls?"

Not wanting to encourage that type of gossip, I smiled, "Not really."

"Well I know you too young to be sexually active so you *must* be jocking?"

I looked at him quizzically, "Jocking?"

"Sunny? You don't know what jocking is?"

I gave a shake of the head.

"Boy, doh ever start dat nah. If you start, you will never stop."

I was forced to ask what exactly he was talking about.

He explained while using his hands to demonstrate.

I realized he was talking about masturbation. I laughed. He then went on to give me some "advice on jocking."

"This what you do. Cut off the wings of a fly. Tie the fly to your shower head. Have the string long enough to reach your dick. Now put the fly on your head and watch him run around on your toti head. It is a wonderful feeling. He nodded his head and laughed.

I had no words. No one had ever spoken to me like this before.

"Have you ever done that?"

"Sure! It does feel nice. But you have to catch the fly first."

For the next two weeks while my mother was away, I took full advantage and would have many night limes with Tomas and the other older boys on the street. Pepe would criticize my behaviour but to no avail.

One night two police officers came to the house. She introduced one as Cliff. They had a chat in the porch. After they had left, she explained that Cliff was an Assistant Commissioner of Police. He was her boyfriend but they had to meet in secret because he was married.

I concluded that although she was an adult, something was wrong with this woman. This was not the kind of conversation you had with children.

When my mother arrived from her business trip, Pepe immediately began reading a journal of everything I had done wrong. Each day was dated. My mother looked at me calmly with a resigned expression. I think at this point she was used to the complaints. I also believed that she had spent half a day travelling and was not in the mood to get upset.

Two days later she would have her own episode with Pepe.

Doing her customary check, in terms of the house cleaning, my mother found the furniture to be dusty. She called Pepe and pointed it out to her.

"But I clean it. It is ok!"

"But Pepe look." My mother then wiped the underside of the chair's wooden armrest, she extended her hand and showed her the dusty finger.

"And that TV is covered in dust."

"No, the TV is fine."

Leila wiped her index finger across the top of the TV. "Oh ghoood! Look at dust!!"

Pepe freaked.

"What are you doing!!?" she screamed. "Get away from that TV. GET AWAY!!" And then she just broke down, sobbing, her head bent and shoulders shaking.

My mother immediately switched gears. "Ok, ok. Take it easy. Sit down. Leila get her some water."

Leila immediately sprinted towards the kitchen.

I myself, had been in the kitchen half hearing the conversation as I made a sandwich. When I saw her blubbering figure, I realized this was not the normal disagreement my mother was having with the help.

I looked at Pepe sobbing away and my mother patting her gently on the back. I realized that this woman was going through some kind of stress. As my mother gave the water, talking to her in a soothing manner, I walked out. This wasn't really my business.

The next day weird became weirder. My mother had told Pepe that things were not working out and she would give her one week's notice.

214

And that she would have to vacate the Maid's Quarters (really a utility room adjacent to the kitchen) at that time.

Pepe asked for a ride into town that morning to go to her bank. As we hit the Morne Coco stretch adjacent to the sea wall, she suddenly ducked down in the back seat. I was in the front and Leila and I just stared at her.

"Cliff's wife will see me. I am hiding."

We continued staring at her.

"What?" I asked, trying to grasp what she was on about.

She pointed to the hills of Cocorite to our left. Looking at houses that had to be a hundred metres away and more, she explained that is where Cliff lived.

I found myself wondering how the Hell could his wife pick this woman out over a hundred metres away in a traffic jam of well over a hundred cars?

"She knows what you look like,"?

"No."

As I watched her laying low in the back seat, I could only shake my head. This woman certainly wasn't all together there.

CHAPTER 34

Not Quite Muhamad Ali

Anyone who knew me, knew how much I loved boxing.

As I got older, I simply became more and more enamoured with the sport and I was sure despite my mother's protests that one day I would train and later become a professional, probably the Heavyweight Champion of the World.

My mind had not quite caught up with reality as yet. However, every day I would shadow box at imaginary opponents. Pretending sometimes to up against some of the world's best.

I really wasn't that good because I had never been trained. But that did not stop me.

Our school carpenter was a pro boxer. His name was Eddie Williams, the Welterweight Champion of TT. He had a record of 10 wins and one loss. He had been used as a sparring partner for some of the tops boxers in the US.

One day I saw a bunch of boys crowded in his work area. The older boys were handpicking younger ones to box each other and Williams would just observe.

They asked for volunteers and I did not hesitate to step forward.

They matched me with another Form I, Teddy Galindez, a tall, lanky fellow. Our fathers were both lawyers and knew each other well.

As we got ready in our respective corners, we each had two older boys as our Coaches.

Williams looked at me, "He frighten?" He unbuttoned my top two buttons and put his hand on my heart. "Nah, he ok."

One of my cornermen shouted at him, "Oh God Williams! You trying to make the man nervous or what!"

Williams laughed.

Actually, I was anything but nervous. I was simply going to box. After all my destiny was to be World Champion.

They sounded a bell and we stepped forward. I had an orthodox stance. Galindez had his gloves apart and I could see a big open space exposing his body. I stepped forward with a one-two combination to the body, followed by a left jab to the face. The left glove in his face obscured the impending right hand which crashed full force into him. He crumpled to his knees and the referee stepped in to check on him.

The boys in my class began chanting, "Go Darsan Go!!"

As the Ref told us to resume, I took my time, jabbing and moving. It was tougher now because he had his guard up.

The first round finished. I sat on my stool as my Chief Corner gave me instructions. But I really wasn't listening to him, I had my own plan. I would do what Muhammad Ali had done with many of his opponents. I would let Galindez punch himself out in the Second and come on in the Third.

That is exactly what I did – in the second round at least. He threw many punches which had the twenty odd boys shouting. The truth is he hardly really hit me as I was moving my head and the full force of the punch was not landing or his shots would be partly parried by my gloves.

What I had not expected was to get so tired. I felt as if I had dust in my nasal tubes. And surprisingly, the more tired I became, the heavier the gloves seemed to feel. Just before the bell, I dropped my gloves slightly just under my chin and Galindez shot a quick jab. My head snapped back and the crowd made an OOOH sound.

As I sat down, my teeth felt as if they had been shattered. I kept licking them with my tongue. I was terrified as to what disfigurement I had incurred. I decided I could not tell my Corner, they would stop the fight. That was too embarrassing. I had started this fight to win it not to be TKO'd like a fool.

I was also curious as to how I had hit him so hard and he never went down but just one jab had done this kind of damage to me.

My Chief Corner looked at me, "What you doing man? Go out there. Use your jab, go to the body and then to the head."

Again, I was not listening. It was time to win. But I was so damn tired.

Galindez had won the second round big and was probably ahead on points. I decided that I had to beat the hell out of him in the third. There would be no holding back now.

As the round began, I kept thinking how long it would be. I was so tired.

I went out after him, throwing my punches and trying to land that right to the head. But he had been instructed by his corner to run. And he did. When he couldn't run, he would just hold on to me for dear life. I punched away as best as I could, dead tired and he hung on whenever he could.

At the end of the round, Williams said, "I give the edge to the black man."

The crowd applauded.

I didn't give a damn. I was worried about my teeth. I took off the gloves and ran to the nearest washroom. I looked in the mirror and realized that one of my lower front teeth had been chipped. I thought to myself, Jesus! I will never get a girlfriend! How can I go through life with this?

The truth is it was barely noticeable. My lips covered my lower teeth and therefore, I really didn't have much to worry about.

We later found out, I had been given the sparring gloves and Galindez, the actual boxing gloves which were much harder. It had not been done deliberately, just the luck of the draw with whomever got the gloves.

As the school years rolled by, we would sometimes reminisce about that day. And I would tell him, "You know you damn lucky I didn't hit you that right with the real gloves."

Galindez would laugh and nod.

CHAPTER 35

The Meat Shop

My father had opened a meat shop in Arima earlier that year. He had written us a letter telling us about it and that he was quite busy working seven days a week.

I was quite surprised that he had even take the time to write us. He had certainly never done so before. However, now that the summer holidays were once again upon us, my mother made sure to shuttle us off.

He and Neelam ran it together, working 8 am to 8 pm Monday to Saturday and 8-3 on Sundays.

We now had to spend seven damn days a week in a meat shop. I thought of all my friends in the Gardens playing and having fun. I on the other hand was being used as free labour my father.

He had one full time employee by the name of "Reds."

Reds was a strapping red skin man with curlyish, brown hair just above his shoulders.

Daddy quickly became impressed with my ability at the shop. I could calculate totals very quickly without needing to write it down. Reds on the other hand couldn't count well and would miscalculate bills more than once. My father could have of course simply purchased a calculator but his cheap ass never grasped that concept.

We would get up at around 6:30 am, have a quick coffee and be off at seven. Getting the shop ready at around 7:45, I would be sent to get sandwiches for everyone which was breakfast. Getting home at close to 9 pm, we would have to bathe in that cold ass barrel water. It was a daily grind and I was fed up after just one week.

There was one upside. I loved RC (Royal Crown Cola). I was an avid drinker and now there it was at my disposal, free of charge.

I would drink about three a day. There was no rush as I was there all day. If I was halfway done, I would put it in the freezer to chill until my return.

By the second week, Daddy would glance at me and my RC. "Sunny, you go break meh yes boy. Yuh go break meh." Alluding to the fact that I was getting a lot of merchandise for free yet failing to mention my unpaid child labour, seven days a week.

My Dad liked to eat and so did I. Working at the shop may have been tedious but he made sure we were well fed. Even if no one else was hungry, he and I had regular appetites. I would be sent for pork sandwiches. We would sit at the back with a cup of coffee or a soft drink and enjoy ourselves.

The one truly bright spot was Saturdays. My father loved the races. Being in Arima he was now quite close to the Arima Racetrack. He would come to the shop in the morning and after a few hours leave with friends for the track, me in tow.

I would be given twenty dollars to bet and usually did quite well for myself. In addition to him buying us something to eat and drink, I would celebrate my individual winnings with a hotdog and a Coke.

With races done at 6:00, we would then go somewhere for dinner, followed by the men having a few rounds of drinks. I would be involved in the daily proceedings like I was one of the boys and thoroughly enjoyed myself.

We would return to the business at almost 9:00, Neelam, Sunita and Leila, quietly waiting in the small car park at the back, sitting in the dark, the shop already closed.

I am sure Neelam was less than impressed at the wait on a Saturday night as my father enjoyed himself with the boys, however, she kept it to herself.

Whilst my friends at the Falls were busy playing and going to the Blue Basin Waterfall, this is how I spent a month of my life. Years before, I would have been pulling out my hair in frustration. However, after years of sufferance in that Caigual bush, the meat shop was a huge step up. We had electricity, there were people to see and speak to, not just the customers but the owners of the premises lived next door, they shared the car park with us and we often had informal chats.

I knew how bad it had been before so I just found a way to live with it and enjoy the few pockets of fun we could have now and again.

One thing I refused to do was to rob the customers. When I had started at the shop, Daddy said to me, "When you are weighing the meat, turn the scale away so they can't see and take of an ounce."

"I can't do that. These are poor people. I cannot rob them."

"Listen. I have to pay extra expenses like the electricity and water, this is how I compensate for it."

However, I refused. Years later, I heard him telling someone how decent I was and on that day, my honesty and kindness had practically brought tears to his eyes.

CHAPTER 36

Farewell to the Falls

My mother had informed us at the beginning of the year that we would be leaving the Falls.

She did not quite know to which neighbourhood but we should be gone by July. When July came around, she said October.

Finally, at the end of July she had decided on a house in Petite Valley about a ten-minute drive from where we were and on the way to POS.

It was a decent three-bedroom house. Nicer looking than the one we had and a spacious backyard. I looked around and saw no children on the street.

"Jesus! There are no children here. Nobody on the street. Who am I going to speak to?"

"Never mind. You will adapt," was the response.

The summer holidays came to an end and it was back to school. I was now in Form II. Many of the boys felt good about themselves as they were no longer at the bottom of the pecking order. Some of them stood up at the entrance of the canteen and would give all the Form Ones entering a slight tap on the head. "Form Ones, take something," followed by the mandatory tap. The poor fellows acclimating to their first day, took it silently. I didn't like bullies. I didn't like it when it was done to me. So, I made sure not to partake in that nonsense.

Life was going reasonably well for me. I had my friends at the Gardens and at Holy Father's. I was truly beginning to enjoy my teenaged years, going to parties, meeting girls and liming with my friends in the Malls.

The mall of choice was the Long Circular Mall, ironically, about a hundred feet from where the original Morgan's had been in my earlier childhood. The boys and I would walk around, look at the other young girls and of course play in the video arcade. I was introduced to games such as Centipede and Millipede. My favourite was Pole Position, racing a car around a track and trying to avoid crashing into other cars. The best players got a ranking in the top 200. Eventually, I was good enough to be always in the top five.

I was dreading moving to the new neighbourhood in Petite Valley. It was called Walter Gardens. My relationship with Anastasia had evolved and we would often have private chats without the other children around.

The fact that she singled me out to spend her time with, made feel that I had certainly progressed socially. She was a nice person so I couldn't be sure if there was an attraction there or not. And I simply did not have the skills to adequately find out.

Although Christmas was usually a fun time for most kids, I knew at some point we would be packed off to Caigual. I got the shock of my life when my mother decided that until further notice, I would be spending my weekends there too.

Fed up with what she cited as my misbehaviour, she asked my father to take me off her hands. "I understand you have problems and I will certainly take him for the holidays but I believe children should be with their mother."

I thanked God for his response. I knew the truth was he just did not want the added responsibility of having to take care of me, listening to the constant bickering between Sunita and myself not to mention the laborious drive to POS every morning to my school.

If she could not get rid of me for good, at least she could get rid of me on weekends. I thus, started my weekly trips to Sangre Grande every Friday afternoon after school.

Ryan and his siblings no longer lived in Trinidad. Ryan had married the daughter of one of my father's friends. His father encouraged him to return to Georgetown and help run the family business, a bakery, which was actually quite successful.

Socially and financially, Ryan would do quite well, living in the house that belonged to his mother in one of the better neighbourhoods and managing his father's business.

In terms of matrimony however, he would not fare so well. The story I got from his mother which may have been biased was that Jameela, his wife had mental problems. She would burst into fits of rage when they had arguments and try to attack him, once breaking a huge bottle of cologne on the back of his head. They lasted three months.

After living a very mediocre life in TT for two years, Gary and Zara begged their mother to return to Guyana where they would not be "poor."

Aunty Farina, aware that they had a comfortable house waiting for them in Georgetown and that their father would see to their needs decided not to be selfish and to allow them to return.

What I could not understand is why she insisted on staying in TT when she seemed to have an upper-class lifestyle waiting for her in Guyana.

With Aunty Farina's children no longer there, these trips were a little more difficult for me. However, it was only a weekend so it was a quick in and out.

I remember returning home one day, walking in the house to see the neighbourhood kids, Leila and my mother watching a VHS movie on the TV.

All I could think was she's getting rid of me but having the other children over to watch TV.

The roller skating phenom had taken over Trinidad & Tobago earlier in the year. There were kids all over the world roller skating and coming up with fancy, acrobatic tricks. There was an American movie *Roller Boogie*, the year before starring Linda Blair. A lot of kids were asking for roller skates. On the weekends, you could go to Roller Parties and just skate in a circle with loud music playing.

Some of the kids would go just to lime with no intentions of skating just to enjoy the atmosphere.

My father explained to my mother that he had some "obligations" for the first two weekends of October and would not be able to take me. I used this as an opportunity to lime.

St. Athony's College which was not too far from house was having one of the Roller Parties that Saturday. Anastasia came with me. I felt kinda cool about it as if we were having a date.

As we entered, she saw some of her friends from St. Joseph Convent. I was introduced. Her ex-boyfriend, Sean was also there. He gave me a sort of suspicious look. I could never understand why a beautiful girl like her had been with Sean. He was a tubby white fellow with blondish, brown hair and his face was shaped like a dog.

I would walk around from time to time and chat with a few of the boys from school. At one point, I went up to a balcony to have a different view. I then decided it was time to go back downstairs and find Anastasia.

As I was halfway down, there was Laura Kanhai coming up. We stopped in front of each other. She looked at me and I looked at her. After a few seconds, I looked away and motioned with my hand for her to walk past me. We never exchanged a word.

Despite her silly behaviour earlier that year, part of me still liked her. There was even a part of me that hoped we might still have something together. I was angry with myself and allowed my pride to dominate the situation. Unless she apologized and explained herself, I would never compromise my self-respect.

As I reached the bottom of the stairs, Anastasia was waiting for me. She had seen what had happened and realized by my body language something was up.

"What happened there?" she queried, glancing towards the stairs. I explained what had happened and my subsequent behaviour.

"She probably did that nonsense at the party because she likes you."

I could not see the logic in it. But she could look at me with Anastasia and understand her basic irrelevance in my world.

We moved on the first Saturday of November. I had no interest in going so I did not help.

Three men came, one was the Mr. Trinidad & Tobago, the other was the Middleweight Mr. T&T. They were brown skinned, well-muscled men.

As they moved our belongings into a truck, I played football in the field opposite our house.

The new adobe was certainly nicer than the one in the Gardens. My room was bigger and we had unfettered access to a TV signal.

For some reason, the TV was put into my room and Leila and I enjoyed ourselves watching the wonderful colour and clear picture.

As I had expected there were no kids to play with. I would visit the Falls on some weekends and on occasion the Douglases would visit us.

My mother left us at home on New Year's Eve as she had a party to go to. This was not the first time but it certainly was in this neighbourhood. No kids to ol' talk with but we did have our TV.

Leila went to bed before midnight. I sat there and looked at a movie on the one channel TT had as 1982 slowly commenced.

I found myself contemplating on the possibilities of the new year and the rest of the decade. The majority of my childhood had already finished and before the decade's end, I would be a full-grown man. I contemplated what could happen in 1982 and in this very new neighbourhood.

I didn't know it but this would be the year that would have an irrevocable change on my childhood. The tensions in my family had been bad and being around my father had been a negative experience for both Leila and me.

However, I could not in my wildest imagination perceive what was yet to come.

It would only get worse.

CHAPTER 37

A Tubby Boy No More

As I settled into Walter Gardens and became totally used to having a proper functioning TV in the house, I nevertheless, found myself looking for reasons to visit the Falls.

Many of us had dreamt of the day when we could leave, have proper TV reception and not live in such an isolated place. However, now that I was living "the dream," I found myself returning to my old neighbourhood. I could play football and cricket, go to the Waterfall. Basically, I could have fun.

The Douglas family would visit us at least twice a month.

I had put on a bit of weight because of no one to play sports with but I enjoyed being able to see the kids of the Falls when I could.

Morgan's was having its annual Sports Day just before the Easter Holidays. I was looking forward to this. I could once again reconnect with the students from my class.

I showed up on a Saturday with Leila and greeted my old teachers. Gordon and I had not seen each other since the previous Sports Day when he and his brother had had a 1-2 finish. With his older brother not bothering to come, the rest of us knew we had a better chance of placing in the top three.

Laura Kanhai was also there. Her younger sister and Leila were in their final year at Morgan's. She seemed alone standing by herself. We saw each other and I calmly looked away.

• • •

Gordon, I and the other boys spent the next few hours, checking out the girls, speaking to some other ex-students and teachers. Then came time for the Old Boys Race.

I was wearing a black sleeveless T Shirt with yellow trim and matching shorts. I looked quite buffed and with my moustache, those who did not know me, would have sworn that I was 17.

Seven of us lined up. We were all nervous and it was apparent. Mrs. Skeene's husband was the starter.

"Alright fellahs. Calm down. Breathe. Take it easy."

We breathed, jumped and ran on the spot. Trying to warm up like the pros did on TV.

Then it was time to get into position. Some ass took off early so we all broke formation and had to start over again. He wasn't really an ass. It was just the nerves that we were all feeling.

Back into position. We waited for the Starter.

"On your marks. Get Set. GO!!!"

And we were off. I had no idea what was happening with the other runners. My eyes were a concentrated squint. All I could see was a semi blurred vision of the green field in front of me.

At the 50-metre mark, I looked to my left. The only person I could see was Gordon. We were neck and neck.

I could not believe that after all his years of dominance at Morgan's and me usually holding up the rear that I had reached such heights. I decided to go for it. Maybe I could win. Maybe I could beat Gordon.

The moment I thought it, I felt a little weakening at the back of my knees. I was a few inches behind him as we pounced on the line. If I had stretched forward, we might have tied. Instead, I was so happy to reach that far, I raised my hands above my head as if I were the winner. It was the way the superstars did it on TV.

Thirty odd feet beyond the tape, we both crashed into the fence. Everyone else closing in behind us. We looked at each other, smiled, gave each other a hand wrestling handshake and hugged.

My days of being the tubby boy at the back of the pack were now firmly over. I was a little overweight because of the new neighbourhood and I wondered how different the race might have been if I had been in peak form.

We took our places on the podium and once again I knew the feeling that had never descended upon me during my time at Morgan's.

As I looked into the crowd, I saw Laura looking at me. I held her gaze for a second and then looked away. Our names were announced on the loudspeaker and the crowd cheered.

As Gordon and I walked off, proud of the ribbons on our chests, I glanced in Laura's direction. She was still looking at me. I walked off and never saw her again.

CHAPTER 38

The Married Man

Despite no longer being in the Falls, I was happy that we could maintain contact with the Douglases.

Our families had spent the Carnival weekend in TT together in Barbados.

We stayed at a bed and breakfast place just on a beach. It was an old colonial house with about five rooms upstairs. Aunty Jane still had family in Barbados so in addition to taking in the sites, we visited them as well.

We would occasionally take a local bus for a short trip as Aunty Jane knew the ropes. I was in awe as to how fast these little buses moved on such small roads. If you were not sitting, you had to hold on for dear life to one of the metal posts.

We eventually rented a six-seat minivan with an 800-horsepower engine. At one point driving past some sugar cane fields, a bus simply sped past us and left us in the dust. It wasn't much for speed but it got us from here to there. It was a great trip seeing the sites and of course swimming in the sea. And then it was back to reality.

At the beginning of the Easter holidays in March we visited Aunty Annete. She lived in Curepe but had a beautiful country home in Cunupia.

Aunty Annete had befriended my parents during their university days in London. She had also met a young Indo Trini, Dick, whom she eventually married and the four of them would become the best of friends.

They had actually lived about a hundred metres away from us on Old Southern Main Rd. during our Curepe years.

Both couples divorced within a year of each other, my parents first. Dick and my dad would continue to be close and so would their wives. The ex-wives just never mingling with the men and vice versa.

Aunty Annete was now married to a tall, strapping Portuguese fellow, Mason. He was a few years younger than her, perhaps not as sophisticated but friendly and down to earth.

After my parents' divorce and with no child support coming from my father, my mother would often borrow money from Annete, pay her back at the end of the month, only to borrow the same money again the next month. They had remained very close and in later years Mummy would reminisce about her kindness.

We arrived at their country home which was nestled at the bottom of a hill. Aunty Annete's family owned a gas station in Curepe and one in Cunupia as well. The house was about a hundred feet behind the station.

The Douglases were already there, playing small goal in the very long porch which ran halfway around the house. I was surprised to see them as they certainly did not know Aunty Annete that well, I assumed my mother had invited them.

The adults spent most of the day in the back chatting next to the bar. We played our football in the front. I noticed a tall white, bespectacled, blond fellow but did not pay much attention as he was on of twenty odd people there.

We left at the end of the day, me pleasantly surprised that I had had such fun in the bush of Cunupia.

That Monday in the evening, I saw the white fellow calling out at our gate. I told my Mum and the two of them chatted for a few hours in the porch.

She explained that he was French and that his wife and children were away on holiday. He had simply come to say hello.

He must have had a lot of hellos because he came every night, the two of them chatting for a few hours in the porch.

We were supposed to go to the Santa Flora Beach Camp the following week for a few days. My mother explained that the Frenchman would be coming with us. I thought nothing of it until two days later when she told us that she, the Douglases and the French fellow would be going to Santa Flora but not Leila and I because we had to visit our father.

I could not understand what the hell she was talking about. Why organize a trip, invite the Douglases and then decide we should not come and the rest of them would?

"But why would you do that. You know we like Santa Flora!"

"Don't you want to visit your father? He's your father."

Leila and I continued to remonstrate and then it hit me.

"You mean you trying to get rid of us so you could take a married man to Santa Flora!!"

"I don't' know what you are talking about. He is your father. Don't you want to visit him?"

"But why can't we go after?"

"He is your father."

That was the only logic she seemed capable of.

For the next two days my anger simply escalated.

"What kind of an ass gets rid of us to take a married man on holiday with the Douglases and their children? Are you so stupid? You not fooling anyone!!"

On one occasion, she actually changed her response, "And your father did it?"

"THAT is your excuse!!!"

When my father arrived, he simply smiled as I explained her reason for trying to get rid of us.

She quietly responded, "That is not true."

One would have thought he would have some sympathy for us and perhaps most fathers would have but he certainly was not like most.

As we arrived at Caigual, he made sure to tell Neelam the situation.

The family had graduated to a nine-inch black and white TV which was powered by a car battery. As we watched it, he began to laugh.

"So yuh mother get rid of allyuh for a married man."

And he cackled.

"You all are really not important. Imagine she going to Santa Flora and left you behind to take a married man."

I had always known he was not much of a father but I thought even he had his limits.

After a few minutes, I could take it no more.

"Why yuh don't shut your ass!"

The snicker immediately came off his face. "Who you talking to?"

"You! Why yuh doh shut yuh ass!"

In a flash he was off the bed and slapped me across the head.

Perhaps if I had been in a civilized, populated, area, I might've cursed at him and run out of the house. But outside there was nothing but bush.

I simply had to take it.

I cried and kept quiet for the rest of the night. I made a decision right then and there. Any relationship we had was over as far as I was concerned. One day many years from now, he would want his children around him and we would not be there.

The next day as we got up, I heard Neelam, sucking her teeth, "Steuups." But it was not one of anger.

My father looked at her. "What happened?"

"I am just thinking about what happened last night."

His tone was one of surprise and insensitivity, "You letting *that* bother you!" And he walked away.

It would be the only time she ever showed any kind of pity towards the way we were treated.

It would only get worse.

CHAPTER 39

The Birthday Party and the Fight

We spent the next week in Caigual doing the best we could. My father did not tease us anymore. But I refused to speak to anyone. If at the house, I found a far corner to be away from everyone.

I simply would not speak. If we went out, I sat in a corner quietly. My father was unfazed and apparently unashamed.

To my shock, a week later, he told us that we were going to return to our mother's.

"Actually, I wanted to send you home earlier. But Neelam said not to."

I was confused as to why Neelam should insist that we stay. How was it any of her business and why the fuck was he listening to her?

So, we went home and we would go to Santa Flora after all.

When I asked my mother why she changed her mind. The response was "I felt sorry for you all."

It turned out that it wasn't sorrow but rather shame.

Richard explained that when his parents heard that she had sent us to Caigual, they made it clear to her, "You can't do that to the children.

You can't do that. How could you send them away and take us to the Beach Camp? Nah man you cah do dat Cintra."

So, she capitulated.

The Frenchman was duly uninvited. Apparently, she had some shame after all.

I enjoyed the Camp as best as I could but my relationship with my mother would not be the same. I could not believe that someone who was always preaching proper behaviour, could be such a vulgar public ass herself.

If she tried to speak to me, I would curse at her and walk off.

However, I did discuss the matter with Richard and Gary. It was shocking that an adult could be so low class and stupid and inconceivable that it was my own mother.

In my subconscious, I realized that the two of them would probably go and tell their parents what we had discussed.

After Santa Flora, we were once again sent off to Caigual. I put up with my father and his family as best I could.

School was actually a semi relief. Although I hated school and homework and could not wait for the day for high school to end, I knew at least we would not be in Caigual putting up with low class, racist, Indians.

One morning as I entered our Form II Class, Michael Bacchus was waiting for me. The school was offering a Summer Camp in Guadeloupe.

I made it clear that I was not that good in French and did not see the point.

"Dat doh matter. We will be together. We can help each other out and we could meet some nice French girls."

Within about twenty minutes I had been persuaded and we signed up along with Carl Ball.

I went home and told my mother. "If your father is willing to pay for it, I am ok with that."

A letter was sent off and miraculously, he said he would pay.

I found myself a bit excited. I had only been to Barbados and now this was a chance to see another country.

Two months later, my mother threw a party to celebrate her fortieth birthday.

She did not throw birthday parties often, probably due to her limited financial situation. However, when she did, there was LOTS of food.

Most of her friends were of a different race and they loved Indian food. So, she made sure that there was a good variety. Although a good cook, it was too much effort to prepare for the 50 odd people that would come.

She would find an Indian woman to do most of the cooking and do some herself. Leila and I were always delighted at these affairs. In true Trini style my mother would cook more than enough food, meaning that we had serious leftovers. For the next two or three days, we would be in some kind of Indian food paradise, finishing off the curry mango, curry goat and whatever else there was.

The week before the party she made sure the that the house was spotless. Helping her was Coreen, our latest housekeeper. She had joined the family just after our Carnival trip.

Coreen was from Grenada and like many of the people from the smaller islands had come to TT for a better life, leaving her two-year-old daughter in the care of her parents.

She was 20 years old, black, slim, short and pretty with her hair tied in two short pig tails. and would often have casual chats with Leila and myself.

She was also a big fan of Dallas, an American TV series that was very popular in Trinidad. The main character being a fellow called JR Ewing who was a bit devious and shameless.

I always credited Coreen as the person who got me into watching Dallas.

Together she and my Mum made sure the house was spotless prior to the party.

There was a major boxing fight that night, June 11, 1982, Gerry Cooney vs Larry Holmes for the Heavyweight Championship of the World.

It had been decades since a white man had won the Heavyweight Title and Cooney had been dubbed as "the Great White Hope."

The day of the party I was unconcerned about the guests but rather the fight. Both boxers were exciting and this seemed like it would be an action-packed affair.

As the guests trickled in after 7:00 pm, many of the men came into my room and deposited themselves on the floor and my bed watching the undercard.

By the time of the Main Event more than half the guests were squeezed in watching. My mother would later complain half-jokingly, "You took over my party."

Gerry Cooney eventually lost in a valiant attempt, TKO'd in the 13th round.

In the midst of the fight, there was almost one that broke out in my room as well. Uncle Gerard had made a bet with Burt Chandleur.

Burt had been one of my mother's colleagues at the Ministry until she left in 1979. Not surprisingly, there were quite a few of her ex-colleagues there. He and Uncle Gerard had made a bet on the fight, five dollars, Uncle Gerard backing Holmes.

As the rounds wore on it became obvious that the Champion was dominating Cooney. Uncle Gerard then decided to give Burt some *picong*.

"I betting, you ten dollars, twenty dollars, a hundred dollars." He just kept going on and on and after a few minutes, he got a reaction.

"Why don't you shut up!! Burt retorted. "Why yuh doh shut yuh mouth. Shut your blasted mouth. Shut up nuh!!"

"Why you don't go fuck yourself?" was Uncle Gerard's response.

The whole room went silent. Everyone's eyes slowly moved from the TV to the two men to the right of it.

Burt looked at him, glanced at the other people, "Look at you. You have no respect for yourself or anybody else in this room."

"Cuss me back nah," said Uncle Garth with a very serious look.

They locked eyes for a few seconds and then Burt just continued looking at the fight.

The *picong* was ended and Burt duly paid his bet after the fight.

At that point, the guests left the room and began their dancing and feting. I continued to look at the post-fight report and then went to eat some of that delicious food.

CHAPTER 40

Loose Thighs

One of the happiest times of my life was early July. It meant the end of the school year and the summer holidays. This was indescribable joy for me.

In addition, I would be going to Guadeloupe later that month.

Around the last week of June, a black fellow showed up at the gate one night, asking to speak to Mrs. Darsan.

He and my mother chatted for about twenty minutes and he left. She explained that he worked at the office.

The next night he showed up again and they chatted for about an hour. For the next week, he continued coming at night.

"Does this man have no home?" I asked my mother. "Is every night this man coming here. Is he homeless?"

Coreen would flash a broad smile and my mother would remain silent.

He then started showing up during the day on weekends. His name was Marvin Crawford.

I got the impression he had designs on my mother. I wasn't surprised. Despite being forty, she was still slim and exceptionally beautiful. Even the teenaged boys would stare at her. Marvin was six feet tall, fit with an afro and a beard but considering he was a bit on the ugly side, I couldn't see him getting anywhere.

I was wrong.

Less than two weeks after meeting him, she invited him to come to Santa Flora with us and the Douglases.

We took his car. Richard's family following us. The two of them holding hands and smiling away. I now had to watch these two asses for the more than 60-minute ride to the Beach Camp.

Of course, I once again confided in Richard. "She met the man just the other day and now she bringing him here." I looked at him and Gary, "What de ass wrong with she? She did not even say anything to us. Just bring him here and start sleeping with him in front of everyone like it's normal!"

The man was so ugly, he looked like a gorilla. I did not think this because he was black. It was because he was *that* ugly. I had always thought it strange that he wore shades at night. On our first day at the Camp, he took off his shades to wipe some sweat from his forehead and I noticed his right eye was a bit *cokey*[14] looking.

"Jesus!" I thought to myself. "This man does not look like a gorilla. He looks like a *cokey eyed* gorilla."

Unlike the previous visit to the Camp, there had been no attempt to get rid of us. Presumably because this one was not married.

If I had been disrespectful before, I was even worse now. I enjoyed the Camp and swimming in the pool as much as I could just having nothing to do with my mother.

If she came around me and tried to speak, my response would be immediate, "Fuck off!"

On one occasion at dinner, I was raising my voice, wondering why we had to eat rice and vegetables with no meat.

Uncle Peter shouted at me, "Sunny!! Sunny!!"

---

[14] *Cokey eye*: someone who is cross eyed aka cock eyed.

I looked at him, "Sunny WHAT!! Sunny WHAT!! "

Prior to that moment, the thought of me ever giving him back chat especially with his imposing physique was unfathomable. But I was so vexed by what was happening, I was actually crazy enough to take him on.

I think the only reason he tolerated me on that day was because both he and Aunty Jane realized what I was going through.

We returned home after a few days with me now waiting to go to Guadeloupe in less than a week.

Marvin was simply there every night now. On one occasion he and my mother left the house at 11 p.m. to go "window shopping."

I was just glad she did not have him sleeping over at the house. I would have been so embarrassed for Coreen to see loose she had become with her thighs.

CHAPTER 41

The Guadeloupe Experience and Peeing on a Nightgown

In the third week of July, I was off to Guadeloupe.

I knew nothing about the island other than it was a French colony and that the capital was Point-a-Pitre.

I met Michael and Carl at the airport. There were a bunch of Form I boys there as well. I had travelled to Barbados on my mother's passport as I had been only 12. But now I had my own.

We saw Uncle Shirvan in a police officer's uniform, guarding the Arrival's Exit.

I saw him and waved.

"Mummy, Mummy. Look, it's Uncle Shirvan."

She just frowned and continued walking.

"You don't want to talk to him? Let's go and say hello"

"We have no time for that. Come on you have to check in."

After duly finishing my check in, she wished me a good trip and gave me a kiss on the cheek.

Before entering Immigration with our Holy Father's Group, I felt a hand on my shoulder. It was Uncle Shirvan.

He had a quick word and a smile with me and wished me well.

I was curious as to why my mother was uninterested in greeting him. But a year later, it would all make more sense.

We entered the Departure Lounge and saw Ms. Laurel. She was a French teacher for the higher forms, with her was a white woman. Apparently, she was French and taught the language at the French Institute of Trinidad & Tobago. Her name was Simone Claudel.

We saw Ms. Laurel going back and forth between us and a group of six girls. "I think those fellahs with us too," said a slim Indian one.

"Eh eh, birds in the lime boy," I told the boys. We later found out that they were from St. Theresa's Convent. A top girls' high school from the South of TT. Some had finished Form IV, and the other three had already completed Form V.

There were six Form Ones and four of us from my class, the other being Jason Jackson. He was called "Cockson" by the fellows in our class because he was considered a slacker. During the first few months of Form I, he would walk up to the many of the boys and just grab their crotch. I could not figure out if it was some kind of joke or he was gay. When he did it to me, I should have hit him but I was just so shocked that I did not know how to respond.

There were also two younger kids a brother and sister. I was shocked when I looked at their parents to see an Asian woman and my mother's French acquaintance. I noticed he and my mother were not as eager to speak on this occasion.

The boy was bout 12 and his sister three years younger. They were good looking kids with a hint of their Asian ancestry around their eyes.

We were separated on the flight but it was only two and a half hours. Arriving in the Guadeloupe airport, we were bunched together and met outside by four men,

Jean, Henry, Pierre and Michel.

Jean was a tall, broad shouldered, fair skinned fellow with curlyish, black hair.

He was the boss of the organization that had planned this trip.

Henry was a tall, handsome, black man with a low-cut afro and a fit, bronzed, body.

Pierre was short and black with glasses and lastly, Michel, was a slim, East Indian fellow. It was weird for me to watch an Indian speaking French as a first language. They had all been born in Guadeloupe.

We were taken to an old, long, wooden building. It wasn't exactly luxurious looking and then we slowly realized it was a school that was obviously closed due to the holidays. We were sectioned off to about four to a room, the girls and the boys well segregated. We had dinner in a sort of canteen, chatted the night away and awaited our first real day in this French colony.

For the next three days we saw the sites, some old historic forts and visited the beach. Point a Pitre didn't seem as big as POS but it wasn't too shabby by Caribbean standards. One difference I did notice was that quite a few women had hairy legs and armpits. They seemed to enjoy a kind of bread that was long and cylindrical – not sliced. It was normal to see the women walking with it unbagged, clutched under their armpits as if it were a newspaper. I had to wonder about the hygienic consequences regarding this method of transportation.

On the fourth day, we were told that we were moving. We arrived at a huge, high rise apartment building of twenty stories. This was certainly impressive by TT standards. We were put in groups on different floors. Michael, Carl, John and I were placed on the fifteenth floor. Carl and I shared one room, John and Michael, the other. It was sort of cool to have our own apartment with very little supervision.

At this point we had gotten to know the six girls a bit better. Jennifer was a pretty fair skinned girl with soft, blondish, brown, hair. She had just written O Levels. Two of her friends were Maureen and Lisa. Maureen was short, black with a low Afro. Lisa was pretty, with a copper toned skin, glasses and shoulder length hair, tied back.

Rounding up their group, were three Indians from Form IV, Karen, Joy and Jean.

Karen had somehow hooked up with Michael on the second day, they would walk with arms around each other or holding hands. Joy was a bit overweight with glasses and long hair. Jean was a pretty Indian girl, slim, with long hair as well.

We were enjoying the atmosphere of this French island. Ms. Laurel was very friendly and easy to get along with. Ms. Claudel, who seemed to be at least in her late forties, was a bit sterner and less amiable. Behind her back, Ms. Laurel who was in her mid-twenties did admit that the French woman was a bit stiff. Engaging in a piece of gossip, she told us that Claudel had married a black man in Paris in the fifties but life had been difficult for them as a mixed couple. She was now a divorcee.

On our seventh day we moved again. We were taken to a collection of buildings on a hillock overlooking the sea. We were put in a building with three huge rooms with showers and toilets at the back. The boys were given the first room the girls the second and the Ms. Laurel and Claudel the last one.

There seemed to be a hundred kids running around and playing also staying there. It was apparently some sort of summer camp.

One of the beds in our room smelled of urine. Obviously, the previous occupant had had a problem of sorts. The mattress was put outside to get some sun.

We were given a quick tour of the camp and told we could go swimming. We had a great time in the sea. At this point I had gotten to know Jennifer better. She was about to enter Form VI after the holidays and was two years older than me. When her hair got wet in the sea, she looked really cute and reminded me of a young Julie Andrews, the English actress. She would sometimes sing a song I really liked *Puff the Magic Dragon*.

It was a pretty song but as I did not know all the words, I would have her sing and join in.

Around the third day at the Camp, coming back from an excursion, many of us fell asleep. Jennifer was next to me and we took turns sleeping on each other's shoulder.

Our relationship for the rest of the holiday became more intimate as we would hold hands or just rest on each other whilst riding in the minivan provided for us.

Trouble seemed to follow me wherever I went and Guadeloupe was no different.

Ms. Claudel seemed a bit on the grumpy side. And at times would shout at us for simple things like wondering off a bit on excursions or talking too loudly at night. Ms. Laurel on the other hand was much more laid back and sympathized with us regarding her colleague's negative demeanour.

Things came to a head a few days before the end of our visit. We were taking an afternoon nap and we were awakened by the two ladies to get ready for dinner.

Me being deep asleep and to the far end of the room did not hear. I continued sleeping. I slowly awoke feeling a sensation on my face. As my eyes opened, I saw Ms. Claudel repeatedly flicking a towel on my face as if trying to get a horse to gallop. It took a few seconds for my senses to grasp what was actually happening. Once I did, I exploded.

"What the fuck!!"

"You gone off!"

I jumped off the bed. "You is a fucking mad woman or what!! You hitting me on my face??"

Everyone was outside waiting for me and a few stragglers. When they heard the commotion Ms. Laurel came bounding in.

"No! No! You cannot treat them like that! You have to show them some respect!!"

Ms. Claudel looked at her with a condescending smile, "You are so stupid."

I was a bit shocked that the two adults were behaving like this.

But I was not finished.

"You must be mad no ass!!" I walked outside past the group and made my way towards the canteen. "No wonder yuh man leave your ass and divorced you. You dumb bitch!!"

Ms. Laurel tried to pacify me. "Ok Sunil. Ok. Relax."

The girls just giggled.

I shouted off a few more obscenities and eventually calmed down.

The incident was a talking point amongst the group for the rest of the night. We were all pissed with Ms. Claudel. Later with just my classmates around, Michael came up with an idea.

With the others outside enjoying the sea breeze and relaxing on the grass, he hatched a plan.

He went to the room where the teachers slept. He grabbed Ms. Claudel's nightgown and took it to one of the toilets. "I am going to pee on this and then everybody will take a turn. Close the door so we don't see you."

All four of us took our turns and that nightgown was truly drenched in urine. We laughed and ran off leaving it there.

We spent the next 24 hours waiting for Ms. Claudel to explode but she never said a word.

Two days later as she walked through our room to the Exit. I mumbled "Pee."

She turned around and looked at me. I gave her a blank stare.

"Yes, pee," she said and left the room.

We laughed quietly. She had figured it out but kept it to herself. We were quite proud of our revenge.

That night we were informed there was a party and we were invited. There were about 10 men, the girls in our group and the boys and I from my class.

Had we not come there would have been no females at this "party."

They played nothing but Zouk, a type of French music local to the French islands of the Caribbean. They seemed to love it, we did not.

We sat there for about 45 minutes just watching them. They then played a catchy score from the movie *the Sting*. In Trinidad we would have ignored this song or even laughed at this old-time tune at a young people's party. But we were so happy to hear an upbeat tune that we recognized, we got up and danced our hearts out. When the song finished we cheered and clapped.

Then came the slow music. The girls anticipated that they would be asked by the Guadeloupean boys. They made sure to tell us "If they ask us to dance. Ask us too so we can politely say no to them."

As a boy made his way towards Maureen, she said "Sunny make sure to ask me eh."

He asked and he was refused. I then stepped forward, "Would you like to dance?"

"No thank you."

I was stunned. What the hell did she ask me to step in for?

She said no to four boys in a row. When I asked her the reason for my rejection, she explained, "If I said no to you and to them, then it's obvious I just don't want to dance and I don't look rude."

I shook my head at her logic. So, I had to look stupid to help her out?

The next few days were pleasant enough. Sophie was the French man's daughter, she had no idea I knew her father. She had taken a liking to me and would always try to sit next to me or put her arm around me. She was a cute girl. However, she would try to jump on me in the sea which was a bit too much. The others laughed as they realized she had a bit of a crush.

On the last night we went to a nightclub. I was curious as I was only 14 and had never been to one before. We grabbed a corner and had a lot of fun.

Jen and I sat next to each other. We slow danced and it was a great last night. I did it find it strange to see a few men dancing slow music together and one or two even asked me for a dance while I was sitting. As strange as it seemed, I chalked it up to the local culture.

After the club, we returned home and spent a lot of time in the girls' room. Jen and I lay on a bed far from the others. A few photos were taken of us that I would see later. We knew it was our last night and we tried to enjoy it as best we could.

The next day we made our way to the airport, reasonably satisfied with our Guadeloupe sojourn with certainly none of the boys having improved much in terms of French. Jean made a short speech bidding us farewell and apologizing for the occasional hiccups in our accommodations. He explained that we had been the first group hence a few problems and it would probably be better in the future.

Maureen volunteered to exchange seats with me so I could sit next to Jen and she and I enjoyed our last few hours together.

The Trinidad airport was not exactly the most efficient, it could take two hours to get your bags and then another two to stand in the line before they were checked and you could exit.

Some of us got our bags in an hour but were in no hurry to leave each other so we sat waiting for the others to get their bags before we entered the final line.

I sat with my arm around Jen chatting with the group and was shocked to see Marvin greeting me.

"I am here to pick you up."

I found myself wondering why the hell my mother needed to send him to meet me at the airport.

But I really had no choice but to go with him.

I bade everyone farewell and surprisingly we skipped the baggage check line because he had "a friend" working there that day.

I wondered how much more of this man I would have to put up with around me.

I had no idea what was coming.

CHAPTER 42

"Your Mother is a Nigger Lover"

When Marvin and I arrived home my mother had a great meal waiting for me, rice, callaloo, stewed beef and plantain.

She seemed concerned that I had lost weight. But really, instead of being stuck in a neighbourhood with no one to play sports with, I had been constantly on the move for the last two weeks.

I enjoyed the food and tried to put up with this man that now seemed to be much more in our life than before.

I went to bed early that night suffering from jet lag.

I got up around eight the next morning and sat relaxing in the living room reading the newspaper. I heard someone coming down the corridor. It was Marvin, apparently, he had spent the night.

The next morning, I saw him exit the room again. It was only after he had spent four consecutive nights that it dawned upon me that he was living with us.

I pulled Leila aside, "Is Marvin living here?"

She nodded.

"When did this happen?"

"About a few days after you left for Guadeloupe."

I looked at Leila. "Are you friggin serious? She knew him for less than a month and just brought him here to live."

Leila looked at me with a helpless smile not really knowing what to say.

"Did she say anything to you when she brought him here?"

Leila shook her head.

"You mean she brought him into the house and didn't even explain anything to you?"

Again, she shook her head.

All I could think of was that while I was in Guadeloupe she had brought this uglito into our home. I found myself wondering if my mother was experiencing some kind of midlife crisis.

About a week later my father came to pick us up. Mummy had explained that he and his family were now living in St. Anne's. When we asked why the drastic change of location, her response was "Ask him."

Although we now hated the thought of seeing him we at least knew that St. Anne's was part of the capital and for sure, we would have access to electricity and TV.

He had closed the meat shop. Apparently, he had made enough money and was moving on in life.

He arrived, chatted with Mummy for a few minutes and was introduced to Marvin.

Within seconds of departing the house, he exclaimed, "Yuh mother is a Nigger lover??"

We looked at him in shock.

"Your mother is a nigger lover! Seriously??

We just kept staring. After my last experience with him in Caigual, I knew I dared not give him any chat. He would simply take advantage of me.

He laughed all the way to his new home that "You mother sleeping with a nigger."

As we arrived at the one-bedroom apartment his family was now living in, he exclaimed to Neelam, "Imagine Cintra have a nigger!"

"What?"

"Cintra! She have a nigger man. She actually brought the man into the house to live with her. They have a nigger father." He pointed to us and laughed.

She looked at us and smiled but in a somewhat daze obviously surprised by the news.

I realized if I cursed at him, he would hit me. If I got angry that would be playing right into his hands.

"Well he might be a nigger but he does not spend his days lazing about. He is a former National Scholarship Winner and has three degrees."

"Eh eh, you defending your nigger father. Well he is your father. I supposed you have to defend him."

I realized it was best not to respond no matter how difficult that would be.

I had given up on him having any class but his idiocy was beyond the scope of my imagination.

It would only get worse.

CHAPTER 43

Idiot Mother, Idiot Father

The rest of the summer holiday was a sort of nightmarish hell for Leila and me.

Within a week of my return from Guadeloupe, my mother explained that she and Marvin would be getting married and later that year would be buying a house so we would be moving.

I looked at her smiling at me and begged God to deliver me from the shit that I was hearing.

"You have only known him for a month and you are getting married?"

"Yes, we are in love. We are a family now and we will move to another home to live."

"You must be out of your fucking mind. You bring this fucking ass in here and telling me he is my family. Now you are saying that you are getting married and we are going to move. I eh going nowhere."

"Well what are you going to do?

"Fuck you. I am not going to another house."

I knew I could not really derail this crazy shit I was hearing but I was determined to go down swinging. I just could not grasp how she could meet a man and in just a matter of weeks make such massive changes in all our lives. I realized that like any adult she needed someone in her life. But after all the suitors she had had, how did this ugly bitch just show up and have such an effect on her?

We now had to put up with this man who was in our midst every day and night.

Worse yet it was obvious to the neighbours because they had eyes.

My mother was now eager to get rid of us on a more regular basis because of the proximity of our father, especially me as I was "the troublesome one."

Any morsel of respect I had had for her previously was now gone. I would use the worst possible language when speaking to her, unimaginable words that I never thought any son could use to his mother.

Coreen had gone to visit her family in Grenada whilst I was in Guadeloupe. She had said she would return in two weeks but never did. Although I liked her, I was sort of glad. It would have just been an additional embarrassment to have her witness my mother's foolishness.

We had a maid who came in August and left two weeks later because she could not tolerate my constant flow of profanity.

We saw the Douglases from time to time. I told Gary how the Frenchman's children had been on the trip to Guadeloupe and how his daughter had taken a liking to me.

"So why didn't you do something with her?"

I looked at him, "You mad? She's only nine years old."

"So? That would have been good revenge for you."

My eyebrows furrowed together, "With a nine-year old? I am not that sick."

He laughed.

If it was difficult for me, it had to be worse for Leila. She was the youngest and the least able to defend herself.

My father had destroyed our relationship years before. But now things were infinitely worse.

My only release of tension was at the house so I fought with Leila even more frequently now. I also knew that my mother found this stressful and I was determined that her life was going to be anything but blissful.

If she thought she could spread her legs at will and embarrass me, I was going to show her how difficult life could be.

There were times I would overreact with Leila, hitting and kicking her. She would go screaming and bang on my mother's bedroom door until she opened it. The more I fought with Leila the more stress she would have.

However, deep down my conscience bothered me. I knew none of this was Leila's fault. My father may have encouraged us not to get along but she was my sister and I did care for her. But somehow, I could not stop arguing with her. I decided it was just best not to be in the same room with her. If we were not together, we could not fight and at least her life could be easier.

Sadly, it would get unimaginably worse for her, my father being the culprit. I had managed to dodge a few visits to him. However, one day he sent Neelam to fetch me.

I did not know how to say no. School had just started and I was hoping to just relax on that weekend.

I sat in the apartment making it clear, I had no interest in them. I kept looking at the clock on the wall.

"When am I going home," I asked.

"Are you in a hurry?" queried my father.

"I have homework to do."

"Why didn't you bring it here?"

"Well I did not know that I was coming here. It's at home"

I was lying as best I could. I had no real interest in the homework but I was trying to leave as quickly as possible.

They mentioned that Leila had visited the week before. My father then explained that he had told her, "You can spend time with your new nigger father. You can play with his hair. How do you like your new nigger father?"

When she could take it no more, she began to cry, screaming, "STOP IT!! STOP IT!!"

He and Neelam had a good laugh.

Now that they had told me the story, they laughed some more and looked at me. They were probably expecting a sign of weakness so I laughed along. They nodded and enjoyed the moment, grinning like chimpanzees.

Inside my heart was breaking, I did not want them to know or they may have taken advantage of me as well. I could not understand how a man could look at his helpless daughter and do such a thing. I reaffirmed my pledge to have nothing to do with him as an adult.

I thought of poor Leila not capable of any kind of cruelty or malice and being treated like this by the only father she had ever known.

All of this behaviour was openly exhibited in front of Sunita by two idiots who obviously did not know how to bring up a child.

CHAPTER 44

Blows, More Blows and Alone at Christmas

Entering Form III was a reasonably big deal in TT. At the end of that year you would pick your subjects for O Levels. This was part of our British colonial heritage.

The Caribbean in an effort to have their own identity introduced the CXC (the Caribbean Examination Council) Exams which they believed was better suited for its students.

I was determined there would be no clowning around in Form III. It was important to do well and get the subjects that I wanted.

I had a rather infamous reputation in my class for getting into trouble. I had been beaten my Mr. Ali in the first week of Form I and thereafter, he had gotten to know me quite well during the next two years.

Sometimes it was for minor nonsense such as talking in class or not having done my homework. However, there were more serious moments.

Around the third month of Form I, I was walking around with a Divider in my hand. It had two extremely sharp pointy ends. Just for fun, I threw it up into the ceiling to see if it would stick. And it did.

I laughed for a few seconds, I was about to walk off and then I realized that at some point it would fall out of the ceiling. It could fall on someone and do serious harm. They would probably ask who had thrown it up there. That would be blows for sure. I decided to retrieve the Divider. But it was high up on the ceiling.

I ran to the canteen which was right next to my class. I looked at Ms. Lyon, the Canteen Manager and asked "Could I please borrow a broom. I want to clean up a mess next door."

I returned quickly and started hitting the Divider. All the boys around me started shouting encouraging me to get the job done. With my luck at that exact moment, along came Mr. Ali.

He looked at me in mild horror. I looked at him and then pretended that my duty to retract the Divider was much more important and it was not that unnatural to have it sticking in a ceiling.

Once out, all the boys cheered and Mr. Ali approached me.

"Mr. Darsan, what is this??"

"Well Sir, I was walking and it slipped out of my hand and went into the ceiling." I demonstrated with my right hand.

"What!! Mr. Darsan how is that possible? How could it slip and end up in the ceiling??"

"Yes Sir. I know Sir. I was very concerned because it could hurt someone. So, I got a broom to knock it down."

"But look at it. It was right up in the ceiling. It CANNOT slip out of your hand and go that far up a ceiling."

"I know Sir. It was very dangerous and I was worried. That is why I got the broom. I didn't want anyone to get injured."

"Mr. Darsan you always seem to be getting in some kind of trouble. It's always you. Look! Tell your parents I want to speak to them."

I duly told my mother who gave me that resigned look as it was not the first time she had heard this request nor would it be the last.

I walked her to Mr. Ali's office two days later. I left her there wondering what her reaction would be that afternoon when I saw her. It was not that bad.

When we met at home that afternoon, she explained that she did her best not to laugh as Mr. Ali spoke.

This is what I am missing work for, she said to herself as he explained the situation.

"I kept picturing you with a broom trying to hit it out of the ceiling and all the boys around you shouting and waving their hands," she laughed out loud and I knew I had dodged this particular bullet.

Our French teacher in Form II was a young Indian girl, Ms. DaSilva, petite, attractive with long slightly curly, black hair halfway down her back. She was a graduate of St. Augustine Girls' High School. She had written her A levels and was in her gap year waiting to attend the University of the West Indies (UWI).

On her first day, she wore a nice, short, red, skirt about two inches above the knee with a slit right up the middle. For the 40 boys in our class it was heaven. She never made that mistake again.

After a few months I had gotten a little tired of her. She seemed like nothing more than a little girl who had been put there to teach us. I had no interest in French. I was from Trinidad, what the hell did I need French or Spanish for in my life or future? Years later, during my many travels, I would realize the folly of my ignorance.

I was not aware of it but when she spoke to me, I would sarcastically but quietly look away, suck my teeth and then answer her. She had become tired of this and took me to the Dean to complain. I misunderstood and thought I was being punished for not doing my homework. She left me outside his office, spoke to him and then left as I was called in.

Mr. Ali looked at me. "Mr. Darsan, what do you have to say for yourself?"

As Ms. DaSilva had not actually voiced to me the exact nature of her discontent, I thought it was regarding undone homework, I tried some psychology on Mr. Ali, "I have no excuse Sir, I was wrong."

His eyebrows raised in unison. "You admit it? You are wrong?"

"Yes Sir."

He opened his left, top draw. I knew what this meant. Out came the strap.

You will be benched. And you will come to me for the rest of the week at lunch time for a benching.

A benching meant you did not receive the blows on your hand. You had to bend over the desk and get it on your ass. It was the norm to have an adult witness it so the school could not be sued for unnecessary abuse.

He called in a teacher and I was given seven.

"See you tomorrow at lunch time."

I left his office thanking God that it was Tuesday and not Monday. That was one day less of licks. Wednesday and Thursday were not as bad as I had thought they would be. I did consider wearing extra pants and underwear but Ali might anticipate this and ask me to pull down my pants and embarrass me. So, I refrained.

It was not easy trying to relax at lunch and after school knowing what was to come.

When Friday came around, I decided to wear triple underwear. It was the fourth consecutive day and my ass was not made of steel.

Ali was eating his lunch when I knocked on this door. "Wait outside," and he continued eating.

Within seconds he called me back in. "Mr. Darsan I do not like doing these things. I take no pleasure in it. So, after today try not to have to come here again. Now go out and wait until I finish my lunch."

I walked out thinking, Yuh lie, it doesn't bother you at all to beat me.

A mother came to visit him and he asked her to witness. I found myself jumping on the second, third and fourth blow. This time it really hurt!

He looked at me, "It hurts. Good. That's good," he said in his Pakistani accent."

Fuck you, I said to myself.

He finished the usual dose of seven and I walked with some difficulty out of the office. I had problems sitting for the rest of the day. After school, I was playing table tennis under the pavilion and was still in pain. I pulled down my pants and realized the area behind my thighs, was very sensitive.

When I went home that afternoon, I looked in the mirror, the area was red and swollen. I was pretty sure that I should not have been hit there and with two parents who were lawyers something could be done about it. However, there was a chance they would have simply scolded me. As beating kids in school was the norm in TT in those days, I just let the matter rest.

Mr. Ali had made it clear that I was a problem case and that no one in Form I and II visited his office as much as I did. Walking out of his office that fateful day in January of 1982, I made it clear to him that he would not see me again. And he didn't.

Now I was in Form III, despite the distractions in my life, I was determined to buckle down and get things right.

Our homeroom teacher was Colin Nieves. He was the Geography teacher and we didn't know it yet but a bit of a character.

At this point I was dodging visits to my father as much as I could and trying to do some form of studying at the weekends. In addition, there was a more serious if not perfect attempt to get my homework done.

About two weeks into the school year, Michael arranged a date with the girls from St. Theresa's. Marvin drove us to Independence Square and showed us how to get a taxi to South TT. He assured us he would pick us up later that afternoon at 6:00 pm.

From San Fernando we got a taxi to the Gulf View Mall. This was the only mall in the South. It was a bit different from the two we had in the North. There was a cinema, nightclub and bowling alley.

When we arrived at Gulf View only Joy was there. We chatted with her, had something to eat and looked at each other's photos including the ones they had taken of Jennifer and I on the bed on the last night.

Jennifer had not bothered to come. We had exchanged letters during the Summer. Hers was quite platonic. I was shocked when my mother gave me her letter to see that it was opened. "It was mailed that way," was the reply.

I knew she had opened my mail and I had even less respect for her.

I would never see Jennifer again. Twenty-five years later, a friend on Face Book would send a group message trying to raise funds for a lawyer in his firm who had Cancer, her name was Jennifer Stuart. She had achieved her dream of being a lawyer.

I gave a donation and even had a chat with her via FB. She was married with two young boys. She was adamant that Cancer would not get the better of her. "I am not going anywhere."

A year later she would be dead.

We had put all of our photos in Michael's bag. Later in the day, I told him to hand mine over to me, I would carry them. He looked in the bag and said, "They are not here."

"What do you mean?"

"They are not there. They are gone."

"How?"

"I don't know."

It was obvious that he was lying and that he wanted to steal my photos. But instead of making a scene, I accepted it. For years, I would question my apparent stupidity.

A little more than a decade later, we happened to mention the girls and I reminded him of how he had stolen my photos. He giggled and covered his face, embarrassed. Apparently, he did have some shame.

Amazingly, just a few months later, he would steal from me again.

• • •

I tried to get through Form III as best as I could. I continued to avoid visits to my father whenever possible. However, my mother had made it clear during the summer holiday that it would be my last year with her. Upon my return from Guadeloupe, my complete lack respect for her and the constant profanity had become too much.

The thought of living with my father's family was too much to bear. But my pride would not let me back down and I figured I had a year anyway.

Marvin had done his best to be friendly to me. Within a month, he was comfortable enough to scold Leila if he thought it was necessary. He would not dare speak to me like that.

My mother now brought him to stand next to her whenever she wanted to speak to me about any topic because she knew I would just curse at her and push her away.

On one occasion, as I was leaving the house on a Saturday, she asked what time I would be coming back.

I refused to answer and was tying my shoelaces in the porch.

"You mother is speaking to you," he said solemnly.

"Fuck you!!" was my response.

"Nobody here is speaking to you. Shut to fuck up!"

One of the changes I experienced during this time was having to shave. I had had a full moustache by the age of 12. Despite having facial hair, I had never felt the need to shave. However, within a month of starting Form III, I was beginning to feel like a werewolf. The hair was now hanging off my face and neck. I bought a shaver and shaving cream. I also purchased some kind of shaving cologne that I was told to put on my skin post-shave.

I found shaving to be a bit itchy and couldn't help but scratch. This resulted in razor bumps. After a few weeks, my mother tried to give me some advice. "Don't scratch, this could become a big problem. Look at Marvin, he had to grow a beard because of his razor bumps. I looked at him and he nodded his head very slowly and solemnly.

All I could think was Jesus! You mean without that beard, you are even uglier than you already are.

For the first time since the divorce, my father celebrated his birthday with Leila. I had ignored him for a month and did not got to his celebration. Leila got some token attention because they were now living within a few miles of each other. She always seemed willing to forgive no matter how badly she was treated. It was surprising that he did not have some pride in her, although I resembled him and had his voice, it was Leila who had his lean, tall physique, a talent for music and in later years an ability for sport, primarily, Netball and Track.

• • •

On my birthday a few weeks later, I was awakened by my family and Marvin. They wished me a happy birthday, gave me gifts and took a lot of photos. I didn't have the heart to shout at them to leave me alone as I knew they were trying to be nice.

Later that day there was my customary chocolate cake. Marvin understanding my love for boxing gave me an Encyclopaedia of Boxing, cataloguing every world title fight in history up to 1981. It also had a variety of incredible photos. Reading that book was like heaven to me.

A few days later, I was having an afternoon nap. I felt a sensation on my cheek, I woke up and saw a present next to me on the bed and Aunty Jane walking away.

"Sleep honey. Sleep."

I realized she had given me a kiss and a Christmas present.

"Thanks Aunty Jane."

I would not see her again for many years.

I could not help but notice that within just a few months of Mummy meeting Marvin, their visits dwindled eventually to nothing. I wondered if there was a correlation and perhaps, they were unimpressed with the manner in which she had handled the situation with both the Frenchman and Marvin. In the back of my mind, I knew that their sons had probably passed on what I had said, thus, giving their parents a very clear picture of what had been going on.

The first term of school was always football season and this was a big deal in Trinidad. I was never good enough to play for Holy Father's. I occasionally played interclass and even then, I didn't always make the team.

A small goal competition had been organized for the inner court after school. It was seven a side with three subs allowed.

We had a good class team and I was not on it. Michael Bacchus in his wisdom, created a B team. I was on it and would play Defence, Right Back to be exact.

Carl Ball and Jason Jackson were also on this makeshift team.

Our match was scheduled for 2:45 pm on a Wednesday. As we walked out about 800 voices roared. We stopped dead in our tracks. None of us had ever played a high level of football and were certainly not used to the roar of a crowd.

One of the boys looked at us, "Ey, I feeling nervous."

He had echoed our sentiments.

We however, got on with it. Everyone taking their position. Jackson was Last Stopper, I was on the right and Carl was the Central Defender. Michael played higher up. Michael and Jackson were basically useless but this was our side. As Michael had organized the team, he was the Captain.

We were playing a Form II side. Their star player was Gus Julien. He was a bit of a celebrity with the lower forms. He was extremely short and looked like he should be six or eight years old. However, prior to coming to our school he had represented the TT U-12s in both football and cricket.

The turf was wet and is it had just stopped raining. I was wary of him and any advancing player as I didn't want to get dribbled, slip and look stupid.

I would back away and wait for the moment to tackle. The other boys seemed slow to this concept and were slipping and sliding all over the field.

I had put on some weight since leaving the Falls, it had gotten worse since my return from Guadeloupe. Lying around in the new neighbourhood had not helped, the only exercise being at school.

However, now the extra weight was to my advantage, I screened boys off the ball. If I saw someone about to collect a pass, I raced in and slid on the turf, bringing them down and feigning great shock that it was a foul.

I would point to myself in apparent confusion as if to say, Me?

At the beginning I had been conscious of the crowd and was a bit frozen. However, with every five minutes that passed, I relaxed more. By the twentieth minute, I was no longer aware of the crowd, all I saw was the ball, the field and the players.

It was twenty minutes a half. They scored in the fifteenth and I was a bit embarrassed that we were struggling with a lower form even if they were good.

Just before the half, we had a throw high up on their side, I made the signal to give it to me, I jumped above the boys and flicked it hard and down with my head, it missed the post by about an inch. My onlooking class praised the effort. However, I realized if I had aimed for between the last stopper's legs, we would have had a better chance to score even on the rebound.

Julien, tried to dribble a bit too much and in having the audacity to stop and wait for me, I brought him down once or twice.

I did a good job of clearing balls in Defence and curling them in but truthfully, we did not have a good enough offence to make the difference. Their last stopper was not that good but he did manage to put himself in the way of our shots. That was until the thirtieth minute, Brent Camps, perhaps the best dribbler on the side, collected a ball and neatly pushed it past their tubby stopper, one more touch and GOAL!!

269

Our class ran on the field to congratulate him. Five minutes later, three of the boys from the A Team who had been planning strategy decided to sub me despite the crap that Michael and Jason had been playing. I just looked at them. I was unimpressed.

It was explained to me that Michael was the Captain and "you don't sub the Captain."

I pointed out that Karl Heinz Rummenigge had Captained West Germany at the World Cup and he was subbed.

The game came to a draw and was decided on penalty kicks. Despite me being subbed, I immediately volunteered to take one. A penalty in small goal was taken by standing seven paces in front of the goal and with your back turned, you used your heel to kick it in. The opposition scored all of theirs, Michael missed his and we were defeated.

For the rest of my life, I would carry the memory of that game, how I had calmed down, zoned out the crowd, played a good game. Decades later, I could even remember the cheers of some of the boys after I had made a good play.

A week later, as we put up with the morning traffic, my mother was scolding me as I did not seem to be doing sufficient homework or studying.

As she droned on, my response was "Hull yuh ass."

"Don't speak to your mother like that," responded Marvin.

"Fuck You!! Shut to fuck up!! You are nobody and you have no opinion. Fuck off!!"

I then shouted for another half a minute, telling him what I thought of his opinion and presence, using some very colourful language.

My mother looked at the nearby lane of traffic frantically. After years of shouting at Leila and I in the morning traffic, now it was her turn to be ashamed for anyone to notice what was happening in our car.

On Christmas Day for the first time in my life, I did not spend it with Leila or my mother. They had told me that they would be going to (the) South to visit Marvin's family.

"Fuck off," was my response.

On that day, I had no idea if there was the usual ceremony of opening presents or not. I made no effort to get up. At some point there was a knock on the door, my mother wished me Merry Christmas and they were gone.

It was the first Christmas I had ever spent alone. And it was much preferable to the alternatives.

CHAPTER 45

Farewell Neelam and Sunita

As the early months of 1983 went along, I had a feeling of dread.

My mother had made it clear that at the end of the school year in July, I would be packed off to my father's.

I knew he did not really want the responsibility or expense of another child in his house but he put up a gallant front for my mother.

"I believe a child should be with his mother. But if you really don't want him here, what can I do?"

The thought of being around his family every day left me practically suicidal. My only comfort was that it was still quite a few months away.

My mother had mentioned the year before that the only reason he was now living in St. Anne's with Neelam was because she had left him earlier in '82. They had patched things up and he was now a POS resident.

The other reason was that he was "building a new house" in Caigual.

He had simply allowed Pa's home to deteriorate to the point where it was on the verge of collapse. He explained that the new one would be a modern structure with a pool.

I was saddened that a historical edifice had been neglected to such an extent. Although his plans sounded grand, I found it hard to believe that a man who hadn't spent a dime to repair a great estate home was now going to pay for a swimming pool.

I had made an effort to do well in my end of term exams during Christmas. Of all the Form Threes, I had come first in English and History, getting 76 in both subjects. By my standards, I had improved in Math getting 44 percent. My Test average which was usually around 38 percent had risen to 48 with Physics and Chemistry really brining me down. This would have been a bad report card for any other child but for me there was massive improvement. I realized that without the Sciences my average would have been much more and I could take that as consolation as Form IV emerged even closer.

Marvin congratulated me on my progress. "I have to tell you, I thought that 38 was some kind of serial number, it was in every report card I saw."

I could not help but laugh.

My father true to form, denigrated me immediately. "You came first in History and English. So what? What can you do with that?" he laughed.

"All you can do with those subjects is become a teacher."

I started the second term more disillusioned than I had been for the first. The nearer I got to having to leave the house, the nastier I became to my mother. She now made it clear that I would go to my father on every weekend.

"This is my house. And I will not be disrespected like this."

"It's your house but you are still a cunt."

I was now too big for her to hit. To her credit she did not get Marlon to try to put his hand on me and he probably didn't feel inclined to as I was a young man and not his child.

I knew that I could not handle him physically but I had made up my mind that if he ever tried to hit me, at some point he would have to turn his back or sleep and if I did not kill him, he would be mutilated for life.

On one of my weekends at my father's apartment in late January, a group of people arrived at the door. To my surprise it was Aunty Vashti and her children. She was with Vidia and Zeenat.

I was quite happy to see them. I had often missed them as I was not particularly close to any of my cousins on my mother's side. My memories of them were of better times.

Sadly, they had visited TT over the years but no effort had been made by our respective fathers to get us together.

A few years before when at Ryan's house in Sangre Grande, they had mentioned that Vinaya was in town visiting his father. I said that I wanted to see him.

The next day, Uncle Basdeo stopped his car outside the house. He blew the horn.

"This is Vinaya," he pointed to the back seat. "You said you wanted to see him."

Vinaya waved.

I found myself wondering how foolish this family was? No effort was made to turn off the engine and Vinaya did not even have the courtesy to come out of the car and greet me. It was like some sort of pity hello. I waved back and said nothing.

They shouted goodbye and took off.

I never again mentioned having any interest in seeing him.

However, years later, I heard that for some reason Uncle Basdeo did not like Ryan's mother which may have been the reason for the half assed stop.

The following year Vidia and Zeenat came to see their father. Again, I had no idea. It was the school summer holidays and I was being used as slave labour in my father's meat shop. Ryan's mother passed by with them because she thought it would be nice to see the family. It was quite a shock. Vidia chatted with me and tried to catch up for lost time. I was impressed with how pretty she was. Zeenat was rather quiet and did not have much to say. But perhaps after a decade of not seeing each other she may not have known what to talk about. I myself, made no extra effort to speak to her. It was surreal seeing them after such a long time. This was the very first time since their departure in 1973.

Now here they were in St. Anne's and to my surprise, they were not visiting. They were here to live. There was one other fellow with them and after a few minutes Aunty Vashti pointed to him, saying to my father, "That is your son you know."

My father looked at her quizzically.

"This is Vidia's husband."

Our entire family looked at him and Vidia in mild shock.

She was only 19 but she was already married. There had been no forewarning.

His name was Roy. Although married in Guyana, they had not had the formal Indian ceremony and their mother had forbade them to sleep together until then. They had not quite set a date for that event but hoped to have it in July or August.

We did not know him but we accepted him as family. Afterall, he was Vidia's husband.

I was happy to know that they had come to TT. The only cousins I knew reasonably well were Aunty Indira's children and I did not see them often. It would be nice to reacquaint myself with Uncle Basdeo's family once again.

I had never been quite the same after my father's idiocy the previous summer. In bullying and harassing us about the men in my mother's life it had affected me.

When back at school there was a definite change to my personality. People would speak to me and I would sometimes just look away blankly and not answer. I would find myself sitting alone trying not to think about the negatives in my life. I knew the stress was having an effect on me but I did not know how to stop it from doing so.

As the first few months of 1983 progressed, the more I had to visit my father, the more I hated my life and the less interest I had in school. My grades had dipped for the second term exams.

My mother pointed it out to me. Marvin did not dare speak to me. He knew the response he would get.

"Don't worry about it," was my answer. "I will be out of here in July."

"But you are my son. I must worry."

"Worried about what. And you are trying to get rid of me."

"But I will always love you. You will always be my son."

"Well you will always be a cunt."

She walked off knowing that there could be no rational conversation with me.

As the Easter holidays commenced. I awaited my father's arrival to be taken away.

He arrived and sat in the living room. My mother sat down.

He looked at her, "Did you tell him?"

"No, I thought you would want to tell him."

He came quickly to the point. "Neelam and I are no longer together. We have separated."

I looked at him stoically. I could not give a fuck if he and Neelam were together or not. But I was curious as to how it would affect me and where I stayed with him.

We left the house and he explained that he had taken a room at the Hummingbird Hotel in Tunapuna. The Hummingbird was a decent hotel with a nightclub at the ground level and a pool in the back.

The following night we went back to the apartment in St. Anne's to pick up Sunita. He was going to take us out for dinner at the Taj Mahal restaurant in town.

Sunita was ready. She was wearing a pretty white dress to just above the knee, white shoes and white socks pulled all the way up to her knees.

Daddy explained where he would be taking us that night.

Neelam listened sombrely, "Bring her home at a decent hour. We are going to Curepe to visit my family tomorrow."

"She will be home by 9:30."

"Don't start drinking and forget."

"Why don't you shut yuh ass! Didn't I say by 9:30?"

Neelam groaned quietly and looked at the floor. We were all aware that in that little apartment complex with the front door open for ventilation, the neighbours could hear. "Look, I not in the mood for your nonsense. Just go please."

"Well stop harassing my ass with shit!!!"

Now it was Sunita's turn to groan. "Oh God. Allyuh stop it nah," she muttered quietly.

Part of me felt sorry for her. I too had had to witness an unpleasant scene when my parents separated a little more than a decade before. However, I remembered all the cruelty Leila and I had been forced to endure for years and I steeled my heart.

We had a great meal that night. I could see the sadness on Sunita's face. But I reminded myself to be indifferent.

With my father at a hotel, we now had great lunches and dinners at restaurants.

This went on for the next few weeks until we visited Aunty Vashti's family who now lived in Tunapuna as well, Tunapuna Main Rd. to be exact.

I was happy to be amongst them once again. Vinaya was living with them. They were renting the second floor of a building directly facing the main road. Behind the house, was a much nicer one where the owner of the property lived. Between the two homes was a garage and a lawn. Directly opposite Aunty Vashti's home was some kind of ghetto made up of a collection of wooden homes. Therefore, it was normal to see a collection of young black men standing on the main road, speaking loudly and cursing on a variety of topics.

Upon visiting them, I quickly realized that they were experiencing a crisis. Uncle Basdeo had refused to attend Vidia's wedding. This also meant he was not going to pay for it. No one mentioned why and I did not think it was my place to ask. However, I later found out that they had informed many people in TT that Vidia was going to get married. Uncle Basdeo found out about it on the street from family friends and felt insulted.

My father had just sold a few hundred acres of Pa's land. He was obviously in a charitable mood. "I will pay for the wedding." The family looked at each other with a sense of relief and pleasure. They agreed it would cost twenty thousand dollars.

I was happy for Vidia but wondered how could he afford such generosity when for years my mother had struggled to care for us with no child support?

We now visited them every weekend. Zeenat and I bonded and would reminisce upon the old days. I could tell that like myself, she felt a certain sense of nostalgia. The family at the back had a beautiful daughter, Asha. She had a light brown complexion, long, wavy, black hair and a woman's figure at just 14.

Zeenat kept making not so subtle jokes that we would be a good couple. My father would occasionally embarrass me by bringing up my "nigger father" or find some other way to ridicule me which he thought amusing. I knew I could not be rude or I would be beaten. I would say nothing or find other ways to irritate him like bringing up how clueless Sunita was in school and that she was taking ages to learn what other students could do in a month. His face would get serious and he would just look at me. It was hardly the payback I wanted but it was the best I could get away with.

As the school year progressed my school grades gradually went in the opposite direction.

It was around this time that we would be having our Annual Sports Day. I usually entered the sprints as I did not have the conditioning for

278

the long-distance races. We actually had to pay ten cents to enter each preliminary. Michael Bacchus came around with the form. I entered the hundred two hundred and four hundred. He actually encouraged me to enter more than one race "because you can sprint."

I placed in the first five in both the 100 metres and two hundred metres. But it was not enough to qualify for Sports Day. I ran my heart out and just avoided finishing last in the 400 metres.

A few days later, it was as if a light bulb had gone off in my head, I looked at Michael, "Wait nuh. You collected money for the Sports Day. What did you do with it?"

"I gave it to the school.'

It was obvious from the manner in which he refused to look at me, he was lying.

"Oh Jesus Michael. You mean yuh steal people money again!"

He snickered and walked off.

Amazingly, I was the only one in the class who seemed to have the common sense to figure these things out.

I promised myself that would be the last time he would ever dupe me. I did not steal from my friends and it was obvious that he was not mine.

Years later if we saw each other as adults, he would have a pleasant chat with me and give me his telephone number. I would be amiable but make sure to keep my distance.

I had been made Vice Prefect of the class in January. Basil Williams was Prefect and together we kept the class under control in the absence of a teacher. If anyone was too difficult, we had the authority to send them to the Dean.

I tried to be cool and not take advantage of anyone the way I had seen some students do in previous years. However, my life would not be normal if it didn't' have some ruction. And ruction it was.

A young Jamaican Form IV by the name of Gregory Rowe entered the class one day to speak to a friend. His mother was a famous ex

Jamaican model who had appeared in a few British films. Her claim to fame now was that she was married Keith Barrow a sort of media mogul in TT. I explained to him that he could not enter and to leave.

He looked at me, walked up to the desk and ripped up a list of names I had. These were the fellows who had been giving trouble for that period. "Fuck you," he said.

"No. Fuck your mother."

He looked at me and made an approach.

I got up and met him halfway. "Get out or I will throw you out!"

He backed out saying "I will see you at lunch time."

I was not too concerned. He wasn't that big and I figured I could take him.

All teachers had their desk on a sort of podium, allowing them to see the class better. As lunch commenced, I got my papers together and was about to go to my desk when Rowe entered the class followed by four of his friends.

He stood in front of me blocking my way. "Say what you said before."

"Boy! Shut your ass nah!" was my response.

"Say it again!" he looked at me hard as if he thought he was capable of intimidating someone.

"Fuck you!" I replied.

"Say it again!"

"Fuck you!"

He threw two punches at my face and tackled me American Football style. We both went across the podium, knocking the desk and chair aside.

As we hit the ground, I rose up in a sitting position, "You son of a bitch!!" I was enraged. I grabbed his head with both hands and immediately three of his friends lifted me off the ground.

"Let him go," said the biggest of the lot. I really didn't have a choice. I had thought they were there to spectate but in reality, they were his backup just in case things didn't work out. He was smarter than he looked.

I was so angry I would have done some bad damage and probably got suspended or expelled.

Within seconds, Mr. Hart, a Spanish teacher entered the class. He tried to find out what was happening but I was too enraged to let Rowe speak.

"You were very wise to bring these men! I was going to break in yuh ass and break it in good. I am going to see you when you have no protection and I will deal with you."

I then looked at his friends, "Why did you save him? He have all that mouth. That is what you come here for to save him?" I looked at him, "Thank them because if they were not here, I was going to kick your ass all over this school!!!"

Mr. Hart realizing the situation was out of control took us to the Principal, Mr. Manson who had replaced Mr. Pinero who was now a politician.

Mr. Manson listened to both parties and gave us six blows each.

As we walked away from the Principal's office, Rowe shameless in his bravado, looked at me, "I will see you later."

"You will see me with your friends or I will fuck you up and fuck you up good."

Being in Form IV he only had another year and a half in the school. There was no way that idiot was going to get into Form VI. For the rest of his time at HF, he would stare at me intently always making sure to stand next to his friends. The hypocrisy of his bravery apparently eluding him.

CHAPTER 46

She Would Never Laugh Again

As the school year drew to a conclusion, I prepared myself for the inevitable move.

Despite my problems with Marvin, he showed great civility to my mother. He was a bit terse with Leila if he thought her behaviour or grades were wanting. However, he treated my mother with dignity. She was finally receiving what had been missing for so long in her life, support, emotional as well as financial.

The fact that he was around and helping with household expenses not only led to less stress for a woman who had never been assisted by her children's father but simple things like letting her sleep in on mornings while he took us to school or picking us up in the afternoons. He was quite patient with me despite my dismissive way to him. The truth is he had no real authority over me. But he did show great patience and class under the circumstances.

A few weeks before the end of school, my father rented an apartment in Maraval. It was close to town and Holy Father's. It was already furnished and though not posh, certainly comfortable. There was a length of concrete separating our car park from the one next door. The apartment complex next door was actually attached to ours but with each having its own entrance.

I noticed that there were many Indians on the street chatting while the children played. My father later found out that these families belonged to the Indian High Commission.

On my second weekend there whilst leaving to return home, I saw a group of them on the street and there was one girl that stood out. She was beautiful and had an incredible smile. I swivelled my head as the car drove by. She was simply beautiful.

The school year was done. I took down all my boxing posters from my bedroom wall, packed my bags and got ready to move. My mother had been threatening for years that I would go and live with my father and now with a regular man in her bed, I was gone. Of course, I could have simply tempered down and been civil but pride would not allow that. Not with a woman who preached proper behaviour but had behaved like a loose bitch.

The neighbourhood was called Cocoa Gardens due to the fact, that the land had been part of a huge cocoa estate the previous century.

During that same month, I noticed some black discolorations on my back. As the months progressed, they got worse. I was quite embarrassed by it. My parents thought it was some kind of fungus. The locals called it "Lota."

Visits to a variety of Doctors and a Dermatologist concluded that it was not Lota. They were simply baffled. During the next year, it slowly spread up my back. It was terribly distressful. I felt like a freak.

Many years later I would discover that the discolouration was a result of stress which had affected my Immune System. The stress I had experienced during that year and the previous one was obvious. I could only shake my head. Fortunately, about five years later, I lay down on the beach, got blackened by the sun and when the tan wore off, my skin was a much more uniformed colour. But I would never forget those years of trauma and praying to God to please heal my skin.

• • •

I no longer saw Neelam and Sunita. They had moved to Curepe so Neelam could be closer to her own family.

I found the Indians to be strangely rude. If I said good morning or good evening to them, many of them would not answer or even make eye contact. After a week of that, I treated them in a likewise manner.

Vinaya was with us in July of that year. It was fun as I had him to speak with and we would sometimes take my father's car to go to the cinema.

Vidia's husband was Roy, a slightly stout fellow with hair brushed back, a moustache and goatee. He was gregarious and always making jokes. I took a liking him but after just two weeks of knowing him my father commented "but he is always lying."

During the next few months I would have greater insight into both his and Vinaya's character.

The first would come a few weeks later regarding a portable stereo my father had. Neelam had started a business the previous year buying goods in Curacao and selling them to retailers in TT, mainly clothing items. Coming back from one of her trips, she brought a beautiful dual cassette recorder, good technology for the time. One day while being visited by Roy and Vinaya, she pointed to the item still in the box. "Tell Vijay that is from me. He can have it."

A month later, chatting with my father at his apartment, she looked at his stereo. "Where did you get that?"

He looked at her in surprise, "What do you mean where did I get that? I got it from you. Didn't you give it to Roy and Vinaya to give to me?"

"I gave them a stereo but not that. What I gave them was much nicer."

Now it was her turn to look at him in surprise.

They then deduced that the two fools had probably sold the original stereo, bought a cheaper one and pocketed the profit. Strangely, my father did not confront either of them.

However, if we thought they were thieves, we were in for a surprise. It would get much worse.

Neelam's conversations with my father had become frantic and uncivil. She was not getting regular money for Sunita's upbringing and she thought this intolerable.

For years she had giggled at my mother's letters asking for child support. She had thought it funny that a member of the great Darsan family had all this land but did not contribute to his children's education, clothing or matters as basic as food. She had loved him and respected him while laughing at my mother's plight and my sister wearing my hand me downs.

The giggling had stopped.

Just like she did not see the humour in her child being harassed, she also failed to laugh at not receiving child support for Sunita. "What kind of man are you? You don't support your own child. You call yourself a man?"

"I eh carrying right now."

"How the hell you mean you not carrying!!?" she bellowed. "You carrying enough to have alcohol in your cabinet. You know how to gamble on horses every Saturday. So how the HELL you don't have money!!?"

"Check me out next month. I will see what I can do."

"And what am I supposed to do in the meantime. Your child has to eat. I need to buy clothes for her. She is growing."

"You seem to be doing just fine."

"What the hell!!! You have no shame? What kind of man does not look after his child!!??

She would never laugh again.

CHAPTER 47

Problems in Guyana and the End of a Legacy

My lifestyle had changed. No more limes in the Gardens, no meeting my classmates to walk about the Mall.

My father spent a lot of time visiting Aunty Vashti. With some of her Guyanese family visiting, I was surrounded by many Indians from both TT and Guyana.

Aunty Vashti like many Guyanese had left her country due to its dwindling economy. Their President Forbes Burnham had been accused of running a corrupt regime with no democracy of freedom of speech. He had taken one of the foremost economies of the Caribbean and turned it into a joke.

Guyanese were fleeing to wherever they could. Those who couldn't make it to Canada, the USA or England were happy to use TT as their backup. It was certainly a better alternative than a country where basic food and sanitation items had become a scarcity.

It was obvious that life was different in Guyana. One thing the Indo Guyanese would bring up was "the black people," having to put up with them and "being ruled by them."

You would hear comments infiltrate their conversation from time to time. Whilst conversing with my father one day, Aunty Vashti mentioned how prostitution had become more prevalent in Georgetown due to the economic hardship. "And it's your own Indian girls doing it too." My father nodded his head in empathy.

I found the comment strange. Why did it matter what race they were? Would it be better if the prostitution was practiced only by black people?

If there were differences between the Africans and Indians in Guyana it was compounded by Burnham who flagrantly denied many Indians from voting at the National Elections citing a variety of excuses, such as not being eligible, voting in the wrong area or having been recorded as dead.

What made the situation more curious was the apathy of the CARICOM (Caribbean Community) leaders. They were publicly denouncing the Apartheid system in South Africa and insisting that Nelson Mandela the leader of the ANC (African National Congress) should be freed. How could our leaders of democracy in the Caribbean, fight so hard for the Africans in South Africa yet not even mention the chaos in Guyana?

My father had no reservations on the topic. "Is black people! Why else? You think Indians or anybody else could deny black people the right to vote and the Caribbean would keep quiet." He continued "Burnham is black so as long as a black person is doing it, it's ok."

What he failed to mention was that it was a black man Walter Rodney who had managed to pull the Guyanese both Africans and Indians together, explaining that as long as they were united the totalitarian government of Guyana would eventually fall. Rodney was assassinated in 1980, the victim of a car bomb. The government was accused but no tangible proof was ever produced.

I never took what my father had to say about black people seriously because he always seemed to have a convenient excuse whenever Indians were racist themselves. However, as a young teenager, the nonchalance of CARICOM to what was happening in their own back yard made no sense to me. I figured that there was no way they could be so openly hypocritical which would obviously lead to them having no credibility. I concluded that as I got older, I would have a better understanding of it. What was apparent was that Guyana's economy was in a free fall and many Guyanese regardless of race were looking for greener pastures.

As the date of the wedding came closer, Aunty Vashti's family got more excited. I noticed that there seemed to be no one in Roy's family coming. Zeenat explained that Roy had been their neighbour, this is how he and Vidia met. Both their parents had an argument one day and because of this his family would not come.

"What was the argument about," I asked.

"I really don't know. I wasn't there and they don't talk about it. But they are not coming."

I would later find out the true reason for their absence.

A week before the wedding, Pat arrived. She was a light skinned, pretty, Indian girl, slim with medium length black hair and almond shaped eyes. She had been Vinaya's girlfriend in Georgetown. Despite them breaking up four years earlier, Vinaya's sisters had kept in contact with her. She had migrated to New York City with her family at the time of the break-up and was delighted to reunite with his family.

Vinaya was what we called a sweet man in TT. He had done well with the ladies in both Trinidad and Guyana. He was slim, handsome, with thick black, hair brushed to the right, a moustache and a noticeable pot belly. He did not have his father's height or size but women were attracted to him despite his aggressive and somewhat crude ways. He and Pat had gone out for a year. Realizing that she was emigrating to the USA, he simply cut off communication with her two weeks before her departure. He would not answer her phone calls. When she sent him letters the from US, he ignored those as well. His reasoning was simple, she was leaving and the relationship was over.

For the next week if we went out, we would take Pat with us so she could see TT. There really wasn't that much to see in Tunapuna. We took her to POS and to the South. She literally saw the length and breadth of the island. She seemed like a nice friendly girl. She and Vinaya quickly picked up from where they had left off, holding hands and resting on each other's shoulders in the car. Two days before the wedding we took her to Caura River in nearby Tacarigua. Roy and a few of their Guyanese friends came with us. It was nice swimming and having lunch at the riverside.

As we drove back home, Pat sat in the front while Roy drove, four of us scrunched up in the back. Vinaya as a joke started stroking Pat's face. He then put his hand down his crotch, looked at the boys, smiled and continued to caress her face. We all laughed. She looked back to see what the commotion was about. But all she saw was four smiling faces. He did it three times. As he attempted a fourth, she turned around abruptly and saw his hand in his pants. She looked at him and said nothing. However, she would not speak to him for the rest of the day.

Many Trinidad Hindus, especially those in the countryside when having any kind of traditional Indian function, would serve you food on a large leaf. It was common to use the banana leaves, if they were not around, you could use the Sohari leaf. It was huge and grew in abundance in the bush and best of all was free.

Vinaya was given Roy's car the day before the wedding and told go to Sangre Grande and get leaves, enough for three hundred people.

He took me with him. Although agreeing at the time, he sucked his teeth in the car, "Steuups. Where the hell I supposed to get three hundred leaves just so? Anyway, I have an idea." His idea was to find one of the ex-workers from his father's property and have him help us. He happened to live in Caigual.

A mile into Caigual Main Rd., he pointed to a small wooden house partly hidden by high bush. "We will go there later. But first I want to show you the old man's house in Caigual. We may never see it again." He meant we were going to Pa's house.

We drove up the hill, with rugged stones sticking out of the road, evident of the lack of repair over the years. As we turned the final corner, my eyes veered left to look at the house. Except there was no house. It was gone. Completely gone.

I looked at Vinaya, "Where the house gone?"

"Scunt," muttered Vinaya. "Whey it gone in trute?"

I then remembered what my father had said regarding building a new house. We stepped out of the car and walked up to where the porch should have been. We saw pieces of wood, a little longer than a cricket stump with red flags on them in a sort of huge rectangular pattern, which we assumed indicated the parameters of the house to be. At the corner, there was a huge hole, with a sign next to it, *Pool*. Whatever work that had been going on was obviously abandoned.

Vinaya and I looked around in stunned silence. The stables and the rubber house were no longer visible due to the high bush. A few of the water tanks still stood the only tangible evidence of a once great legacy.

"Well," said Vinaya, turning to me, " … at least you got a chance to see the place." He pointed towards the hole, "Looks like he was actually building a pool."

As we slowly made our way down the hill which would be the last time ever for me, I despondently thought of the once great home which had stood there for more than seventy years. The envy of so many now just a memory. I thought of my father who seemed to enjoy lecturing me on having ambition and goals in life and found myself wondering where was his? Lastly, I thought of Rampersad Darsan, an unknown labourer from South Trinidad who had come to Sangre Grande and created a great legacy which now was all but gone. He had cultivated an empire which lasted over twenty-five years only for it to dissolve within a decade of his death.

We found the worker Vinaya wanted. His name was Sam, a short, slim, middle aged, black man. He took us to a spot off the Eastern Main

Rd and within a mile from Caigual, armed with cutlasses, we acquired the three hundred leave relatively easily.

Vinaya then bought Sam a few drinks as a token of appreciation. We returned with the leaves, properly drunk. We entered the house, singing and dancing showing everyone the leaves. My father just looked at us and shook his head at the two drunken fools.

CHAPTER 48

The Wedding, the Slap and the Affair

Vidia and Roy's wedding had been one of great effort.

Newly arrived in Trinidad, they found themselves slowly settling in. Getting a job, a house as well as a car was a bit of a chore for a couple of limited resources, compounded by the expenses of a wedding.

They had been immensely lucky to have a few contacts from our family. They never mentioned it but they got a lot of free groceries from Uncle Basdeo's supermarket in Cunupia. It was in its third year of operation, however, due to his traveling and going to the horse races on Saturdays, it was a bit neglected.

My father had also stepped in and in addition to their wedding had also assisted them with a car.

The bank had explained to them that they could not secure a loan for a car without a guarantor. They had asked my father to do so. The Manager explained to my father that the loan was six thousand dollars and that he would have to give that exact amount as a deposit. They would charge them eight and a half percent.

He looked at the Manager, "Basically, you are taking my money and lending it to them and charging interest." He said to Roy, "I will lend you all the money at six percent."

Roy readily agreed.

Roy had been greeted with open arms by our family and certain members had bent over backwards to help him and Vidia. It would later prove to be a tragic mistake.

Zeenat had stopped speaking to me. She had tried to get Asha and I together. At a party one night, I asked Asha how she felt about it, she just groaned and looked at the floor. I was a bit confused. "What does that sound mean? Is that supposed to be a yes or no?"

She nodded her head in the affirmative which I thought was a good thing. But she then seemed to have nothing to say around me. At first, I thought it was shyness. I pulled her aside one day and asked her why she was so silent. All she could do was watch the floor. "Can't you speak?" She continued looking at the floor. "Just go your way," I said dismissively.

As a result of this, Zeenat simply froze me out. If I did speak to her she would give me a short reply and look the other way. After a week I just didn't speak to her if it wasn't necessary but visiting Aunty Vashti's became more uncomfortable, especially if Vinaya wasn't around to speak to.

I had put on some weight over the last year due to no more sports on the weekends or school holidays. I didn't realize how bad it had gotten until one day Vinaya's friend on meeting me for the first time, said "Who is this? Young Roy?"

I was aghast, some family members would sometimes make jokes about how tubby and round Roy was. I had no idea *this* is what I looked like to people as well. Perhaps I had been in denial but no more. I made up my mind right then and there that I would be eating less and find some way to get more exercise.

The night before the wedding I found myself trying to find a way to get out of it. Asha and Zeenat were the only two people my age I would know there and they were not speaking to me. I told my father I was feeling a bit ill and maybe I should stay home.

"Look, I don't want to stay there long either. We'll arrive at seven and leave at midnight."

They may have been expecting three hundred guests but there were barely a hundred there. The fact that Uncle Basdeo had chosen not to go had obviously had an effect on many of the Sangre Grande guests. Conveniently again for Roy, the wedding was held under their apartment in an empty space which would be used as a supermarket in the future. Asha's father knew Aunty Vashti well and he offered them the premises free of charge.

A few of Aunty Vashti's siblings had come. They had arrived a few days before and were all staying at her house.

One of them was Ryan's father, Aunty Vashti's brother and his second wife along with their two young children. I remembered my father saying that he had met her "while she was practicing her profession."

She was a pretty, Indian woman with long, black, curly, hair and curves in all the right places. I could not help but notice her because in my opinion a lot of Indo Guyanese women were a bit on the scrawny side but not this one. She also had a penchant for wearing tight jeans which accentuated her figure. She was in her early thirties, her husband twenty years older. When she walked around in those jeans, his eyes would sort of bulge out of his head. His glare would follow the jeans and then he would scan the room to see if anyone else was looking. Vinaya and I would quickly look in the opposite direction.

During the first hour of the wedding, I chatted with her and anyone else I knew there. Pat was there as well still ignoring Vinaya.

Indian weddings in TT were a bit infamous for alcohol and violence. This was one would be no different.

Ryan's stepmother was looking quite pretty. At one point she was standing by herself, three of Asha's cousins, young men in their early and mid-twenties walked over and began chatting with her. A few minutes later, one of them offered her a glass of champagne. She accepted it with a smile and continued chatting. Within seconds, her husband had crossed the floor. He swung his hand across the side of her face, SLAP!!! "Since when you does drink champagne, eh!!??"

The men took a step back in apparent shock. Many of the guests looked on in horror. Some had not noticed because of the music. She held the side of her face and immediately exited, going upstairs to the apartment. A few seconds later, her husband exited as well.

I walked outside with my drink speaking to one of Vinaya's cousins who was close to my age. We walked across the driveway standing near to the wall. My father and Aunty Vashti followed and were chatting at the foot of the steps of the apartment. Within seconds, Zeenat came running down the steps, "Mummy! Mummy! Uncle is choking her!!""

Daddy and Aunty Vashti were up the stairs in a flash. They entered the bedroom and saw his wife on the bed, he on top of her, choking away. He was a short but broad-shouldered man and there was not much she could do about it.

Daddy grabbed him by the shoulders, "Come nah man. Come nah man. Don't do that. Come on man. Don't do that." In the meantime, Aunty Vashti grabbed his right hand, trying to pry it loose without much success. Eventually he let go, breathing hard. "You want to be a slut! You want to be a slut!"

"No. No, she doesn't," said Daddy, putting his arm around him and rubbing his shoulder. She was now sobbing uncontrollably. Aunty Vashti took her to the balcony to calm her down. "Zeenat, bring her some water."

Her husband was taken downstairs and we did not see her again that night.

The rest of the wedding went reasonably well. There was the cutting of the cake, speeches and the catching of the bouquet. Zeenat caught the bouquet and was beside herself. Three years later she would be married.

We never did go home at 12. My father and Pat sat in a corner talking and eventually dancing. I didn't really have anyone to speak to. Vinaya had become too drunk and he was put to bed around 1:00 am. One of Vidia's friends visiting from Guyana sat next to me. We began talking. She seemed quite friendly. She told me how much she enjoyed speaking to me and could I continue because there were some extremely aggressive men from Georgetown who kept asking her to dance.

We eventually danced and had a great chat. She left around 4. I don't know how but my father and I did not leave until 6:00 am. It had not been the most exciting wedding I had ever been to but now it was over. I was hoping I could spend more time in POS and not around people I did not seem to have a lot in common with.

Not only was Pat still ignoring Vinaya but now she and my father were going out quite a bit. Vidia and Zeenat seem quite surprised. Vinaya was mum on the topic.

A week later Aunty Vashti and the whole family would visit Guyana. Pat was going as well and my father was invited. I decided not to go. If I was bored at the wedding how much bored would I be in Guyana, it's not like I could have gone home at the end of the day. It may have been illogical but I missed my surroundings in POS, spending a lot of time in Tunapuna was one thing but Guyana!!

My father thought it was silly to miss out on visiting another country. However, "I am not going to waste money on a ticket for someone who is not interested."

Despite my protestations, he and my mother concluded I would stay with her. It was almost enough to make me go to Guyana.

The week I spent with her was reasonably uneventful. I stayed in my room and watched TV. I only ventured out to eat or shower. I refused to speak to them.

Marvin apparently had properly settled in and became a bit more assertive around me. He would knock on my door and just enter, well aware I was not going to acknowledge the knock. A proper cussing did not seem to deter him.

One day as I made my way to the bathroom, he and my mother were speaking in the corridor. I passed in between them. He looked at me, "Don't you see us speaking?"

"Well hull yuh mudda cunt and speak."

My mother grabbed his arm in shock, perhaps worried that he might respond.

"You are standing up in the middle of a corridor. Don't you see someone walking. Move your cunt. You fucking blind?"

I opened the bathroom door and turned to him before entering, "Do I look like I give a fuck about you or anything you have to say?"

He stared at me blankly.

I would mitigate the boredom by going to the mall.

However, the week of just sitting around and hardly doing anything had made me even fatter. I had never seen myself like this. In addition to a huge stomach, I now had rolls of fat on the sides.

Upon their return to TT, there was no longer any pretence. Pat and my father had become a couple. She arrived two days after he did and went directly to his apartment. Whilst Vinaya and I watched TV, they went to the bedroom and we did not see them for a few hours. Vinaya was very silent, glum to be exact.

After a while he pointed his head in the direction of the bedroom. "Look at that. She has a boyfriend in New York and she is doing this with another man." He sucked his teeth ... STEUUPPS ... and shook his head in disapproval. However, he did not seem to have a problem when she had been prancing around with him a few weeks before.

Eighteen odd months prior, I had actually felt sorry for my father. In his early forties, I had thought his life was basically over and that he was like a grandfather. I was obviously wrong. Children often do not see their parents the way others do. In reality, he was a slim, handsome man with a full head of hair and it was the norm for women twenty years his junior to notice him.

Pat spent the rest of the week at our apartment, eventually returning home. I tried to avoid going to Tunapuna with my father as Zeenat was still being distant. However, as there was nothing to do in the neighbourhood and no boys to play sports with, I found myself without a proper reason to say no.

August became September and it was once again a new school year. This was how I lived my life, starting school in September and waiting anxiously for holidays. We lived closer to school so there was less headache with traffic. However, living with my father was not easy. He was prone to shouting for the slightest of reasons such as forgetting to wash a dish. Naturally, the whole building had to hear. He did not seem to care. He was from the bush, this was his way and he was not going to mellow out for me or the neighbours.

Three weeks into the school term, he decided that he would travel. He would visit London and then see Pat in NYC. I found myself wondering how her boyfriend was going to fit into all of this. He would be gone for two weeks. As someone who had not paid taxes in more than a decade, he had no Tax Exit Certificate. However, if it is one thing Vijay Darsan was good at, it was making friends and contacts. Someone working in the Public Prosecutor's Office simply got it for him despite the computer rejecting his name.

Zeenat had become a little less antisocial which was good for me because Daddy had decided I would be with Aunty Vashti's family while he was away.

Those two weeks would be eventful to say the least.

CHAPTER 49

"When it Comes to Money, Family Doesn't Mean Anything"

My father left for England in early October. I tried to settle in as best as I could. Zeenat was a bit friendlier and exhibiting less attitude.

As Asha's house was on the same property, literally about eighty feet behind the apartment, they would see each other a lot. I tried to give them space so that they could have their girl talk. Asha and I no longer had anything in common.

Zeenat and her sister were not impressed that Uncle Shirvan always seemed to be around. He had helped Aunty Vashti move some furniture with his van. He had also come along with us on a river lime when my father was in the country and now he was often at their house. It seemed like every day and the girls were tired of it. Naturally, the suspicion was that an affair was going on or at the very least they were on the verge of one.

When the girls voiced their discontent at his constant presence, Aunty Vashti explained that she was entitled to have friends as well. Seeing that there was no open evidence of an affair with a married man at least in Aunty Vashti's eyes, nothing scandalous was going on.

I had always liked Roy although I found him a bit loud and crude at times. Whenever we would go out and the other boys would flirt with the girls, he would try to participate as well but he seemed to have no skills. And his attempt at lyrics were pathetic even by my fifteen–year-old standards.

I was surprised that Vidia who was so pretty, intelligent and respectable had ended up with a guy who really didn't seem good enough for her. My father's take was that there was a five-year difference between the two. They had met when Vidia was 16 preparing for her O Levels. Roy had helped her practice Spanish and three years later they were married. My father's philosophy was that by 19 she had outgrown him.

During the next few months, I would acquire far greater insight into his character.

The first was about two days after my father had gone to London. Vidia's mother came over and was in a sombre, almost apologetic mood. Her husband ran an import business and would distribute items from Germany in TT, such as sweets, nuts, door handles, etc. He had given Roy a job as a salesman, only to find out a few months later that he was also working for one of his competitors.

He left for New York on business and called the next day telling his wife that he would be back in one week. He instructed her to tell Roy that due to his dishonesty, he would have to leave the house before his return.

Somehow, they found a house in three days' time, a decent three bedroom on Cavalry Hill, St. Joseph. It truly was on a hill and from the Eastern Main Rd. well over a hundred metres.

By that weekend they were moved. Uncle Shirvan showed up with his pickup and along with Roy's car, it only took two trips.

The new home had a front and back yard and because of the altitude, you could see the lights of the town at night.

Zeenat was exhibiting some attitude occasionally, she seemed to think she could raise her voice to people whenever she wanted. I was not one to put up with that but I was a guest in their house so I did my best to be tolerant. I only had about a week to go.

A few nights later Aunty Shanti showed up. She had come without the children and after a few pleasantries she got to the point. Apparently, she had co-signed a loan of three thousand dollars. It was not being repaid to the bank and "my account is being debited."

I realized that this was a sensitive matter and left the room to give them privacy. I sat on the steps of the porch, enjoying the cool tropical night air.

About five minutes later, Aunty Shanti walked by me, "Good night Sunny."

"Good night Aunty Shanti."

I could see that she was in a sad mood.

About a minute later Roy sat next to me. He explained that Vinaya had borrowed some money from her and was not paying it back.

"I don't understand that," I said. "I could never borrow money from other people and not pay it back."

Roy looked at the ground and gravely shook his head "Me neither. I could never borrow money and not pay it back."

I shook my head and wondered out aloud how Vinaya could be so rude.

Years later, Aunty Shanti told me the true account of what had actually happened.

It was not Vinaya but rather Roy and Vidia who had borrowed the money. The bank had lent them three thousand dollars with our Aunt as a guarantor. They had made no effort to pay it back and of course now Aunty Shanti had become concerned.

When she explained the situation to both him and Vidia, he calmly responded, "Aunty when it comes to money, family doesn't mean anything."

Vidia and her mother just looked at her not saying a word.

"But my account is being debited for your loan."

"Yes but when it comes to money family doesn't mean anything."

In a state of disbelief and shock, she simply left.

Years later when told the story, I sat there in awe of not only Roy's complete lack of gratitude but how just a minute later, he could so sombrely bemoan people who did not pay their debts.

I also could not believe that Vidia and Aunty Vashti had just stood there saying nothing while this man insulted our family in response to her benevolence.

Aunty Shanti went to her big brother, Basdeo but his response was blunt, "You should have consulted me before you loaned them any money. That is between you all."

She was never paid a cent.

What we did not realize at the time was that Roy had two objectives while in Trinidad: to use it at as a pit stop to the USA and to suck as much money as he could from whom he could with no interest in repaying the loans. In addition, we would slowly learn that his thieving knew no boundaries.

Roy may have been a crook but he was in good company with Vinaya as his brother-in-law.

About two nights before my father's arrival from New York, Vidia suggested we go to his apartment and clean it for him.

With Vinaya, Roy and Zeenat there as well, it would be a reasonably quick job. A few minutes into it, Vinaya announced that he was going to put gas in the car, "I'm taking Sunny with me."

We never did go for gas. We went to a nearby park in Woodbrook. Vinaya very slowly drove around the park and from behind a tree, a large black man appeared.

He approached the car, it was obvious that they knew each other. He was smiling but seemed a bit frantic. "Boy! I swear I see police circling the park. I think the blasted men looking out for we." He was all teeth as his eyes kept frantically, scanning the park and the surrounding environs.

"Tell the man I have he package. You could deliver it tomorrow."

"Alright," said Vinaya. "I will go meet him now and get back to you."

I got the impression that something was not right. But I couldn't believe that Vinaya had taken my father's car for what I thought he was doing.

A few minutes later, we were at the Holiday Inn. As we slowly drove in, a man emerged from the shadows beside the entrance.

He was a Bajan and a deal was being made.

He made it clear to Vinaya that he could deliver the package on the day that he was travelling because he needed "to pack it." He added, "You have to bring it the day before. It has to be well packed. The last thing I want is problems with Immigration."

I could not believe what I was seeing. This was a drug deal in my very presence. I had seen this in the movies but I never thought I would actually be in the middle of one. I was only fifteen and if apprehended by the police, my mother would be only too happy to believe her son was a drug pusher.

Growing up at that time, most of us had an unspoken code, we did not rat.

I was shocked that Vinaya could take such liberties with me and my Dad's car. However, it explained how he seemed to have money despite never working.

I said nothing to him. I never told my father as he might have killed him. His reaction would have been unimaginable.

Upon his return, he had some pleasantries with the family and then very politely took Roy aside. It was obvious that he was going to talk about Roy's lackadaisical approach to repaying the money he had lent him.

Just one month later, it would be Neelam who came calling for her money but her approach was much more proactive than that of my father or Aunt's.

He had borrowed money from her and despite many phone calls over six months had only made one payment. He was never there when she called and if she came directly to the house, Vidia would explain that he was out. With the car tucked away at the back of the house out of sight, it was a plausible lie.

On this occasion, she had had enough. She arrived at a little after 9:00 pm on a Wednesday night. Roy and the family were watching Vidia's favourite show, Dynasty.

She had hired a pickup van and a driver. She had also brought a dolly for moving furniture and boxes.

She walked into the house, "Good night." She turned off the TV and disconnected it from the VCR. "How much is this TV?" She then picked up the VCR. "How much is this?"

She wheeled both items out to the pickup. She returned and went to the kitchen. The family silently followed her. She unpacked the fridge and loaded it on to the dolly. "How much is this fridge?"

She then looked at them, "Thank you. Good night."

They followed her outside in stunned silence. Roy would not dare speak to her as he had done to Aunty Shanti. Neelam was a very different kind of woman.

CHAPTER 50

The Capitulation of Aunty Vashti

Being around my father and Neelam had been an education in life that no child should have had to endure.

Prior to my visits to them, I had been under the impression that adults were there to show you a better way, to lead by example. The ones who had guided me may not have been perfect but they were not cruel hypocrites.

Around the two fools, I had learnt how petty someone could be to children and enjoy it. Strangely enough they would never dare treat Sunita like that.

I had come to hate my life. I had no respect for my mother and even less for my father. It was now normal for him to bring home a variety of women.

On one occasion at Aunty Vashti's house, one of his cousins, Sarika from Penal, mentioned to him, "Vijay, I know you go have your fun but you think is a good idea to do it in front of the children?"

"I am not inconveniencing myself for my children."

"But that is the whole idea of being a parent. You are supposed to inconvenience yourself for your children."

"What! Not me! I am not changing my life for my children."

She looked at Aunty Vashti, who just stared at the wall.

"But is ok," he laughed. "They have a nigger father. He will mind them."

I could hear her later in the kitchen speaking to Aunty Vashti, "That man will lose his children."

I was disgusted with my life and thought how just less than two years ago, things were so different. My social circle was my school friends and the children from the Falls. I would go to the Mall or class parties. Now I was stuck with country Indians who seemed socially inept outside of their own race.

I was at my wits end. I realized running away was not the answer, I needed to at least finish high school if I were to get a job. I decided that at the end of Form V, just eighteen odd months away, I would leave home and get as far away from my father as I could. I had given up on ever having a normal family life. However, I would grow up, marry and give my children the childhood I had missed out on. In the meantime, the next eighteen months would be like a prison sentence. I just had to ride it out and July of 1985 would be my freedom.

One of the highlights for me during the end of the year was a football match we had after class. It was a Friday afternoon and we split the class into two teams and used the Colts Football Field.

I was playing Defence and doing the best I could, trying to stop the opposition and making some useful passes. I had learnt some years before that I was not exactly gifted. However, if I played intelligently and used my "ball sense," I could have a decent game.

During a scrimmage in the opponent's half the ball came to me. As it bounced, I hit it instinctively without thinking with my left foot. I was a right footer but my left could be accurate if not powerful. The shot took everyone by surprise and entered just inside the right post. The Keeper never even had a chance to move.

Everyone patted me on the back and we took up our positions again. I will never quite understand what happened next. But it was if my body had a mind of its own. I would just play the ball very quickly without planning the move in advance. It was as if my mind was half a second behind my body. I started running and playing the game at a furious pace. I would run and pass the ball before anyone could anticipate what was happening. If I lost the ball or someone else had it, I would just kick it away and run off with it. Even my own teammates were watching each other in wide eyed amazement.

About five minutes after the first goal our Defence cleared the ball from the penalty area and it landed with me just inside the half line. I collected and saw Basil Williams running towards me. He was one of the best players in our age group at school. I leaned on my left foot and started shaking my right foot over the ball. With him about three paces away, I kicked it to his left past him and bolted towards the goal. I could feel someone just behind me to my right but I just kept pushing the ball and running making sure that it was between me and the challenger. I raced towards the goalkeeper who stood crouched at the ready. I could feel someone to my left just outside my peripheral vision, it was Allan Alibey, a starter for the A Colts Team. With just about ten feet left between the Keeper and me, I passed to Alibey. The ball curved perfectly to his forehead. He nodded his head forward and it easily evaded the Keeper who was diving to his right in vain.

The boys went crazy. The first goal might have been a bit of a fluke. But not this one. As my team ran towards me cheering, their expressions indicating half joy, half disbelief. I calmly walked back towards the half line.

The other team was in a different mood. The Forwards glared at the Defenders.

"Allyuh blasted men. Stop the man nah!!"

The Defenders shouted back. "Why the hell don't you come and stop him!!! YOU come and stop him nah!!"

I didn't realize it then but I was in the zone. And only half aware at the reaction amongst the players.

I glanced up and saw a very red-faced Williams looking at the ground and smiling sheepishly at both teams. It wasn't just the dribble that had embarrassed him but whom it had come from. I simply was not usually that dangerous a player.

As 1983 became 1984 my father's patience with Roy was withering. I had begun to call him Rob Roy, after all, he was like a thief taking other people's money when he could.

Uncle Shirvan and Aunty Vashti were now practically inseparable. She had made a short visit to Guyana for Christmas returning on Christmas Day. We were all surprised to see Uncle Shirvan arriving at the house with her. "He picked me up at the airport," was the excuse.

When I saw his passport sticking out of his back pocket, I realized that he had done more than just go to the airport.

Roy was less subtle, "You need passpart, to pick up people at airport bhai," he shouted in his thick Guyanese accent."

The following year all pretences would evaporate.

It was on a Saturday in January of 1984. We heard a knock on the door. Both my father and I went to answer it. We opened the door and Vidia and the entire family came rushing in.

"She have a man! … She said she said she don't want to go and…"

"What?" said my father.

They all started babbling at the same time, "She have a man."

"She said she didn't want to come!"

"He was in the bed!!"

"Hold on!" I shouted. "Stop. What are you saying? Speak slowly!"

This time they took turns telling us what had happened.

The family had decided to go to Maracas Beach. However, Aunty Vashti had said she was not in the mood and would stay home.

They stopped off in Valsayn, to meet another Guyanese family they knew so they could all go together. However, the wife was not in the mood to go with just a bunch of young girls. "I don't want to be the only woman there. Let's go get your mother."

They made the quick trip back to St. Joseph, parked the car at the back and entered looking for Aunty Vashti. As they made their way up the corridor, she stood in the doorway of the room that both she and Zeenat shared. She had a serious look on her face with both hands on her hips.

Their friend looked at her with the brightest of smiles. "We're going to Maracas. Come on. Let's go."

"No. I am not in the mood for Maracas today," she replied, her face dead serious with no hint of pleasantries.

Zeenat tried to enter the room. But her mother stood in the doorway like a rock, hands on hips.

Finally, Zeenat just elbowed her way in. When she walked up to the bed, she realized that a person was wrapped up under the covers. She was discombobulated. She spun around and just walked out of the room.

After a little more cajoling and realizing that she would not come, they left.

My father and I looked at them wide eyed and in shock. It was obvious that more than thirty minutes later, they were all trying to psychologically recover from what had happened. None more so than Zeenat who seemed to be practically hyperventilating.

We went to Maracas that day. However, on the drive there and even at the beach, the topic of Aunty Vashti and her lover continuously permeated the conversation.

During the last few months, her reputation had taken quite a hit. Zeenat and Asha were practically sisters. And despite any previous problems with Roy, their two mothers were good friends. Asha's father was also quite fond of Aunty Vashti.

Just after my father's return from New York, Asha's parents had opened a supermarket at the front of their property. The very place where Roy and Vidia had gotten married. Aunty Vashti had been hired as a

309

cashier. The business had been a great success with all the food being sold out on the first day.

However, on the second week there were problems. They had discovered three hundred dollars missing at the end of the night. The only person who had had access to the money besides Asha's family was Aunty Vashti. Under the circumstances they had no choice but to let her go.

"So Vashti tiefing now?" mused my father.

"You don't really know that," I responded. "Anything could have happened. You weren't there."

He looked at me and smiled.

The following week whilst watching TV, he said to me, "It turns out Vashti stole the money."

"How do you know that?"

"Roy told me."

"How does Roy know?"

Rob Roy as we now called him, had explained to my father that it was confirmed by his brother Rohan who had been visiting from Georgetown.

On the night of the theft, the family had taken a drive to get some ice cream. Rohan had said he would stay at home. While taking a walk in the yard, he could see Aunty Vashti through the dining room window. "She had a stack of bills in front of her and was counting on the table."

It was too much of a coincidence to ignore.

I felt a bit sorry for her. She had come from the mighty Jagan family from Georgetown. Now here she was somebody's outside woman and being branded a thief by her own family.

Although I did not see much of Aunty Shanti anymore, she had also started going out with a married man in early 1983.

I thought of my mother and these two women. They obviously considered themselves respectable people yet they were shamelessly making fools of themselves in public, practicing the very behaviour that years before they had probably admonished.

310

On a positive note, I did not need to feel so self-conscious anymore. Now there were other mothers making fools of themselves.

CHAPTER 51

Emasculating Rob Roy, Farting in Fear and Unbelievable Greed

Vinaya would lime a lot with Uncle Shirvan. It did not seem to bother him that he was socializing with a married man that his mother was having an affair with.

Or if it did bother him, he hid it well.

Despite Shirvan being his close friend, my father spoke disparagingly about him on this topic.

"This is what he does. He likes to run after other men's wives," apparently forgetting that Aunty Vashti was divorced.

He recounted an experience Mummy's sister, Aunty Indira had had with him in the early seventies. He would come around in the middle of the day when her husband wasn't around. After a few visits she had had enough.

"Look, let me tell you something. I don't like men coming around here when my husband isn't home. Don't come here again unless my husband is here. Do you understand me?"

A stunned Uncle Shirvan nodded and never visited her home again.

As my father finished his story, a lightbulb went off in my head. I remembered his visits in Maracas Valley about a decade earlier. Although he would be talking a lot and laughing, my mother would have a very serious look on her face. And then again years later when she simply had no interest in acknowledging him at the airport. He had obviously been trying to make a move in those earlier days and failed as he had with Aunty Indira.

Vidia and her mother were no longer on speaking terms. Zeenat may have disapproved of her mother's behaviour but there was only so much she could protest. She was still a child and her mother would not have tolerated any overly rude behaviour.

Vinaya came to stay with us just before the TT Carnival. He just hung around as he had done the year before. My father did not seem to mind and would use him to do certain errands and to drop me to school early in the morning.

It was the first time since the divorce that my father and I would be together for Carnival. This meant I would meet Steve Cross.

Uncle Steve was a red skin man who had befriended my parents in England. He was nine years my father's senior but they were practically brothers.

Brought up in Port of Spain, he had migrated to London in the 1950s. He explained that in those days if two black men were walking on opposite sides of the street, they would run over, hug each other and start talking.

He had cultivated a shipping business for the early West Indians who needed to send items back home. In later years, he opened a pub which was a favourite watering hole for the West Indians, and the Caribbean cricketers plying their trade in London.

He had been a fair cricketer and footballer in his youth. He had a fete match cricket side which would tour the UK. My father had played for them during his University days bowling his off spin.

Eager to play competitive football when in his early thirties, he lied and said he was ten years younger, playing as a Goalkeeper for a semi pro team. He would reminisce how they had "made it to the final one year," against a team with five Irish internationals. His team was beaten 5-0.

"I cried after that match," he said. "You know what it is to have to take that long coach ride back home and you are the man who let in the five?"

Amazingly, he had two wives. One, a beautiful Irish woman with whom he had a five-year old son. The other was a copper skinned Jamaican whom he had met in his pub. "I explained to my wife that I am in love with two women. And I just can't help it," was his response.

Uncle Steve never missed the TT Carnival. Never!

I had heard from Sunita and the rest of the family about his visits to the Estate during Carnival.

However, now my father lived just minutes from central POS. He would stay with us and it certainly wasn't boring.

He had brought a group of Australians from London to tour T&T. They were two couples and another girl, all veterinarians.

They arrived a week and a half before the Carnival weekend. We took them to see the One Day International, the West Indies vs Australia. Our team was impregnable and hardly ever lost. But they lost that day much to the delight of our visitors from Oz.

• • •

By the time the Carnival weekend had arrived, my father and the single Aussie had become an item. She was pleasant but certainly no looker. Curly, brown, blondish hair down to her shoulders and a bit of a thick set figure, she was good looking in a wholesome way.

I could not understand how a man so many younger women thought so handsome could settle for this.

I did not go out much with Uncle Steve and Daddy so I didn't really care what was happening.

Carnival came and went and so did they.

The Aussie's name was Olivia. She sent my father one or two letters and then that fling fizzled out.

My father had now reached the end of his rope concerning Rob Roy. He simply would not make an effort to pay his loan and only after much pressure would pay a portion of what he should have.

If we visited, he would be "sleeping."

Daddy would walk up to his bedroom door and bang loudly, "Get up! Get up!"

He would come out with a very sleepy face. If he was faking, it was a good one.

I would go into Zeenat's bedroom and we would chat. Aunty Vashti and Vidia would vacate the living room because they knew what was coming next.

At first the conversation would be at a low level but then we could hear my father's voice begin to rise, "You Guyanese come to this country and like to laugh at us. You think we are stupid. But we're not stupid. Is nice we nice."

Rob Roy would look away, occasionally nodding his head.

"Then we help you out and put up with this shit!" He continued, "Look at Shanti. She will never get her money from you. Will she?"

At the time I felt sorry for him, being belittled like that in his own home.

However, we were slowly coming to realize that we had a con artist of immense proportions amongst us.

Eventually we would understand the real reason his family had not attended his wedding.

Rob Roy had had a reputation as a crook amongst his family and peers in Guyana, long before he had ever come to TT.

315

His parents had sent him to Seneca College in Toronto to study Business Management in the late seventies. There was a problem buying foreign currency in Guyana due to strict government controls.

Realizing his family wanted to buy Canadian dollars, he took the money they had given him for expenses in Toronto and sold it back to them at a black-market price. Basically, he had taken their own money and made them buy it back at an inflated rate.

His brother looked at him, "But Roy is Mummy and Daddy!"

"So? When it comes to money, family doesn't mean anything."

It took his parents many years to forget his act of selfishness. In the meantime, he was ignored by them.

Just before coming to TT with Aunty Vashti's family, he would have one final misadventure.

Two nights before their departure, he was driving Aunty Vashti's car through a dangerous part of Georgetown and hit someone on a bicycle. His excuse for not stopping was that it was a dangerous neighbourhood. But it could just as easily have been because he didn't give a damn. The people on the street started shouting at him to stop but he just drove on. They had seen the license plate and because of his medium length hair combed back, they assumed from the back that it was a woman.

As the car was registered under Aunty Vashti's name, the officers assumed she had been the driver.

The following night, just 24 hours before their departure to TT, the police showed up at their home, a second storey apartment. In a flash Aunty Vashti locked the door and she, her daughters and Rob Roy, somehow fitted themselves under the bed next to the door.

The police began banging on the door.

"Open up. Open up. It's the police. Open up."

They kept banging loudly.

They were squashed under that bed not making a sound - except for Rob Roy.

The fear was too much for him and he began to fart.

He just kept farting. The police officers' presence seemed to be having a combustible effect on his bowels. The family dared not make a sound as the police were just on the other side of the door. Zeenat on the other hand could not help but giggle. The more Rob Roy farted, the more she giggled. They were quite angry with her but they could not shout so they just glared at her.

After a few minutes, the police left and they all extricated themselves from under the bed. They harshly admonished Zeenat for her behaviour.

"Is my fault? He hit somebody and drive away," she retorted pointing at Rob Roy. "How is this my fault?"

She was quickly silenced by her mother. But she had made her point.

Now, here was Rob Roy in Trinidad, taking up from where he had left off in Guyana.

As Uncle Basdeo had been known for a fair degree of dishonesty in his youth, my father would say to him, "You get the right son-in-law yes. You really did."

Just after the Carnival we saw another side of him that we would never forget. Whilst staying at a hotel during his breakup with Neelam the year before, Daddy had frequented a particular restaurant near his hotel. He had eventually become quite friendly with the owners. If ever in the area, he would pass in have a few drinks or a meal and chat with them.

They lived in Kelly Village, a semi-rural place not far from the hotel nor where I grew up in Curepe. They invited my father to come visit for a Sunday lunch. He explained that he would be brining Vinaya and myself.

Amazingly, Rob Roy passed by that day. He made a payment in cash but was fifty dollars short, promising to have it in a week's time. Daddy resignedly accepted his explanation.

Vinaya had prior plans and could not make it. Rob Roy on the other hand realizing that we were going out, invited himself.

"Sure," said my father.

As Rob Roy went to quickly use the washroom, Daddy looked over at Vinaya, "That bitch, he know we going for lunch. He just trying to scrounge a free meal."

We arrived in Kelly in less than thirty minutes. Vishen and Pat were the married couple that owned the restaurant. They greeted us warmly along with Pat's mother and sister. We immediately started off with snacks and drinks.

An hour later it was time for lunch, curried duck, rice, dahl and curry mango with a cucumber salad. It was a sumptuous meal and in true Trini fashion we were encouraged to have seconds.

Rob Roy took it even further. He had seconds, then thirds and then fourths.

During his first three meals, the family looked at us and laughed. By the fourth there was a look of mild shock on their faces.

He walked outside and they all looked at us with wide eyed amazement as if we should have an explanation. However, this fat, greedy bitch was not quite finished.

I decided to take a stretch outside myself. I walked around the side of the house and say Rob Roy coming around from the back, he was stumbling a bit and using the wall for support.

He walked back in and promptly helped himself to fifths, sixths and finally sevenths. All the while, the family just stared at him and then us in absolute disbelief and horror.

He finally pulled himself away from the table and rejoined us in the adjacent living room.

"Have you had enough?" my father enquired sarcastically.

He nodded, smiled and patted his protruding stomach.

For the rest of the afternoon the family could not get rid of the look of astonishment and mild fear on their face.

I knew that Guyana was going through hard economic times and there were many shortages. I wondered if he just wasn't accustomed to seeing food or he was just plain lickerish.

There was more to come.

Finally, we bade Vishen, Pat and their family goodbye. As we drove off, we soon stopped at a supermarket to buy some goods.

Rob Roy came out of his car and walked over to us.

"Sunny, do you remember you saw me walking from the back of the house and I was holding on the wall?"

I nodded.

"Well, I went to the back, put my finger down my throat and made myself vomit. I wanted extra room to eat more."

I just stared at him. I had seen greed before but not anything at this level.

"Are you fucking serious?" my father said, staring at him as if he had a hole in his head.

As we drove away, my father shook his head. "Unbelievable. That man is as greedy as he is crooked."

CHAPTER 52

Mother Frog, the Indians and Lost Virginity

Halfway through Form IV, I was only a year away from the CXC Exams. These exams were big in TT because they dictated how much of a future you had. If you failed, you prospects were considered limited.

I had chosen six subjects, Math and English Language were mandatory. In addition, I would write Principle of Business, History, Accounting and Geography.

My parents were not impressed. "Choosing only six subjects is laziness," exclaimed my father.

I had been struggling with Accounting and had decided that I wished to drop it in preference for English Literature. It would mean doing a lot of reading and making up for the months lost. I had been told by the Dean that I had to get the permission of Ms. Harragin who taught it in Form IV and V.

She was a short, bloated, black woman who wore large, black shades. The students referred to her as "Mother Frog," behind her back.

I approached her a few days before the Easter Holidays.

"Come back to me after the holidays," she responded.

"But Ms. Harragin, if you say yes, I can use the holidays to study."

"I will answer you after the Easter," she said dismissively and walked away.

I spent the Easter playing cricket with Vinaya and one of the neighbours in our building. Vinaya and I would go to the cinema and it was enjoyable.

Sunita came to visit. She would try to insult me in front of Vinaya, hoping to harass me the way she had done with her mother. However, Vinaya just looked at her stoically and she soon stopped.

I did not usually go out of my way to denigrate children but in Sunita's case, I made an exception.

Vinaya and I would laugh at her if she could not read a word in the newspaper or if she mispronounced certain words.

The Country Club was nearby and we were allowed to use their facilities. We would go over to swim and sometimes just swim away from Sunita very quickly and leave her alone in the pool. She was hurt and frustrated but it was only a fraction of what she and her mother had done to me in the past.

At the end of her visit Daddy and Vinaya drove her back home.

Neelam was now hooked up with a Doctor, Basdeo Singh. He was a pot-bellied man, balding with salt and pepper hair on the sides, a bespectacled 54-year-old, twenty years Neelam's senior. They were a little more than hooked up, they were actually engaged.

Neelam now had a wealthy lover and her life had become much easier, on many occasions she would be seen driving his Mercedes in the area.

She had cooked that day and offered my father some callaloo to take home. "It will last for days and it's less cooking for you."

My father didn't mind and he noted that it was one of my favourite dishes.

He and Vinaya went in and were introduced to Basdeo. They were offered a refreshment and accepted.

After the normal pleasantries and introductions, they sat down whilst Sunita went to her room to deposit her bag.

Basdeo looked at my father and said, "You know you must make a greater effort to visit this child."

"What?"

"You don't really come around often. You should see her more often."

"You are fast and out of place. That is none of your business!"

"Well, she is your daughter and I am minding her. So, whose business is it?"

Neelam did a sort of knee jerk reaction in the kitchen. She knew my father well and she braced for what was about to happen.

"You need to know your fucking place! That is none of your business and have NOTHING to say to me!!

Basdeo jumped to his feet, "You can't speak to me like that! I here minding this child. YOU know your fucking place boy!!!"

Sunita came running out of her room, "Oh God man!!" she shouted tearfully.

My father never bothered about the callaloo or drink. He turned to Vinaya, "Let's go before I slap this ass!!"

As he walked out, Vinaya behind him, Basdeo followed, "You want to fight me!!?"

Daddy turned around to confront him. Vinaya stepped in front of him to bar any confrontation.

Neelam, ran and put her arms around Basdeo to restrain him. My father threw a punch which missed its mark due to Vinaya holding him back but it did graze Basdeo's face.

Basdeo went ballistic.

"I'll kill him!! I'll kill him!!" he shouted lunging for my father.

Neelam pulled him away while Vinaya did the same with my father.

He made one last attempt to get at Basdeo, "Man give me a chance, let me beat this ass!!" But Vinaya would not let go.

Finally, he left with both parties on rather acrimonious terms. It had to have been traumatic for Sunita. She was simply experiencing some of what Leila and I had been forced to endure for years. Like us she was getting a rude awakening regarding her parents and their fallibilities.

The third and final term began in late March. As we had the usual gathering in the Hall, I approached Ms. Harragin.

"Miss, is it alright if I do English Lit this term?"

"No, not at all. I spoke to your Accounting teacher. She says you do not do well in that subject and it's a lot of work you have to do to catch up."

"But Miss, Accounting is the subject that I want to drop. If you speak to my English teacher, he will tell you how good I am."

She turned away, "No. You will have a lot of work to do." And with that she walked off.

"But that is why I asked you for the Easter Holidays to study."

She never answered.

I was shattered. This was my future. If I wanted to drop Accounting for English Lit., why would she speak to the Accounting teacher and not the English teacher who knew I was his prize pupil?

This fat jackass! I thought to myself and walked away.

Two months later she gave birth to a baby and a month later brought him in to the Teachers' Room so the staff could see him.

The boys were in shock.

"You mean she was pregnant??" We all looked at each other.

"But how she could be pregnant and nobody noticed?"

"Nah!" I exclaimed. "No one gets pregnant and is the same size before, during and after. She is the same fat she always was." I deduced that she must have adopted.

"Sir," I asked a passing teacher. "Did Ms. Harragin adopt a baby?"

"No. Why?"

"So that is her baby?"

"Yes. Why?"

"No reason. Thank you, Sir."

We marvelled at her size and that no one could notice the difference between her being pregnant or not pregnant.

"That woman really is a Mother Frog," exclaimed Michael.

Zeenat's sixteenth birthday was coming up. This was a big deal for girls and her family had planned a party. She went to an all-girls' school, so there would be a fair bit of females there.

One person I was looking forward to meeting was Tammy. She was a classmate of Zeenat's and I had been introduced to her over the phone during my stay at Aunty Vashti's the previous October. She had actually called to speak to Zeenat but after the initial introduction, she would always ask for me when speaking to Zeenat. By the fourth call, there was no longer any pretence and she would ask directly for me.

We would have long chats on almost a daily basis. Upon my return home, we would exchange the occasional letter as my father did not have a phone. Sometimes, I would call her on a pay phone.

Zeenat's birthday was on the second Saturday of April. I arrived early. My father was not staying. He made it clear that I would have to spend the night there and that Rob Roy should drop me home the next day.

If parties started at 7:00. It was normal in TT for people to arrive at least half an hour late. Sure enough, they started trickling in a little before half past seven and by 8:00 there were at least twenty people there with more coming in.

There was a good variety of males and females there. Tammy arrived and she seemed like a pretty girl with a dark brown complexion, long black hair and well made up for the event.

We talked easily enough. She had brought her brother and two of his friends. After about half an hour, I realized they were having a seemingly serious conversation in the kitchen with Zeenat, Vidia and Rob Roy. Within a few minutes Tammy's brother and his friends were gone. Zeenat explained that the party was "invitation only," and that those

324

fellows had not been invited. I realized that with many of the guests from a girls' school, they had been hoping to take advantage of the natural proliferation of females. Sadly, for them, they had failed.

The night went well. Tammy and I danced quite a bit. What I did not know is that there was a fellow there by the name of Sammy. He was medium height with copper toned skin, thick, curly hair and three years older than Zeenat. She had met him through some friends and was hoping to make a connection that night.

Later, there was the usual cutting of the cake. She and her sister made a production of putting all the boys' names in a bag.

Rob Roy, looked at them and shouted in front of everyone, "What you doing that for? Is Sammy you want to cut the cake with."

Zeenat let out a shriek and ran to her room. She had been embarrassed in front of everyone.

It took about five minutes to calm her down, simultaneously, Rob Roy was being berated by Asha and Aunty Vashti. She then returned and went through the ceremony of choosing a name from a box.

She opened the piece of paper and told the girls. "Sammy!!" they shouted.

The cut the cake, kissed and took photos.

I was happy for Zeenat. It was obvious that my cousins and I came from dysfunctional families and we all had our respective burdens to bear regarding maintaining our dignity and sanity in the mess that was called our family. However, on this day she could enjoy her sixteenth birthday just like any normal teenager around the world.

Tammy and I danced the night away. She had a habit of singing the song while we danced but she could sing well so I didn't mind.

There was a very cute, light skinned, Indian girl with beautiful long, black hair, that caught my eye. But with Tammy around me all night, I never really had a chance to say more than a few words to her. She was nice enough to come over to me and say goodbye when she was leaving.

I realized I had a thousand times more interest in her than Tammy but I had not been able to execute an opportunity to get to know her better.

The next day I went home and thereafter, I never really paid much attention to Zeenat. She would occasionally have an attitude which made it difficult to speak to her or want to be around her. But if you gave her attitude, she did not appreciate it.

Aunty Shanti once said that all of Rampersad Sarwan's grandchildren had taken after him, when they believed they were right, they were always right. I would realize in my adult years that it had been an astute observation.

Vinaya was still with us and he and my father would visit Neelam's family a few times a week. She requested that I come to visit because she wanted to speak to me. I had thought it was something important but really she just wanted to chat. She also explained to me that she and Sammy were celebrating their "montherversary." I noticed that she also had his name written all over her jeans.

Although she was my cousin, I could not handle her on again, off again friendliness so I decided to give her some space.

The school year was ending, I still ignored the Indians next door due to their rather rude behaviour. They did not seem to understand that in Trinidad, neighbours greeted each other. I was tired of saying good evening to people who would not look at you or respond.

They certainly had their own social ways. Every night, about 15 or more would gather on the street and have loud conversations while the children played. This would go on sometimes past eight o'clock, on weekends even later.

Obliquely opposite our building was a home that had been turned into a small government electricity station. There were mango trees on the lawn and no wall. It was normal for the neighbours to go pick some. However, with the Indians it was not some. They would walk with a big, black garbage bag and basically ravage the tree. In TT we called this attitude "Never see, come see."

I found it hard to believe that people who had been sent abroad to represent their country could be lacking in certain social graces.

My father's simple explanation was "These are civil servants from India. You can't really expect much from them. The High Commissioner, however, knows how to conduct himself."

Whatever the reason, I decided I wanted very little to do with them. However, there was this one girl that I had seen on my first week. I had never been quite able to describe my dream woman but there she was, long, jet black hair, beautiful dimples and a face that became even more amazing when she smiled.

I tried to ignore her because like the rest she was not sociable. Strangely, her mother was the lone Indian that would smile in greeting to me.

One of the families lived on the ground floor and had a young son and daughter. The boy was about 18, six-foot tall, broad shouldered, with a full head of hair and a moustache. His sister was a slim teenager, with medium length, black hair and glasses. She looked like a quiet bookish type. I was about to get a lesson in never judging a book by its cover.

Vinaya had been claiming for months that the sister was always staring at him. I thought nothing of it. One Saturday in early June, Vinaya and I were washing the car. The family drove by on their way home with the girl and her brother in the back seat. Vinaya looked at me in great surprise. I ignored him and kept washing. As the family walked into their building, he grabbed me.

"Did you see what she did?"

"Who? What? Who did what?"

"The girl in the car winked at me!"

"Vinaya stop fantasizing. She was probably just blinking. Why would she wink at you?"

I dismissed him and his fantasy.

Two days later, he saw her walking on the street. He made sure to stop her away from any prying eyes in our complex.

Her name was Shoba. She had lived in Mauritius for three years before coming to TT. They would usually travel every three years as her father would be posted to various Indian embassies around the world. Amazingly, Vinaya picked her up at school in my father's car the following day and took her to Carenage beach. He could be aggressive when he wanted. And although it did not work with all the ladies it did work with a lot. He was successful this time as they kissed and he then dropped her off a little way from the Indian High Commission.

She would come to visit at our apartment after school or on the weekends if my father was not there. On her first visit, they were sexually active. By her second she had lost her virginity two months shy of her fifteenth birthday.

I could not believe that this librarian looking individual with her glasses could be so bold and outgoing.

A week later her brother walked up to us and started talking. His name was Rajesh. He obviously wanted to make friends. He and his family had no idea what was going on with his sister.

Within a week we slowly began to chat a bit more with the other Indians due to Rajesh being around us.

Form IV came to an end and the beautiful summer holidays was once again upon us.

CHAPTER 53

Sunny and Sony, a Love Story

I had never believed in love at first sight.

I considered it some nonsense that people spoke about or something that existed in the movies.

Then I saw Sonakshi.

Her family and friends called her Sony.

She was beautiful, everything I had ever imagined my dream woman to be. I had had the mental image in my head but could not quite verbalize it. Now I didn't need to. There she was.

For approximately one year, we never really spoke. She would occasionally say hello but like most of the Indians she did not seem very sociable outside her little clique.

Despite our limited social contact, I now had a serous [15]*tabanca*.

Vinaya had opened his big mouth and told Shoba how I felt. In mid-July, he had gone to Guyana to visit his cousins. Shoba knowing how I felt about Sony, would invite me if ever they were chatting outside.

---

[15] *Tabanca* – a feeling of unrequited love causing unbalanced behaviour.

Sometimes, Shoba would make an excuse to go inside for a moment giving us a chance to speak more privately. I had a feeling she might have already known about my feelings because Shoba might've told her. However, if she knew, she certainly showed no aversion to speaking with me.

She was four years older than me. Logically, I had no chance but how did one resist such beauty, smile and intellect.

Her mother had been a singer on the radio in Bengal. Not surprisingly, Sony spoke Bengalese in addition to Hindi, English and French – all fluently.

Prior to coming to TT, her family had lived in Paris for two years. She had done Form VI at a local Polytechnic school in TT and after graduating was simply at home. I was curious as to what her ambitions were or was she planning to just marry off? Arranged marriages were not uncommon amongst the Indians and her parents had met that way. She made it clear that these marriages were not forced upon the girls and that if she were to go that way, her parents would not approve unless she did.

My appearance had changed considerably in the last year. Referring to me as "young Roy," had been the impetus for me to lose weight. I had shed about 15 pounds and was now a fit looking fellow.

I was saddened to know that Sony and her family would be leaving in late August. Her father had been posted to the United Arab Emirates.

After two weeks of chatting, I couldn't take it anymore. I had to say what was in my heart. I knew there was no reason for her to say yes. But I had never felt like this before. If she was going to leave the country, I wanted to know that I had told her. I did not want to spend the rest of my life regretting that I had never voiced my feelings to the first woman I had every truly fallen in love with. Rejection or not, she would know how I felt.

I had always been a bit shy when it came to girls I was actually attracted to. If they were just friends, I was a chatterbox.

I had never had to have a conversation quite like this before. I was a bit nervous but my attraction for her overrode those emotions.

I told Shoba to let Sony know that I needed to speak to her. She met me at 7:30 pm that night. I took her to the entrance of my building away from prying Indian eyes and ears.

I was sure Shoba had told her. She did not seem at all surprised by the subterfuge.

"Do you know why I want to speak to you?"

She shook her head.

"I wanted to say I know you are older than me. I know you will leave in one month's time and I will probably never see you again … but… I really like you. I care for you and I want to be with you."

She looked towards the floor then she looked at me. I braced for the rejection.

"You are very nice but I am leaving in three weeks so it's not possible."

Although not a yes, it did not sound like a definitive no.

"So what are you saying? What would happen if you weren't leaving Trinidad?"

"Then I would say yes to you."

I could not believe that I had reached that far.

She looked at me with her beautiful smile, and apologetically said "I am very sorry."

"Sony, I have to be honest. Three weeks with you is better than nothing."

She looked at me for a second and slowly smiled, "Ok. Yes."

"Yes what?"

"Yes, I will be your girlfriend."

"Really? But why did you change your mind?"

"Because you said three weeks is better than nothing. It's a very nice thing to say. So yes."

I could only half grasp her logic. But I figured there was no need to ask too many questions. She had said yes.

The next day she and Shoba came to visit. She was too innocent to go to my room. So, it was Shoba who sat in my room with the door closed and Sony and I chatted in the living room.

I was shocked that I was her first boyfriend.

I couldn't understand how someone so beautiful who had lived in both France and TT for years had never had a boyfriend.

"I never wanted one."

"There is a Muslim family we know here. A month ago, the son asked me to marry him but I said no."

I couldn't blame the guy. If I had known her for years and she was leaving the country, I would have asked her to marry me too.

"I was never interested in boys. But you are very nice and polite. Not like Vinaya, he seems a bit crude."

This was a smart girl.

"Now I am thinking of you all the time. I don't want to eat. Then I am hungry but then I see the food and I am not hungry."

No matter how much I had liked a woman, I had never lost my appetite. I couldn't help but feel a bit flattered.

Vinaya returned two days later. Naturally, he was surprised at the progress made in his absence.

For the next week Shoba and Sony would come over. Sony would bring some letters. The idea being if anyone saw her exiting from our building, she would use the letters as an excuse saying that they had been sent to our apartment by mistake. She had been informed about the letters and was simply retrieving them.

She and I would go to my room and Vinaya would take Shoba to my father's.

After just one week with Vinaya, Shoba had told him that her family would leave TT in two years' time. However, she would stay behind and they would get married.

Vinaya just stared at her.

"Why are you staring at me?"

"Oh. No reason."

"So, we will get married. Ok?"

"Ok."

She had no idea of how little she meant to him.

Sony and I had our fun in my room. But we never had sex. She wasn't ready. I loved her and was more than happy to wait. I certainly wasn't interested in impressing people like Vinaya.

We kissed and loved each other. We talked about our lives. She noticed the variety of women my father had coming in and out of the building. She also realized that Vinaya was aggressive and a bit coarse.

"Honestly, for the last year, I did not want anything to do with your family. Your father looks like a real playboy. But my mother always says you look like a nice boy."

She explained that the reason she had never greeted me was "because the High Commission people love gossip and they would have made a big deal about it."

For the first time in years I had someone I could open up to.

"You have to understand, I did not ask to be born into this family. I did not choose my father. I have no control over my situation.

"The last year of my life has been like some kind of hell. But you know if I had not come to live with my father, I would not be here and I would not have met you. So, I guess the suffering was worth it. If I hadn't gone through it, we wouldn't be here now and I would not know what it is to be in love."

A few days later Rajesh and his sister decided they wanted to go South, to visit the Gulf City Mall. Sony, her little brother and I were invited.

We went to the mall, walked around and enjoyed some Kentucky Fried Chicken. On the way back, Sony saw a Mandir and told Rajesh to stop so they could pray. I had no idea of the ceremony involved and she and Shoba showed me how to light the diyas and do the prayers.

Sony looked at me in surprise.

"What kind of Indian are you? You don't know these things?"

"You have to understand, I did not grow up around Indian people. So, there are a lot of things I don't know."

As we drove home. Sony got sleepy and fell asleep on my arm. A shocked Rajesh just kept staring at us in the rear-view mirror.

One day while relaxing on my bed, I lamented that Vinaya did not take Shoba seriously yet "I love you so much and I can't have a relationship with you."

"Thank you Sunny. That's what I wanted to hear. Now I will continue with you even after I leave Trinidad."

"What?" I couldn't believe my ears.

"I needed to understand how honest and sincere you are … that I could trust you. Now I do. So, we will continue even when I am in Dubai."

I was thrilled. There is perhaps no greater feeling than loving the love of your life and having those feelings returned. The joy is indescribable.

During her last two weeks we would meet at my apartment or at the Long Circular Mall. If we held hands, we made sure it was in a position where we could see everyone coming and going so that no High Commission people would catch her. Because if they did, they would immediately go gossiping to her parents and there would be negative consequences.

My father realized something was up. I was now showering, two or three times a day as opposed to my normal once. I did not discuss the situation with him but I was sure Vinaya had.

The final week was bittersweet. It was wonderful being with her but our days were now numbered.

She would smile at me, "Sunny and Sony. That would make a beautiful love story. They should make a movie about us."

I smiled, "The movie has just begun."

On Sony's last night her family was invited out for dinner. Before leaving she sent Shoba to call me. I was to meet her at the side of the building. She was wearing a sari, her face was all made up and her hair was tied up in a style like the beehive of the sixties. Anyone else may have looked stupid with that hair. But not her. She looked like an Indian movie star.

We talked about how much we loved each other.

"My father told me not to pine away for you. But my father is an idiot. He does not know anything about relationships. I have no intentions of listening to him."

"I hope not."

We kissed. I held her in my arms trying to feel every ounce of the moment. So that it would last with me when she left.

Her apartment was actually next to mine, coincidentally her bedroom was on the other side of my bedroom wall. We would sometimes knock on the wall just before going to bed as a way of saying goodnight to each other.

She came home around midnight that night. And a little after 1:00 am, I heard a knock on the wall. I knocked back. Fifteen minutes later, I decided I would go to her window. It would be a quick goodbye because I knew she shared a room with her brother.

Vinaya and my father were watching TV and as I put on my slippers to go outside, my father asked, "Where the hell are you going?"

"I am just going outside for a second," I mumbled.

Vinaya laughed, he knew exactly whom I was going to meet.

"Going outside? To do what? At this hour of the night!?"

"I am just going out for a second," I said, walking away.

"Sunny stop!! Listen. That girl's parents are going to catch you. They are going to catch you!"

"Oh no. I am just going out for a second. I'll be right back."

No one believed me.

He wagged his finger at me. "They are going to catch you!"

"I'm coming back now," I said, dashing out and closing the door quickly.

I walked around to the back of the building, praying none of the Indians were up that late to see me because surely, they would know something was up.

I knocked on her window and she answered immediately. The Gods must have been smiling on me because her brother wasn't there. He had decided to sleep with his parents that night.

We held hands through the glass louvres and talked about our life, love and aspirations.

I would find a way to visit her in Dubai. We would one day marry but what about her parents? I was not exactly what they had in mind.

"They will accept you."

"How?"

"I will explain to them that you are a good man with a good heart and that you are not like your father.

"But Vinaya cannot live with us."

I nodded in agreement, "Ok."

At one point we laughed too much and our hands pressed down on the louvres, one of them broke and that crash sounded overly loud at that hour of the morning.

I dashed.

Hiding at the side of the building, I came back five minutes later, surprised to see that all was reasonably well.

"My Mother came but I told her that I was closing the window and it broke."

"She believed you?"

"Of course. We cleaned up the mess and she went back to bed."

We talked for hours that night. All the while there was a dog in someone's backyard that kept barking at me. Thankfully, the neighbours seemed uninterested in the noise.

At a little after 5:30 am, the sun slowly began to emerge. I knew it was time to go.

"Understand this. I have waited for a girl like you all my life. You are the woman I have asked God for. I will not forget you."

"Me neither. I love you."

It was impossible to kiss with the burglar proof and the louvres so we just kissed each other's hands. And finally, it was time to go.

I slid into bed, Vinaya, fast asleep in his. Sony's family would leave at 9 for the airport so I set the alarm for 8:50.

I stood at the kitchen window as the Indians gathered in the car park to say goodbye. Everyone gave them hugs and kisses. Sony looked over at me and smiled.

As the car began to pull away, she looked at me and waved, she never stopped, I waved back and we looked at each other until the car disappeared. Normally, we would have been wary about being so obvious in front of the Indians but not on this day.

I went back to bed exhausted and tried not to think about the void in my life and how I would have to cope with it.

CHAPTER 54

Perverted Guyanese and Being Related to Fools

That afternoon, a few hours after Sony's departure, Shoba, knocked on my door. She spoke to me in the corridor and explained that Sony had asked her to say goodbye to me and give me a kiss. She then leaned forward and kissed me on the cheek.

I found it hard to believe that Sony would ever ask her to do such a thing.

A week before leaving, Sony mentioned that Shoba was very impressed with me. She thought I was so well mannered in comparison to Vinaya.

"Perhaps, I chose the wrong boy."

Sony looked at her.

"Now I am a little jealous. Why is she saying such stupid things?"

I found myself wondering if Shoba had decided to flirt with me before Sony's flight had even landed.

The next day Ryan came visiting with two friends. The two men, Alvin and Ivan wanted to see TT. They offered Ryan a free ticket in exchange for taking them around.

These men were from a wealth farming family. They lived outside of Georgetown in a village "over the river."

The screamed and shouted at everything as if a country bookie seeing New York City for the first time. It was a bit embarrassing watching them point and shout in the Mall or harass female workers and shoppers.

As we walked past a sort of kiosk selling jewellery, Alvin said to buxom white girl, "You are sweet like a mango."

I cringed and looked in the opposite direction.

"You are sour like a lemon," she responded.

The boys laughed and kept on walking.

Ryan was his usual civilized self and perhaps this is why I always liked him.

That night we went to a popular bar in Woodbrook, the Loft.

It was the norm for the boys to take turns buying a round for everyone. However, I noticed that Ivan refused to buy one for Rohan, every time. Other than that, they seemed to get on well enough.

As Vinaya and I walked into the washroom together, he grabbed my arm and smiled. "You notice Ivan doesn't buy a round for Rohan?"

I nodded.

He continued grinning like a chimpanzee and explained.

About a month before, liming in a rum shop with a group of friends in their village, Rohan had made a bet with Ivan.

"I bet you can't suck this, pointing to his bulging crotch. I bet you a thousand Guyanese dollars," which was roughly one hundred and sixty US.

Ivan looked at their friends and laughed. "Buddy, you don't know me. Let's go."

He got down on his knees and performed his oral duty with the onlookers laughing and screaming.

Finally, he said, "I'm done. Give me the money."

"I was just joking," said Rohan walking away.

339

Ever since that day, Ivan never trusted Rohan.

I looked at Vinaya in shock, "Man! Fuck off nah!! Who the hell does that!!

"I swear to you, it's true."

"But why?"

Vinaya just continued grinning from ear to ear.

After that night I never saw Rohan or Ivan again and I was glad.

The very next day was school, Form V. This was a big deal. We were practically at the end of our high school years. I knew that no matter what happened in the CXC Exams, I would not have sufficient grades to go to Form VI. There were too many boys doing more subjects than me and they would have the priority.

My mother had already said I would go to Canada and use the Grade Thirteen system as a short cut to University. I could not believe that I would actually go abroad. Although my father had agreed, I knew he always made grand plans that never materialized. As a child he had told me that I would one day go to Boarding School in England after Form III.

I realized however, that if my mother was involved there would certainly be a possibility.

I had no interest in school and started Form V in the hope of finishing it as soon as possible.

I walked in on the first day and saw Mother Frog as my homeroom teacher. I remembered how because of her I could not do English Literature. I will deal with you, I said to myself.

During the first week, I would just try to find a place to sit by myself on breaks and think of Sony and remind myself that no matter how bleak my existence was, there was a beautiful girl out there that loved me.

That following weekend Vinaya's family passed by to invite us to Maracas with them. My father declined but Vinaya and I went with them. It was a great day. Of course Vinaya opened his big mouth and told everyone about Sony.

"Oh. He must be so sad," said Vidia. "I am so sorry."

I just swam and enjoyed my favourite beach.

Vinaya went home with his family that weekend.

The next day I was introduced to the family that had taken Sony's apartment. They had been in New York and now with their youngest son who was my age, they would be in TT for the next two years.

He was a light skinned fellow with light brown, curly, hair, his name was Suresh.

The next weekend Vinaya passed by with his family. "I will be staying with them so I came to get the rest of my things."

I was chatting outside so I threw him the keys for the apartment.

About five minutes later, he and Rob Roy exited and the keys were returned.

A few days later Mummy and Leila came to visit. I didn't care for my mother's visits. She had moved heaven and earth to get rid of me when I lived with her. She had brought some uglito into the house and had no problems asking me to leave. Now that I lived with my father she wanted to play the part of a caring, concerned mother.

"You know," she said looking at Leila and me, "I would like to take some photos of us as a family. Next time I will bring my camera."

"But I have a camera right here," said Daddy. I bought a great one in New York."

"Sunny, go get it."

My father kept it in a special camera bag, hidden under some T-shirts in his closet.

I went to get it only to discover the bag empty.

I checked and rechecked the closet.

"Daddy, it's not there."

"It has to be there."

"Well I checked and it's not. I never touched it. Did you?"

He came and we looked together. Mummy and Leila followed.

The camera was gone. No one had broken into our home. No guest could have entered his bedroom without us knowing.

However, there was one person who knew where it was hidden and who had been in the house in our absence.

We looked at each other. Our eyes mutually communicating that the camera had been stolen and by whom.

I could only shake my head.

Vinaya had lived with us for almost a year, paying no room and board. Yet, his final act of departure was to steal from us. This was the gratitude we received for basically taking care of a man too lazy to look for work.

His father had a reputation as thief and apparently, Vinaya was no different.

He would steal from other family members in the future. Sadly, this was part of the burden of being related to fools.

CHAPTER 55

Life After Sony

I got through the first term of Form V as best I could.

It was not easy putting up with my father's temper tantrums. He seemed to think that the louder he was the better life would be. I did my best not to have much to do with him which was quite difficult in a two-bedroom apartment.

If I wasn't watching TV, I would simply stay in my room reading my boxing magazines or whatever I could find.

It was my job to clean the apartment. However, in typical Vijay Sarwan style, this cheap fucker would not buy a vacuum cleaner. He had the audacity to give me a cocoyea broom. Cocoyea was a long slim piece of wood found in coconut branches. It was common in Trinidad to tie many of them together and use them as a broom.

It could also be used as a pretty good tool for beating a child as many of us found out during our youth.

I would clean, only for him to be screaming later because there was dust in the carpet. It took me a while to understand that if I swept too hard, the dust raised and then gently resettled. I had to develop a gentle sweeping style. I marvelled at how this man could find money to gamble on horses every weekend but could not invest in a vacuum cleaner.

On one of my mother's visits, I mentioned that I would be seventeen in only a matter of weeks and that I should go for my Driver's License.

Never in my life had I seen my parents agree on any topic so quickly.

"License!! License!!," they both shouted in unison, jumping off their chairs, a look of panic on their faces.

"No! No! Wait until you write your exams next year and then you can go for it."

I thought that was fine. After all, I had no car, what difference would another eight odd months make.

Shoba would come over sometimes to speak to me, on other occasions, she would knock on the door and invite me to chat outside.

Sony and I had told no one about our plans to continue our relationship. Shoba could not understand why I still had her on my mind.

"You should move on. Really! You will never see her again. You guys are finished."

I thought her just a bit too eager for me to forget about Sony.

However, in early October with no letter from Dubai, Shoba was nice enough to offer to send one for me via the Diplomatic Pouch.

One Saturday, while oversleeping as I often did, I woke up with a start to find her sitting on my bed, gently shaking me.

"Get up Sunny. Get up."

"Ey. How did you get in here?"

"Your father let me in. He said I could go wake you up."

I wondered who told this stupid man I wanted her waking me up.

"So, what is really going on there?" my father enquired one day.

"Nothing."

"Is she making a move on you?"

"I don't know."

"Well don't you want to do something?"

344

"No."

"Why not?"

"Because I said so. Don't ask me stupid questions."

"You must be a horn child,"[16] he muttered, shaking his head.

A few days later, he picked me up from school. As we made the five-minute journey home, with just a hint of an amused smile on his face, he said, "You received a letter from the United Arab Emirates today."

The letter had arrived less than a month after I mailed mine. I tried to be calm.

"Really?" Where is it?"

"On the dining room table."

As we entered the house, I picked it up, admiring the colourful stamps from Dubai. I went to my room and opened it.

The letter started off nicely enough with her telling me how different Dubai was and that she now had to cover herself up when she left the house.

Then around the fourth paragraph, things took a turn.

Sunny, I have something to say to you and I am afraid it will break your heart.

Two weeks after we arrived, my mother found one of your letters when she was cleaning. Sunny, it was terrible. They shouted at me and I couldn't leave the house for two days. I cried so much.

They said I can never see you or write to you again.

I am very sorry. Please forget me. I know you are a good man but there is nothing I can do.

I took about half a minute to get over the shock and compose myself. For the rest of that afternoon I just allowed my mind to absorb what I had read.

She had given me a friend's address in Dubai to which I could write and the next day I sent off a letter.

---

[16] *Horn child*: a woman giving birth to a child as a result of cheating on her partner.

I made it clear to her that she was the love of my life and I would not give up.

I love you. Please do not give up on us. I will try to find the money and maybe I can visit Dubai in a year or two as I will be in Canada. Maybe it can be birthday gift from my parents.

In the meantime, Shoba continued her visits. She gave me a letter for Vinaya which I duly passed on to my father as I was no longer visiting the family. She made it clear that she had broken off things with him.

She came over one Saturday and sat next to me on my bed. After a while we seemed to run out of things to speak about.

I glanced at her and then aimlessly around the room, eventually my eyes settling on the floor. "Looks like we have nothing to talk about."

"Why talk she said, kissing me and lowering my head onto the bed.

I thought about Sony and how much she meant to me. But then again I thought about that letter.

I allowed the moment to happen.

After a few minutes of kissing, Shoba stood up and very quickly dropped all of her clothes on to the floor. And then lay completely naked on the bed.

She looked at me waiting for my next move.

I had never met a girl so willing to undress herself. I took my time but eventually my clothes were on the floor.

It was not bad but it was not great. I thought of Sony the whole time. I kept thinking what a bad person I was.

She was still unaware of our communication so she was confused as to why I would still think of Sony.

She came over twice more that week and I allowed myself to enhance my sexual experience.

Just before my seventeenth birthday, I received what would be my final letter from Sony. Praising me for not being angry with her. Complimenting me on my good heart but sticking to her decision to end our relationship.

I once again sent her a letter pledging my love for her.

... I don't know how many people are lucky enough to actually fall in love and be loved in return but I don't want to lose this. ...

I would wait for her next letter but she never did respond.

My father had gotten a telephone at the end of the summer and now I was having conversations with Tammy.

I had developed a relationship with Suresh who now slept in Sony's room. He seemed to be a poor man's Vinaya. Always talking about women and perpetually horny.

He, I and Rajesh would spend a lot of time chatting in front of the building.

Shoba hated him. He had tried to flirt with her and hold her hand so if he came around her she would just go inside.

Tammy invited me to a Divali celebration her school was having. I was happy to go to an event at an all-girls' school.

Suresh was more excited than me. "Man! Man! Does she have a friend? Introduce me to her friend man. Don't you know any other girls?"

I promised to ask on his behalf.

Tammy did have a friend, Cindy.

My father drove us to the event and I waited outside the front gate to meet Tammy as we had planned. I had explained that inside would be too crowded to locate each other.

After half an hour, I was starting to get antsy. I did not like to wait on people. More than five minutes doing so, eventually drove me up a wall.

"Let's just go inside," urged Suresh.

"Listen, if I go inside and she comes here then she will wait for me not realizing I am inside."

After another ten minutes, I realized it didn't make sense to keep standing out there and we entered.

To my shock as we walked through the crowd admiring the girls in their Indian dresses and the bright lights of the diyas, there was Tammy standing next to Zeenat.

Tammy walked up to me as if nothing was the matter, "Hi,"

"What happened? I was waiting outside for forty minutes."

She explained that Zeenat did not want to stand there alone so she asked her to stay with her.

"But didn't you know that I was outside waiting on you?"

"Yes but Zeenat said eventually you would come in and look for me."

"But after half an hour didn't you think I was out there waiting for you?"

"Yes but I knew eventually you would come in."

I explained why I had hesitated to come in order not to confuse her when she eventually arrived.

"Yes but Zeenat did not want to be alone and I knew you would come in after a while."

I found myself wondering what the hell was wrong with her. This was Zeenat's school. Couldn't she stand alone for five minutes? I needed to respect a woman's intellect and already at the beginning of the night I found myself not impressed with Tammy.

However, rather than ruin the night, I decided to salvage what I could.

Suresh was introduced to Cindy. She was a tall, leggy girl, with long brown hair down to her butt. Certainly not displeasing to the eyes. After a while, I made it clear to him that Tammy and I would be taking a walk.

I was not quite aware of what an ass Suresh was but given time I would grasp it, that night I got more of a clue.

Ten minutes later, we saw him and Cindy. The two girls pulled apart to have a little chat and Suresh turned to me.

"Man! Nothing is happening. She doesn't want to kiss me!"

"Ok?"

What am I supposed to do? I have to spend all night with her.

"Well, you just met her. Not all girls kiss right away."

He continued to complain.

"Look!," I said firmly. "You wanted to meet a girl and she is nice, pretty, girl. Not everybody is a slut here for your convenience. I haven't kissed Tammy yet. Do you hear me complaining?"

We walked off leaving them to continue their night.

Tammy was laughing, "Do you know he tried to kiss her?"

"Really?" I said, feigning ignorance.

"Yes," but she pulled away and told him, 'No hanky panky on the first date. I don't do that.'"

We stood up under a tree chatting away. I could tell from the look in her eyes she was definitely attracted to me.

Finally, perhaps unimpressed with the pace at which I was moving, she asked "Sunny, do you like me?"

"Of course."

"As a friend or more than a friend."

I realized where this was going. I paused for a moment and then answered, "More than a friend."

"Then you can kiss me if you want to."

We spent the next half hour kissing.

We then went to a bench and sat. Opposite us sat a classmate of hers. A pretty, Indian girl with short hair who was obviously involved with a young black man. That was quite a sight in a school full of Indian girls, many of whom were Hindu.

I tried to explain to Tammy what to expect from me if we had a relationship.

"I just want a nice intelligent girl, I can communicate with. I talked for about two minutes. Her only response being, "Ok, alright. Yes. Sure."

We finished the night and promised to try to see each other soon.

Suresh complained all night that he had gotten nowhere with Cindy and that he had spent the last hour alone because she told him she was going to be with her other friends.

I was quite unconcerned. It was not my duty to supply him with women.

Tammy and I would speak every night that week. However, it was on the following Saturday that I got a better picture of her personality.

In the midst of our conversation, she queried, "So where do you see this going? What kind of relationship do you want?"

"Really? You don't know. Don't you remember what I said at the Divali celebrations."

"No."

"Remember, we were on the bench and I was telling you what kind of girl I was interested in."

"Oh *that*! No. I wasn't listening to you."

"What?"

"You were talking but I wasn't listening to a word you were saying. I was maccoing[17] my friend and the black guy. I just told you 'Yes. Uhhuh, ok,' but really I was paying attention to the two of them."

I said nothing but I thought to myself well this is someone I won't be taking seriously.

I never bothered to call Tammy after that. She phoned for another month, complaining that I never called anymore. I simply explained that I was busy with schoolwork. It took about a month but eventually, she stopped calling.

---

[17] Maco: verb/noun, a person who is nosy, excessively curious about the affairs of others.

CHAPTER 56

The Hypocrisy of "Nigger Neal"

Your seventeenth birthday is usually a big deal in Trinidad. You are old enough to get your Driver's License and although not legally an adult, you're practically there.

Mine was one of my more uneventful birthdays. I got up that morning and got ready for school. As I entered the dining room area, my father shook my hand, "Happy Birthday. Here," and handed me a hundred-dollar bill.

No card, no gift. But I was ok with that. A few of the boys at school wished me well. On the way back home, I decided to treat myself. On some occasions I had to walk home, approximately a mile and a half, I would often break it up by stopping at the Long Circular Mall which was the half-way point. I went to the video arcade and spent an hour. Then it was on to the Food Court and bought myself a maxi hamburger with chips and a coke. Then back to the arcade. At that age it was as fun as a day got for me.

I got home at five and as I entered the car park my mother and Leila arrived. I groaned. Now I would have to put up with them. My mother would often ask why I seemed so angry and negative as if amnesic about her past behaviour.

They had brought me two gifts and a huge chocolate cake. I just looked at them and had very little to say. When I got tired of my mother's babbling, I turned on the TV. I pulled the chair about two feet in front of it making it very clear that I had no interest in speaking to them. After a further ten minutes they finally left.

I never saw my father that evening, which probably meant he was out drinking somewhere. It was typical of him, that alcohol should take priority over his son's birthday. Whereas this may have been disappointing by another person's standards, I was actually relieved. It was preferable to spend it that way than with people whose company I didn't care for.

Living with my father meant I was introduced to some additional characters from his life. One of them was Neal Ramjohn, a middle-aged accountant whose business was just a few hundred metres away from our apartment.

There was actually a hotel with a bar in our neighbourhood so Neal and his friends would invite my father to go drink with them. On some occasions I would arrive from school to see them drinking in the living room. I would try to stay in my room away from the drinkers.

One day as I was getting a drink in the kitchen, I heard Neal complaining. "Imagine my son tell me he have a girlfriend and he bring home a coon."

They all looked at him enquiringly.

"A nigger. Well actually red skin but she still have black in she!"

There were only Indians in the room and one of them said "But boss, ent your wife has black in her?"

"My wife family name is Chen. That is Chinee".

"But your wife *does* have black in her, doesn't she?"

"Her family name is Chen," he responded with a bright smile, obviously aware but unashamed of his hypocrisy.

I went to my room and even with the door closed it was not difficult to hear their conversation.

A half hour later Neal left and his two friends freely vented their opinion on his previous comments.

"Is he some kind of an ass? His wife is blacker than me. He watching dem big, thick lips and saying she is Chinese??"

My father never commented, not wanting to speak ill of his friend.

For the next few months if they were chatting at our home, I would hear Neal make the occasional comment, "You notice nigger does only eat with a big spoon never a knife and fork. How the hell a woman could watch a black man with dem pubic hairs on he head and find him attractive?"

I would shake my head. I had heard my father or his friends make derogatory remarks about black people before but this was unreal.

My father as usual would not comment, maybe slightly smile at the silliness of the statement considering the source.

His friends were less polite, they facetiously referred to him as "Nigger Neal," behind his back.

I wondered if he made these comments in front of his wife.

One day my father offered the group some lunch, stewed beef in black bean sauce with sweet peppers and rice.

He put a knife and fork next to each plate.

"No, I want a spoon," said Neal.

I could only shake my head some more.

CHAPTER 57

An Uneventful Christmas, Uncle Duggie and the Best Village Olympics

Christmas Day in TT is a time for being together with family, friends, neighbours and eating lots of food.

However, for my father, Christmas Day of 1984 meant to just eat and lie on the couch watching TV.

The previous Christmas we had visited a few friends and Vinaya's family as well.

I wondered how he could have me just sitting there with nothing to do. I was not aware of anybody in the country being so lazy and anti-social on this day of all days.

We ate a lunch of stewed pork with red beans and rice. We then looked at the one TV channel in the country.

I was watching the story of Scrooge as I had done on many Christmases before when he turned to me, "You'll go and wash the car, right?"

"On Christmas Day!!" I exclaimed.

"Well you know I will want to go out tomorrow. So, I need it clean."

"But it is Christmas Day. Who washes a car on Christmas Day?"

"Well I have to go out tomorrow so you need to do it today."

Being bored wasn't enough, now while everyone was enjoying time with their family, they could look out of their window and see the one ass washing a car on Christmas Day.

He never went anywhere the next day. For some reason, I was actually surprised.

Despite not going anywhere on Boxing Day, we did receive some visitors. We heard someone screaming on the street "Darsan!! Darsan!!"

My father and I jumped and looked at each other in shock.

"Who the hell is that?"

"Who do you think it is? Obviously one of your damn country bookie friends!!"

He ran to the window and saw his friend from Sangre Grande, Duggie and two other Indian men.

"We're in Apartment 2A. And why are you shouting like that?"

"Well you know I from the country. I eh know any better!"

The entire building had to know some country bookie ass was visiting us.

Despite his sometimes lack of finesse, Duggie adored my father. They had been students in high school. Daddy would always laugh and sometimes recount Duggie's deviance in class.

Mr. Mohamed was their Mathematics teacher. He had a habit of putting the better students at the front of the class and the less inclined at the back. If Duggie was too talkative, he would say to him, "Sit in the back of the class."

Duggie would rise, look at Mr. Mohamed very seriously and shake his finger at him, "The sins of the father shall be visited upon the sons."

Mr. Mohamed would give him a bemused look. My father would laugh at Duggie during the lunch break. "You are talking in class so he sent you to the back. Why did you say that to him?"

"The sins of the father shall be visited upon the sons," he said watching my father with great intensity.

Duggie came from a poor family and would come to school barefoot. This bothered my father so after a few weeks he approached his mother one day and said "My friend is too poor. He has no shoes. He always comes to school barefoot, I want to buy some shoes for him."

His mother fished five dollars out of her purse. "Here. Go buy some shoes for him."

The next day my father handed Duggie the five dollars. "Here. Go and buy some shoes. When I see you tomorrow, I want to see you with shoes on your feet."

Duggie was shocked. He looked at my father in disbelief. "Ok boss," was all he could say with a grateful smile.

The next day he approached my father with a broad smile, "Look," he said pointing downward.

My father looked and his eyes widened. Duggie was wearing two right sided shoes.

"What the hell is this!!"

"What happen?"

"You wearing two right shoes boy!!"

Duggie looked down at the shoes silently as if trying to process the information which he had just received. He then looked up at my father queryingly.

"Oh God Duggie!! They sell you two right sided shoes!! You couldn't see that!!??"

No Duggie couldn't. He had never owned shoes before. He was just so proud of his brand new, shining shoes.

"Duggie, after school we going to the store that sell you this!" bellowed my father.

They walked into the store together and Duggie pointed out the salesman whom he had dealt with.

"Did you sell him these shoes yesterday?" asked my father.

A slim, young Indian man with glasses and a moustache looked at my father as if a fly had just landed on his shirt. "Yes and what about it?"

"You sold him two right sided shoes. Sell him the proper shoes."

The salesman and the Manager looked at this precocious youth telling them what to do unaware that he was the local MP's son.

"I don't know what you are talking about," said the salesman calmly. "I sold him a normal pair of shoes."

"You sold him the wrong pair. Now get it right. We are not leaving here until you sell him a proper pair of shoes."

"Boy!! Catch yuhself!!" shouted the Manager. "He was sold a proper pair of shoes. Now leave!"

An old man who had been trying on some black, leather shoes and was observing the drama, looked at Duggie, "Did that man sell you those shoes?"

Duggie nodded in the affirmative.

He looked at the Indian, "Sell him a proper pair of shoes. Or I will go to the Police Station and make a statement about you and I will take him with me."

The Manager and salesman were shocked. They had not expected this.

"Alright," muttered the Manager, "Let's see what we can do." He took the shoes and came out with a proper pair. "Here see if this is alright."

Duggie tried them on, walked around and then looked at my father with a bright smile. "It's ok." And with that they left the store.

He now worked as a clerk in the Postal Office. Although he hardly ever saw my father much, he had never forgotten his kindness. When leaving that day, he gave me a firm hug. "Remember, I am your Uncle Duggie. If ever you need anything, let me know."

The Best Village Olympics

Indian culture was strong and alive in TT. The indentured labourers had brought it with them and it was prevalent in all areas of the country. There was a weekly television program on Saturdays called Mastana Bahar where Indians from all parts of the country would showcase their talent.

There would be elimination rounds with the top three going to the next round and eventually a grand final with amazing prizes; the first prize, usually a brand-new car.

For the Africans, there was Best Village. This was a weekly program where African culture was showcased.

However, it went one step further, the Best Village Olympics was shoved down the country's throat in January of every year.

The different villages/communities got together and displayed their talents. This was seven hours a night, finally finishing at 3:00 am. This would go on for seven consecutive days.

We only had one TV channel in the country – state owned. You learned to go read a book, chat with the neighbours or watch a few minutes of limbo dancing, African songs or whatever else was on. I say a few minutes because no one was really interested in seven hours of this. Even on the weekends, the government was insane enough to foist this on the public all night.

There would be complaints by the students in my class but we had gotten used to this, year after year.

My father was less accepting.

"Jesus Christ!! You think any Indian could do this seven days a week!"

One night in a rage, he called the local station, "Get those fucking people off my TV!!"

"What people?" asked the employee.

"Those fucking black people. Oh fuck man!! Is every fucking night. Get them off my fucking TV!!"

"Why don't you turn off your fucking TV!!"

My father paused for a moment in shock. "Fuck you!!!"

"Fuck you too!!!"

And they both slammed down the phone.

CHAPTER 58

Galindez, Sandy and Juvenile Slackness

I started off 1985 with anticipation and excitement for a variety of reasons.

This would be my final six months of high school. I hated school. I always had. It had been tolerable in Morgan's. But in general, I *hated* it.

I was now seeing the light at the end of the tunnel. The only reason I had been able to somehow handle living with my father was that I had promised myself that 1985 would be the end of my sentence. As much as I had detested living with him, running away prior to my graduation would have just been a huge detrimental blow to my future.

I had suffered in silence and my reward was nigh. It now seemed obvious that I would be going to Canada. My mother had taken me to meet a woman who linked students with schools in Toronto. The school chosen was Prudem College in Guelph, Ontario. It was a small town but within driving distance from Toronto.

Aunty Ana, mum's friend from high school lived in nearby Hamilton with her husband and two sons. I had actually met them when they returned to live in TT in 1979. She adored my mother and they were practically sisters. However, life in TT was not the rose garden they had hoped and they returned to Canada around the time my mother met Marlon.

Visiting the following year, my mother raved to her about Marlon. "He is a very intelligent man and so handsome like your husband Lenwin."

Lenwin was indeed a handsome fellow reminding many people of the singer, Marvin Gaye. Well into his mid-forties, it was not uncommon for his female students thirty years younger, to flirt with him.

After meeting Marlon, I asked Aunty Ana, "So do you think he looks like Uncle Lenwin?"

"No."

"Do you think he is handsome?"

"Why do you ask me that?"

"Because Mummy said he is handsome like Uncle Elwin."

She laughed and laughed, "He is a very nice man. A very nice, smart, man."

Aunty Ana when informed about my impending arrival made it clear that I was welcome at their home anytime. It was some degree of relief to know that I would already have friends there.

With the CXC Exams and Canada ahead of me, I decided to try to stay out of trouble and finish Holy Father's as quietly as possible. By my standards, the previous two years had been serene. However, it was obvious that I would never be destined to be one of those students that had an uneventful school life.

Teddy Galindez and Carson Sandy sat behind me in English. Both were amongst the top 400 metres runners in the country. Galindez and I had always remained on friendly terms after our boxing match in Form I. Sandy, was my height, but had strong, broad, shoulders and a thickset physique like a heavyweight boxer. His skin was as black as oil and he had a thick afro. He was also an aspiring batsman and had once hit 5 fours in an over of a cricket match, quite a feat in the Schools' League.

One day just before lunch they approached me with a sly smile. Galindez turned to Sandy, "Let's invite him.'

Sandy's face was all teeth and I knew whatever it was, it was not going to be boring.

However, I could not have in my wildest imagination, guessed what was coming.

Woodbrook was an old neighbourhood that was easily within walking distance of our school. It was an old middle-class area where some families had been living for as much as three generations.

During my high school years it was also known to house one or two houses of ill repute.

Galindez and Sandy explained that they had gone exploring about a month ago and visited a place called the Haven at around lunch time. "If you go to the back, there is a space between the air conditioning unit and the wall. It's less than a quarter of an inch but it's about six inches long," he laughed … "and sometimes you can see some action going on," now he was practically panting.

I looked at them as if they were insane. "But what if you get caught?"

"Well we go run," was the immediate response from Sandy.

"Steuups, you all know how to run. I eh not athlete."

They explained that once a week about four of them would go and nothing had happened so far.

"Dem people in they own world. They have no idea we are there. Just keep your ass quiet. And we know you cool. So, come nah."

I found myself intrigued.

The Haven's gate was wide open. The front door was firmly shut as they were not open during the day. My two guides quickly scanned the building and then we walked to the right side of it. At the very last room, there was an AC unit making its customary noise. The boys slowed down and gave me a serious look, putting their index finger to their lips.

You would have sworn that Galindez was some kind of secret agent, the way he eased up to the unit as if peeping around a corner for a perpetrator. He looked to the side of it, then turned, smiled and winked at us.

Sandy immediately stepped forward and stuck his head under Galindez's. I, curious and wondering where the hell my head was going to go, stuck mine under Sandy's.

I looked through the small crevice between the unit and the wall and saw a huge, black man on top of an Indian woman. Their bodies meshed together, the bed heaving and creaking and she making noises as if she were being killed, "Aaagghhh … Aaagghh … Oh guuuuud … Aaagghh!!"

I wondered for a moment if she was actually enjoying herself or if she was in some kind of pain. The fellow was huge with massive arms. I could only see the bottom half of their faces to just above their waist.

The pounding last about a minute and a half. He bellowed like some kind of beast then rolled off of her, both of them covered in sweat.

He went to the shower and a minute later, she joined. "Eh eh, you come to bathe," we heard him say as if surprised.

I could hear both Galindez and Sammy breathing hard and truthfully my heart seemed to be pounding in my neck.

They returned to the bedroom. He sat on the bed and you could literally see it sink a bit and creak in protest. She dropped to her knees in front of him and bowed her head in his lap. We were all breathing hard now – in unison.

The man's head tilted to the left, his eyes glazed over as if drugged. Very, very slowly, his head began tilting to the right. It seemed to stop, his eyes pointed to the minor crack near the AC. And then very slowly, his eyes began to focus. He looked at us and we stared right back.

"Ey," he muttered, his face going from heavenly ecstasy to complete shock.

"WHAT THE FUCK IS THAT!!!" he bellowed rising up but unable to do it fully due to the woman's impeding head.

As one, we swivelled and ran. As we hit the gate, we heard shouting behind us. Two huge men were running after us. Galindez and Sandy pulled ahead, a good fifteen feet ahead of me. I was a decent runner but these two guys were the very best in POS. I brought up the rear doing my utmost to keep up. I would occasionally turn my head and thank God, the men may have been huge but not as fast as me.

"Come back you fuckers. We will kill you!!!"

We chose not to heed their invitation and as we hit the top of the street a hundred metres later, they gave up. We never broke stride and jetted into Holy Father's covered in sweat.

There was no running allowed in the school compound so we half walked, half ran to the other end of the facility, peeping around the corner of the canteen.

Our clothes were drenched as if we had been in the rain. After a full minute and realizing that no one was still after, us the adrenaline began to subside. We looked at each other and giggled hysterically.

I shook my head, "Allyuh men mad yes."

We laughed at what we had seen and our narrow escape.

I didn't know it at the time but an even crazier scenario was just around the corner.

A week later they approached me at lunch time, again with those broad smiles on their faces.

"Darsan, we going on an adventure after school."

"Not me and that shit!!" I shouted. "You want me to get kill. Last time we get away by the skin of we teeth!!"

"Ssshhh!" They hushed me and looked around to see if anyone was listening.

"This is different," said Sandy. He looked and smiled at Galindez, "Tell him."

Galindez explained that his father's office in Port of Spain was on the fifth floor. The building next door only had three floors. There was a fire escape to the roof. Galindez bored one day at his dad's office climbed up the 25 odd feet to investigate what the roof was like. He was walking along it and noticed a hole. Looking in he saw a beautiful, big breasted woman sleeping naked on a bed. She had thick, long, black hair, cascading over her shoulders and arms. He ogled her beautiful, thick, brown lips and a tanned brown physique. "Boy if you see that flat stomach, dem big breasts and nipples and those thick thighs. She is like an Olympic athlete."

Way at the back of my head there was a voice that said, No.

However, the mental picture was too much. And it wasn't like we would have bouncers to worry about.

I smiled resignedly. "Ok, let's go."

School finished at 2:15 pm. We were at the office before 2:35. Mr. Galindez was at court. We were taken to the empty office and saw the roof from two floors up. The hole was only partially visible.

"Boy I really hope she taking a nap today," said Galindez.

"But something doesn't make sense," I said looking at them, processing the situation. "How can she have a hole above the bed. What does she do when it rains?"

"Oh God man Darsan!!" shouted Galindez. "You is a lawyer? Why you have to analyse so?"

"Look! She does move the bed when it rains. Alright?" said Sammy, holding my arm and guiding me out of the office and towards our mission.

I had a problem with heights even something as simple as standing on a table. However, on this day I manned up and followed my friends up the ladder.

We gently walked across the roof to our objective. As we got closer to the hole, we could hear some kind of gasping. I thought maybe someone was doing aerobics.

It wasn't aerobics but it could be categorized as some form of exercise.

A beautiful black woman with copper toned skin, high cheekbones and long, thick, luxurious, black hair, was gasping away, her eyes closed and mouth wide open. Her magnificently, toned legs, high in the air.

On top of her was a white man. He was pumping away, beads of sweat covering his back. I was sure if the woman looked up, she would have seen us but if she did, her eyes seemed only half open at best and in some sort of hypnotic state.

Within about ten seconds, Sandy, who was standing between Galindez and myself, whipped out his member. I glanced in shock, at this big, thick, black beast between his legs.

I refocused my gaze on the couple below. But you could not help but see what was in your peripheral vision.

As the white man pumped, Sandy pumped. The white man pumped faster, Sandy pumped faster. Then the white man started ramming like a jack hammer. Sandy kept pace. Finally, the white man let off a loud groan as if dying… "AAAGGGHHH" Sandy, simultaneously, let off a scream like some kind of mad Tarzan, "HHAAARRRGGGHHH!!!" And jetted a huge glob of sperm up into the air and down the hole, splashing on the white man's back.

He and the woman looked up at the ceiling in horror. For one second their eyes locked with ours.

In a flash, we turned as one, we literally glided towards the ladder, Sandy, managing to insert his member back into his pants as he ran. Galindez met the ladder first, grabbing the side with both hands and swinging himself onto the rungs. I was second practically sliding down the ladder. I thought to myself, I am going so fast if I hit Galindez's head, tough luck. Just as Galindez hit the ground, I leaped to his right so as not to block his path of exit on the left. Sandy seeing the space between the two of us just dropped like a rock. I rounded him like a footballer going past a defender. We hit the main road and veered left and then left again into the Mr. Galindez's building. We didn't bother with an elevator, we leaped up the stairs and dashed into the office. Not wanting to be seen through the window, we sat on the floor, panting, our school uniforms wet with sweat.

After a few minutes, my breathing gradually returned to normal, streams of perspiration running down my body.

After about half an hour, Sandy and I left Galindez. We scanned the street carefully before stepping out. We made our down to Independence Square, gave each other a bounce of the fists and a smile and walked off to get our respective taxis.

The next day they walked by my class before the start of school. They looked at me and smiled broadly.

"Stay to hell away from me. And never ever invite me to that kind of shit again. I will make a jail or worse yet get a beating."

They laughed and walked away.

Many years later upon my visits to TT, I would see them in clubs or on the street and they were still giggling. A decade and more later, I too allowed myself the luxury of a laugh at our juvenile slackness.

CHAPTER 59

"The Husband and the Outside Woman Always Treat the Wife the Best"

Uncle Steve came for his usual Carnival visit. He was a popular man so it was normal for the house to have a variety of guests during the week or for my father to shuttle him around to meet different people.

On the second day after his arrival, I came home from school and walked into my room to see an Arsenal Umbro T-shirt laid out on my bed. Arsenal was my team in England and Umbro was a much sought-after product by footballers and fans in Trinidad. This was certainly not being sold in TT.

I came out and looked at Uncle Steve and my father.

"Did you see your surprise?" asked Uncle Steve.

"Yes," I responded still in delighted shock.

"Boy," said Uncle Steve, I had to stop at the store on my way to the airport, it was pressure. But I knew you are an Arsenal fan."

I smiled and shook his hand, "Thank you Uncle Steve."

I was flattered that he had remembered me.

After his usual two weeks, Uncle Steve was gone and our life was more serene.

My father had stopped visiting Aunty Vashti's family. He had simply had enough of Rob Roy. He would make the occasional call for his money but the multiple visits had now been reduced to zero.

I looked at him one day, "I don't understand. You are a lawyer. Why don't you simply take him to court?"

"You have to understand this is family."

"First of all, he is not family. So, people could get away with your money because they are family?"

"Well its Basdeo's children living in the house. He is married to my brother's daughter."

"Well he is family and he has your money. Maybe you should stop lending to family because you don't seem to know what to do when they don't pay."

Neelam was even more direct. "You supposed to this bigtime lawyer. You win all kinda case. And he come from Guyana to take your money just so? How come I get my money? Your problem is you want to treat dog like cat. You treat a dog like what it is, a dog!"

My father did not bother to respond, possibly because regardless of the response, he was still waiting for his money.

Vidia passed by in early March with Zeenat and a visiting cousin from London, a pretty, slim, fair skinned girl, with medium length, curly hair.

There was no Rob Roy probably because he would have had to discuss his debt.

We chatted pleasantly. When we asked how Aunty Vashti was doing, Vidia and Zeenat rolled their eyes. She was still seeing Uncle Shirvan. They were not impressed.

"Can you believe he brought is wife over to visit for the Christmas season. And he and Mummy were so nice to her," said Vidia.

"Yes!!" added Zeenat. "You wouldn't believe it. They were serving her tea and cake and talking to her nice-nice."

Daddy smiled, "Well you know how it is. The husband and the outside woman always treat the wife the best."

"But they were so nice to her. Speaking so sweetly and politely," said Zeenat.

"Well you know how it is. The husband and the outside woman does always treat the wife the best," he repeated shamelessly.

I don't think he understood how crude it was to refer to their mother as an "outside woman," in front of her daughters.

Rob Roy may have failed to visit but we would still have to put up with more of his antics.

CHAPTER 60

Confronting Nieves and Mother Frog

Throughout my years at Holy Father's I had been known as a class clown. And if there was a certain teacher I had a problem with I could be witty and facetious.

I had promised myself upon entering Form V that there would be no shenanigans, my goal was to pass my CXC Exams and move on to the next chapter of my life.

However, there were two individuals that made me deviate from my oath.

The first was Mr. Nieves. He had been my homeroom and Geography teacher in Form III. An outspoken individual who had no problem dressing down students, we had had our verbal barbs.

He was a fit, balding, black man in his early forties and for many years the fastest teacher in the school, easily beating colleagues ten years younger than him in the Teachers' Race on Sports Day.

Behind his back many of the boys called him, "Totie Head," due to his bald spot. If his eyebrows ever raised in shock or surprise, we called it an erection.

I had started the year determined to be a well-behaved fellow in his class. However, three weeks in, I was leaning forward to ask the boys in front of me a question. Nieves saw me and queried, "Yes Darsan. What is it?"

"Nothing Sir," I said, quickly reversing back into my bench.

I thought he would go on with his class but instead he looked at the class, "Darsan does not was his ass when he bathe so he have to sit halfway off the bench."

The class broke out in raucous laughter.

I just looked at him. Had he forgotten who I was? Did he not know that I was capable of giving as good as I got? I said nothing but in my mind I was thinking I will deal with you.

The very next day we had a chance to see classic Nieves in action at the expense of Robert Govia.

Govia's father was a well-known insurance broker. He managed one of the biggest firms in the country which advertised in the newspaper and on TV. His name was always listed on the TV ad.

Govia answered a question. Nieves confirmed that it was correct. Just as he began to sit down, Nieves confirmed, "Your name is Govia.?"

"Yes Sir."

"Your father is the man who does be on TV begging for business."

While the other 39 students laughed loudly, Govia, looked away with an irritated expression.

With more than just a tinge of aggravation, he responded "It's not begging Sir. It's called advertising."

We all continued laughing.

Nieves got up and walked around to the front of the desk, "It seems to be if a man had to go on TV and ask people for business, he begging. But you want to call it advertising, Ok," he said with a shrug of the shoulders.

The class laughed some more and a bemused Govia sat down.

After my mini humiliation, I initiated some classic Sunil Darsan behaviour. I would answer his questions slowly as if not sure what he was talking about.

"Can anyone tell me what kind of soil is prevalent in Canada?"

"Darsan?"

"Sir?"

"What's the answer?"

I would slowly look up at the ceiling as if deep in thought. "Are we talking all of Canada Sir?"

The class would laugh, well aware of what I was doing.

"Don't be an ass boy!"

"Ass boy?" Is that some kind of baby ass Sir?"

Again, the class laughed.

"Bring your book. "

I knew what this meant. He would point out to a few pages and you would have to copy it onto a piece of paper as a penance.

On another occasion, he was the teacher during study hall. This was a free period which was used to study or do homework in the Assembly Hall.

At the beginning of the period, I put my head behind a History textbook and was speaking to a student.

Nieves spotted me. "Sarwan, if I see your head behind that book again, you will have a problem."

I picked up a smaller textbook also for History, "Is it alright if I put my head behind this book Sir?" I could not stop myself from smiling.

His eyebrows went into erection mode, "What?"

I repeated myself, all the while the other students cackling away.

"Bring it," he said pointing to the book.

He pointed out four pages for me to copy.

I hated doing penance but the anxiety I caused him was worth it.

Nieves could be a sneaky fellow. He would give a student a penance and a few days even a week after it was due, he would suddenly remind them that it had not been handed in. The student would look at him silently or lie badly. He would then double or triple the amount of penance.

I never once gave him a penance. They slowly accumulated over the school year. I would walk around the school my shirt pocket bulging with all of Nieves' penances.

I refused to hand in any of them. I was sure he was waiting to catch me and jam me good. I wanted to present them all with a smile on my face.

Although he would catch many of his students this way for some reason he actually seemed to forget every penance he ever gave me and I had to endure the discomfort of that bulging shirt pocket until the end of the school year.

From the first day that Mother Frog walked into Form V as my homeroom teacher, I knew she and I would have some fun. I had been unfairly denied English Lit. because of her and she would understand whom she was dealing with.

I would make smart aleck remarks from time to time and in general she seemed to handle it well but matters came to a climax the week after Carnival had concluded.

I had acquired a habit of anytime I wanted to throw away a piece of paper, I would scrunch it up into a ball and try to shoot it into our large class dustbin as if I were a pro basketball player. One day whilst she was taking the Attendance after Lunch, I saw some garbage in front of my desk which coincidentally was also in front of hers.

I picked up the paper, balled it up and bent my knees and prepared to shoot doing my best NBA impersonation.

"Sarwan, stand by the door," said Mother Frog who was observing me.

I was still lining up my shot so I finished it, scored and walked to the door.

I was looking down the corridor when I hear her say sternly, "Pick it up."

I looked at her.

She looked right back at me, "Pick it up."

I looked behind me and then back at her, "Are you talking to me?"

"Pick it up," her voice becoming a little louder.

I looked around, "Pick what up?"

"Pick it up!!" now she was shouting.

I again looked around, confused as to what she was talking about. There was no one next to me so I knew she was talking to me.

After two more times, I finally realized she was talking about the garbage.

"You want me to pick up the garbage?"

"Pick it up!!"

"But it's garbage. How can you ask me to put my hand in the dustbin take garbage *out* of it?"

"Pick it up!! Pick it up!!"

"But Miss, it's garbage. How can you ask me to put my hand in the dustbin?"

She continued shouting her one line.

At this point, I was no longer confused. This mad bitch expected me to put my hand in the dustbin.

"Like you eh hearing me or what!" and with that I turned my head and looked down the corridor.

PICK IT UP!!

I continued to look down the corridor.

At this point the forty odd students in the class were laughing loudly as one.

This short toad of a woman jumped off her seat and made her towards me. I think she knew I would not pay any attention to her so she grabbed my elbow and took me further into the corridor away from the class.

"You want to play the fool with me, eh?"

I was now concerned not because of her but the Vice Principal's Office was two doors away and he had the authority to beat students.

I became my passive in my response. "But I can't put my hand in the dustbin."

She began shouting even louder and got what she wanted. The VP came out of his office asked what was happening and instructed me to retrieve the paper. I did so.

"Come with me," he said and together we walked to the Principal's office.

Principal Manson heard what I had to say, left me standing in his office and went to Mother Frog to get her side of the issue.

I stood there looking around the office. During my school life, it was very rare that I ever entered that office for anything other than a negative experience. I was sure that this would end in blows.

He came back in a sombre mood. He explained that Mother Frog was angry because I slowed down the action of going to the door by taking my shot.

I of course feigned ignorance.

You know Mr. Sarwan, you are writing the CXC Exams in a few months. When you leave this school, you will want a Letter of Recommendation. So, you need to think about how you behave. You may go.

I was shocked. No blows.

I re-entered the class. Seeing a piece of paper near the dustbin, I picked it up and very slowly placed it over the bin, dropped it and began dusting and blowing on my fingers. Mother Frog looked at me in a peeved way and the class laughed.

The next day as she did the Attendance, I was still getting that look. She called off a student's name and realizing that he was not there, said "Not here."

Without looking up, I said "Not here? Absent. Can we not speak the English Language? Are we barbarians?" She looked at me in shocked anger. The class laughed away, the fact that she was the English Lit. teacher making it more comical.

However, in a few weeks Mother Frog would be the least of my problems as I would find yet another way to put myself in hot water at school.

CHAPTER 61

The Pervert in the Savannah and Mummy Saves the Day

Breaking biche had become sort of semi normal during my last two years of high school. I would simply leave early, go to the Mall or even home.

Another option had become the home of William Clauzel AKA Sidney. His middle name was given to him because of his parents' fondness for the actor, Sidney Poitier.

He was a talented footballer and cricketer. Clauzel had started breaking biche right off the bat in Form I. We would marvel how he never seemed to come to class. However, his prowess in sport seemed to give him special dispensations.

He would miss school for two weeks and the day of a football or cricket match just arrive and be placed on the team.

Mr. Rivas was the Dean of Form III and IV and when we were in those forms, Rivas would go to Clauzel's house in middle of the day, pick him up and drop him to school – no punishment whatsoever.

Rivas was known for his stern nature and for his willingness to beat if necessary. We were in awe of his benign nature towards Clauzel. I would joking refer to him as Rivas Jr. or Mr. Rivas being Clauzel's fairy godfather.

He and I had become friendly in Form V, primarily because his family had moved from Belmont to nearby St. James. His home was now less than 10 minutes' walk from the school. It was normal for some of us to leave prematurely and watch videos at his house.

A few days after the Mother Frog fiasco, I looked at him. "You feel like going after lunch?"

He smiled and said no.

"You sure? We could play some video games and watch a Betamax."

He refused again and I laughed. "Imagine you want to be in school."

I left immediately after lunch, visiting the Video Arcade in the Mall and then going home for an early afternoon nap.

I came to school the next day. Minutes before the first class was to begin, Mr. Rivas called me into the corridor. "Sarwan, where were you yesterday after lunch?"

If you were going to not do homework or break biche as much as I did in Holy Father's, you had to know how to lie and lie well. I was considered legendary for my ability to do so, to the point where boys would come to me for an excuse when having not done their homework.

When questioned by Mr. Rivas I did not hesitate for a moment, "Well Sir, my mother had to go away on business so I went with my father to drop her off at the airport."

"Tell one of your parents to come in and tell me that. Don't come back to school until they do."

Damn! He had put me in a corner. I decided to see if I could ride it out.

I had the end of term exams in two weeks and I knew that if I showed up at home too early and my father was there, I would not be able to adequately explain it. I went directly to the Queen's Park Savannah and took a bench obliquely opposite Queen's Royal College (QRC). I immediately pulled out my Principle of Business textbook and began studying. I studied for a few hours, went over to QRC at lunch time and bought some food at their canteen and at 1:30 pm began making my way home.

The next day Rivas was waiting for me. As I sat down waiting to take the Attendance, he walked up to the doorway, "Sarwan, I did not meet your parents. Get out."

And so I did.

I was now in a pickle. I didn't know quite what to do. I passed by a shop, bought some snacks and it was on to the Savannah. I would study for my impending exams, intermittently, turning on my radio to listen to the New Zealand tour of the West Indies.

A black man came up to me and said hi. He was in his early thirties, slim, with a medium afro, blue jeans, sneakers and a blue shirt. We chatted casually and he asked me what the score was.

The next day he showed up again and we chatted. Whilst doing so, an Indo Guyanese man approached us and showed us a tennis racquet.

"You fellas interested in buying it?"

We told him no.

"You sure. Only twenty-five dollars."

After refusing a few more times, he went up to a nearby dustbin, broke the racquet on the side of it and threw it in.

We both looked at him in shock.

His response was "I was staying at a nearby hotel and I just checked out. So, if nobody wants to buy it, it going in de bin."

As he walked off, the black fellow looked at me, "I think that is a tief."

I shrugged not really caring.

The black man's name was Tom, he chatted very pleasantly with me. By the end of the week, I knew I couldn't just keep coming to the Savannah. If I told my father, I would probably get a terrible beating. As I pondered what to do, Tom came by again. He was his usual friendly self. Then all of a sudden, he became too friendly.

As we spoke he put his hand on my knee. Then very slowly with a sly smile on his face, his hand moved slowly up my leg. I tried to be cool and moved his hand away.

"You don't want to play?" he asked with that stupid smile on his face.

"No."

"Come nah. We could have some fun. Nobody is watching."

I had heard about men like him. Sickos. I always thought they would look kind of gay or deranged. But he was a normal looking man and there he was trying to sexually harass a teenager. I moved to the far end of the bench and put my head into my book. He tried to continue speaking but I just ignored him.

Finally, after many attempts to have a conversation, I told him, "I am studying. No time to talk." And walked off to another bench with my books.

I had now been out of school for five days this was getting serious. I went over to Leila's school at lunch time. She was now attending Bishop's Anstey High school, an all-girls' school in POS.

I had never ever visited her at her school before so she must have been surprised. I made it clear to her that I was to speak to Mummy and that when she came to Daddy's house, she should send her to call me outside. She agreed and surprisingly, did not ask me any questions.

I knew that Leila finished school at three and my mother work at four. I left my father reading the newspapers, went outside at 4:20 and just sat in front of the building waiting nervously.

My mother arrived, Leila sat in the back while I explained to Mummy what had happened and that she would have to speak to Mr. Rivas.

She agreed that she would but first she would explain the situation to my father.

"No. Don't tell him. He will beat me. Just go and speak to Mr. Rivas on your own.

Every time she tried to open the door, I would lean over and shut it.

"Where are you going?" I asked, holding her arm.

"We must tell him. He is your father. And you must understand that you must face the consequences of your actions."

"I agree you are right," I replied, holding her handbag tightly, knowing that she would not leave without it. "I must face the consequences. Just don't tell him."

At this point Leila was giggling in the back seat.

Finally, I had to accede and wait outside while she spoke to him. I was a bit terrified, I hadn't gotten a beating in years. And my father's licks was the stuff of legends.

She came out ten minutes later and said "It's ok, I spoke to him. Tell Mr. Rivas, I will come after school tomorrow."

I waited a few minutes and then went inside with trepidation. He sat silently, watching TV. I went into my room and began studying.

The next day Mummy visited Mr. Rivas. They spoke while I waited outside the office. I thanked God that it was after 4:00 pm which meant a lot less attention from anyone else. Eventually, they called me in and the Rivas I saw was not the man we at Holy Father's were used to. Instead of the shouting beast, I observed a very soft-spoken man, smiling and speaking to my mother like the gentlest of gentlemen. The matter was resolved and we left.

For the next week there was not a better-behaved person in the world than me. I studied diligently, leaving my room only to eat, shower or watch the sports report on TV. If in the car with my father, I said not a word, I had a book open and studied. For most of that week I tried not to make eye contact with him. I thanked God for dodging that bullet. Despite my problems with my mother, she had come through for me that day.

CHAPTER 62

"How the Hell Can It Be C?"

With the Easter holidays upon us, Sunita came to visit.

Life was now very different for her. She had to endure watching her mother have a variety of lovers. She hardly ever saw her father and had to listen to her mother constantly complain about his lack of child support.

She didn't have Neelam to partner with her to harass me and I was happy to exact my revenge from time to time.

She was telling us that how much she had enjoyed visiting the Caura River the previous weekend.

"We went with Uncle Bobby."

"Who's he?"

"She hesitated for a moment, "That's mummy's new boyfriend."

"Wait, I thought that was Uncle Frank," I said, looking at her and feigning ignorance.

"No, that was before."

"What about Basdeo, the Doctor fella?"

Her face screwed up uncomfortably, ".... Ahhm ... that was before."

"So, wait nah, how many uncles you have girl?"

"And what about Marvin?" she retorted.

"That is one man. How many does your mother take in a year?"

"Don't worry about that," said my father, looking at her a little sadly. "That's not important."

I looked at him, "It's not important."

"No," he said giving me a bland look.

Apparently, it was humorous when my mother had a man in her life but not with Sunita's.

However, there was one area in which he was dead firm and that was education.

Sunita was due to write her Common Entrance Exams in a few months. She had never been a good student and I did not see how she would succeed. Surprisingly, her parents had never sent her for private lessons as most parents did.

"So, CE is coming up. Are you practicing?" I asked.

She nodded her head but not convincingly.

"Are you practicing your Vocab, Spelling and Math?"

"Yes."

I decided to have some fun with her.

"Spell knife."

She looked straight ahead as if thinking it over.

Daddy looked over at her, "Sound it out."

"Knife ... knife. C .."

"C?? HOW THE HELL CAN IT BE C? AND IS KNIFE YOU SPELLING!!??"

Her face crumpled and she seemed on the verge of tears. She did not speak for at least three hours.

For the first ten minutes I would glance at her and smile. That will keep her in her place I thought. However, part of me felt sorry for her. More importantly, she had CE in a few months, what was she going to do?

With Sunita there, Daddy made an extra effort to go out and took us for dinner at the Taj Mahal. On another night, we went for coconuts at the Savannah.

As she had gotten older, Sunita was perhaps beginning to understand that Leila and I were more than just targets for her parents' pettiness. She would ask about Leila and even asked me for a photo of myself for her album.

When Neelam came to pick her up at the end of her visit, she didn't just chat at the door. She came in and looked at my father, an extremely concerned look on her face.

"I need to talk to you about something."

Daddy looked at her with a hint of apprehension, "Ok."

She sat down on the couch next to him. I had no idea what the problem was but I could tell from the look on her face it was serious.

She explained that in February she had left Sunita with one of her aunts while she went on business to Curacao. She would buy clothes and resell them in TT.

Sunita had boasted how her father owned a lot of land in Sangre Grande and who her grandfather was.

The woman went off on Sunita, "Your father? The man who does run down woman all over the place. He selling land and is a nobody. You mother is a next one. How much man she have? Imagine your name is Darsan and look how you living, poor, poor so."

Pathetic. You are Rampersad Darsan's granddaughter. Your father is a Darsan and a lawyer and you might as well be a nobody."

If she tried to talk back, she was shouted down and reminded whose house she was in. She was then berated for the next two weeks on how "sad and pathetic" her family was.

Unable to defend herself or handle the daily abuse, Sunita would go to the washroom, lock herself in and cry.

I could hear the conversation in my room. I went to the kitchen to make a cup of coffee and enhance my maco position.

384

"That woman is obviously suffering from a complex," said my father. His face was dead serious.

"When Sunita told me what she had to experience, I can tell you that it was very hurtful," bemoaned Neelam, her crestfallen face looking straight ahead at the floor.

"Never send her there again," he said.

"Of course not," said Neelam, rising to leave.

"I cannot tell you how upset I was when Sunita told me these things."

The expression on their faces was palpable.

I thought of how they had harassed us in the past. How he had teased Leila until she cried and they had both laughed about it. However, with Sunita it was different. They were aware that a child had feelings and how hurtful it was.

With the holidays done, I was on the home stretch. The CXC Exams were in three months' time. We would have a Mock Exam one month prior to it.

I had started attending private lessons in January in a school in Belmont. The teacher, Mr. Hines would focus on English, Math and Accounts with me. English was never a problem, my accounting seemed to improve, however, Math would continue to the be the scourge of my life.

Mr. Hines would look at me, "But you are creating your own formulas. Are you some kind of Doctor?"

I quickly got the nickname Doc in his classes.

Although classes ran from 4-6 pm, he would often finish after 6:30 as he never believed in having a lesson "half finished."

Once or twice my father was too busy drinking and after waiting until almost 8 pm, I would simply have to walk the two-mile journey to our home. At that age, I could handle the walk but with a full book bag slung over your shoulder, it was a tedious experience.

CHAPTER 63

Rob Roy Adds Insult to Injury and Goodbye to High School

Aunty Vashti and her family were no longer a part of our lives.

Rob Roy would dodge my father as best he could rather than pay his debts.

Daddy had simply given up. He had chatted with him, encouraged, shouted and humiliated him but to limited avail.

I pointed out Neelam's effective method of reimbursement. He repeated that it was not that easy with family. I then politely pointed out that perhaps he should stop lending as he did not seem very successful in dealing with his debtors.

To add insult to injury, Daddy had imported some goods from Germany the year before, canned sweets and door handles. He had formed a company, VS Investments and Trading Ltd. and give Rob Roy business cards, assuring him of a commission if he sold the items. He did but never gave my father his money.

There was more insult to be added. My mother came by one afternoon in mid-May.

"I want to talk to you," she said to Daddy very solemnly.

She then explained that Rob Roy was working for a company called Laughlin Brothers, they specialized in selling refrigerators and air conditioners. He had been accused of stealing from the company and selling their products on the side. He was using my father's business cards. In other words, the customers thought they were purchasing from my father's company and he could now be implicated in the mess.

He looked at my mother blandly.

"You notice I am not surprised."

"Why not?"

"Unfortunately, that is the kind of man he is. This is all he has done since he has come to this country, scheme, lie and steal."

"But does Vidia know this?"

"Everybody knows this. His reputation as a crook is well established."

"But how is Vidia staying with a man like this?"

"Well she got married young and is trying her best to make her marriage work."

"Well this looks bad. It looks like you are involved."

They continued talking for a while and amazingly he never confronted Rob Roy. I found myself wondering what was the point of having a law degree if people could get away with this? But I knew asking the question would not really get an acceptable answer.

If by chance he and Rob Roy were in the same building he would simply run. On one occasion Daddy attended a wake in Sangre Grande. When he walked in, he saw Vinaya. He was laughing, his shoulders shaking up and down.

"Roy was here, wasn't he?"

Vinaya nodded, laughing away.

"When he saw me, he ran out through the back door?"

Vinaya nodded, his head, shoulders and belly shaking as he laughed.

When I wrote the CXC Mock Exam, I managed to pass English, History and Business. I failed Accounting, Math and Geography. My average was 56 per cent, nothing glorious but the best I had ever done. My father went off on me.

I was lectured by a man who only worked when he felt like it, owned no home and was paying rent at the age of 44.

"Your life is obviously laid out for you, isn't it? You don't need to work. You just go outside in the back yard and pick money of the money tree!"

I sat silently in the car and listened to his pontification, reminding myself that in a few months he and I would not be in the same house.

Like tens of thousands of students around the country I had been studying, preparing myself. With two weeks to go, I went into overdrive. I not only studied all night but I was at the school until 6:00 pm. I would then go to school on the weekends to study more. There would be other students doing the same. I avoided my home for most weekends as there were too many distractions there.

Between the private lessons with Mr. Hines and my studying, I believed I had a shot at passing my subjects even Math.

My father may have had his faults but the stepped up the week of the Exams. He made sure I had good dinners ready and waiting every night. I came out of my room only to eat or watch the Sports Report. As I exited the car every morning he would say "Good luck son."

I had never heard him call me son before.

I went into the Math Exam pumped and ready. The boys had developed a technique for the Multiple-Choice part, the first four fingers would indicate the letters A-D. We simply had to communicate which question. I found that section to be easy and was all smiles. The rest of the exam left me befuddled. I was not the only one. I was sitting at the back of the auditorium and as we exited, we all looked at each other as if to say what the hell just happened?

I owned the English Exam as I expected to. History was also not a problem. However, I stumbled in Accounting and Geography. I was only able to finish two of the three required questions in Accounting.

I did not think to turn the last page in the Geo Exam to see more questions. I therefore missed out on easier questions in terms of choosing which to answer. Why did I not think to look on the other side of the page?

The exams were over and life became more relaxed. The teachers reviewed past material and did activities with us.

There was a tradition amongst the prestige schools, the boys would wear the girls' uniforms and vice versa and we would then visit each other's school. I had no intentions of wearing girls' clothes and I doubted I could find my size. However, in the last week of school, I saw a bunch of boys slowly walking in and looking unsure of themselves, they looked different somehow. It was then that I realized some of the Holy Name Convent girls had borrowed our school uniform and invaded us. All the boys came out to watch and cheer them and then they were politely shooed away by the priests.

On the last day of school, we signed each other's shirts. Some of us went to the Mall and did the usual of walking around, looking at the girls and visiting the Video Arcade.

And just like that high school was over. No more.

No more getting up early in the morning. No more traffic. No more blows from the Dean because of misbehaviour. I would be furthering my education in Canada but I was sure it could not be as dreary as school life in TT.

CHAPTER 64

Rob Roy Again and an Inconceivable Future

I started July having nothing but fun. Tomas Romero lived in Federation Park not too far from my neighbourhood. He had repeated Form III in our class because he "did not get the Sciences." We had become friendly as we would walk the same route to home and sometimes with the other boys would stop off at the Long Circular Mall for the usual lime.

With more free time on our hands we would see each other, usually at his house or the Mall. His father was the Permanent Secretary of Foreign Affairs in TT. He had got Tomas a job as a clerk until his departure for the US at the end of the summer. The idea was he would prep for the SAT Exams and use that as a short cut to University instead of the Form VI route.

Tomas' first day was an eye opener. He did some basic clerical work and acted as a Messenger Boy if necessary. He had lunch at 12 pm with the other workers. However, just after 12:30 he saw everybody get up and run. He was confused. He wondered if it was some kind of fire drill except, he had not heard an alarm.

He discovered the reason for the mini stampede towards the end of lunch. All the workers would finish their meal and then run to find an office to sleep in for a few hours. If you happened to walk into an "occupied office," someone would shout, "Ey!! Get out of here!!"

We laughed that a Ministry could operate in such a way.

Zeenat and Sammy were full on in their relationship. I had not seen Sammy since her birthday party the year before. Zeenat's family liked him. They were surprised at how quiet and reserved he was but they figured with Zeenat's assertive and at times aggressive personality, they probably complimented each other. Aunty Vashti and her children now lived on the second floor of a house in Tunapuna.

Uncle Shirvan came to visit with his brother in mid-July. He and Aunty Vashti were still an item. He explained to us that Sammy wanted to marry Zeenat. She had not said no but asked him to wait for a year. She was only seventeen and was not sure of what she would be doing after school. She and her mother had discussed the matter and agreed that she would take a sewing course and perhaps be a seamstress.

"She will be eighteen next year and working. It would be appropriate to wait a year and get married next July."

Sammy's response was "If I don't get married, I will die."

At the time of this conversation, Vinaya was driving home. What he saw was Sammy jump from the second-floor porch, land in the yard and start running down the road without even breaking stride.

A concerned Vinaya drove after him. Wild thoughts were running through his mind, had someone been injured, had the house been robbed?

He pulled up next to the sprinting Sammy and screeched to a halt.

"Sammy! Sammy! What's wrong? What's wrong?"

Sammy looked at him, eyes red and on the verge of tears, his face etched in distress, "Nobody love me!! Nobody love me!!" he shouted and continued running down the street.

Vinaya rushed home and up the stairs to find his mother and Zeenat in a daze.

"We only asked him to wait a year," said a befuddled Aunty Vashti.

Uncle Shirvan laughed and looked at my father, "I didn't know man does die if they don't get married."

They both laughed and continued drinking their rum.

When Uncle Shirvan left, I looked at my father, "I don't know this fellow and he seems popular with the family but any man who can't wait a year to marry a seventeen-year-old girl and is jumping off the second floor of a building has some issues."

Daddy laughed and shrugged his shoulders.

I continued, "What if that conversation had taken place on the fourth floor? What about the next couple of years, they get married and have a terrible argument, what might he do then? Has Zeenat thought about that?"

"Boss," smiled my father, "that is not my concern. Thank God he eh go be my son in law."

Amazingly, we received a visit from Rob Roy in late July. He presented my father with a cheque for three thousand dollars. With a broad grin he said "Here you go Doc. I know I was a bit late."

My father gave him a wary look, took the cheque, scanned it and nodded, looking at him as if he were a suspected drug trafficker.

"Well I have to go. Take care. Sunny bye bye."

The next day as my father made his way to the bank, a little voice told him to go to Rob Roy's bank. He walked up to the clerk, "Please tell me if this cheque is good for the amount written."

The clerk punched a few keys on her computer, paused then looked at my father with a wry smile, "Sir, this account was closed two days ago."

My father shook his head, "Right there that is three criminal offences."

He went home that afternoon trying to contain himself. "If I lose my temper with this fat bitch, I will give myself a heart attack."

He called Aunty Vashti that night asking for Rob Roy.

"Well he and Vidia left for the USA this afternoon. They are going to live in New York City."

"Well he wrote me a cheque but he actually closed his account before writing it and it's no good."

"Well I don't know what to say. They are not here. They left for the US."

"Do you have a telephone number for them?"

"No, I don't."

"Your daughter has gone to New York and you don't have a telephone number for her?"

"No."

"Vashti, are you a lying bitch just like your son in law?"

She put down the phone.

Rob Roy had left Trinidad just as he had arrived, lying, stealing and shamelessly taking advantage of other people's generosity. He had milked TT for what it was worth and now he was gone.

God help New York City.

One of my regrets about leaving TT was that I would no longer be able to see the sports. For the first time I would miss the high school Intercol Football League. I would also miss the boxing and cricket.

We were leaving on August 15, I made sure to squeeze in a boxing card at the Jean Pierre Sports Complex on the fourth. Local hero, Leslie Stewart successfully challenged Lotte Mwale for the Light Heavyweight Championship of the Commonwealth.

My mother and Marvin had bought a beautiful home in Maraval not far from the Moka Golf Course. Although they lived less than five miles from us, I never visited them. I had no interest. However, a week before leaving, I was brought over by my mother to pick up some shirts she had bought for me. I was impressed at how well decorated and posh the house was.

She and a neighbour were chatting away as I folded the shirts and put them in a bag. My mother was speaking in a critical tone of a woman who had numerous lovers.

I looked at her, "It seems to bother you."

"Well of course. What kind of woman parades herself like that?"

"Really? Tell it to the married men you lime with," I said walking out of the room.

I could hear her telling the neighbour, "He likes to drink."

She was now trying to paint me as an alcoholic to cover up her own foolishness. Sadly, it would not be the last time she would do that.

A few days later she had a dinner for me as I was leaving the country and invited some close family friends. I did not want to go but I knew that if I didn't, she would complain to my father and I would be made to. So, I simply said yes. I could not help but notice that Mr. Uglito was nowhere to be seen.

Just prior to my leaving TT, I asked Leila what had happened to him.

She explained that he had been married before and that his ex-wife and daughter lived in New York. Although he was separated, Mummy had been waiting for his divorce to be finalized so they could get married. After three years, she wasn't in the mood to wait any longer.

"Damn!" I said to Leila. "She was really eager to marry Uglito."

The Murrays, Mohammeds and Khans were there that night. I was happy to say goodbye to them as they had been such an important part of my childhood. They had stepped in on so many occasions when my mother had needed assistance with her children or other matters.

Two nights before my departure my father actually spent some money and we went for dinner at the Kapok Hotel. We ate on the top floor and enjoyed a beautiful view of the city.

I got up on the day of the flight nervous and excited. I made sure that I was packed and that my passport and money were in my pocket. My father came in the room and showed me how to tie a tie.

Not surprisingly, he was not going to the airport with us and made sure a taxi came to pick us up.

My mother arrived a half an hour before the taxi. She repacked my bag as she found it too disorganized.

"The taxi will cost seventy-five dollars" she said looking at Daddy.

"Oh, you want me to pay for it?"

She looked at him blandly, "You expected me to pay for it?"

He gave a sheepish grin and fetched it from his wallet.

As the taxi arrived, he shook my hand, "See you for Christmas."

As we made our way across the Beetham Highway, I looked to my left at the green hills of the Northern Range. I was excited at the prospect of living in Canada. I was nervous about the unknown. How would I make friends? How would I adapt to a foreign culture? I thought of Sony and how our romance had been extinguished almost as quickly as it had ignited. Would I feel that kind of love again?

I could not conceive the changes that were to come.

My mother would accept a job in England three months later, taking Leila with her. Ten years later Leila would graduate as the third lawyer in our family.

She would marry a Frenchman in Paris in 2002. A year prior to the wedding, she would call my father and ask him to walk her down the aisle. He promised to do so, telling everyone that his suit would be tailormade.

I warned both my mother and her not to rely on him.

"That man never drove across Trinidad for her. Do you really think he is going to cross the Atlantic?"

"But he is her father," said Mummy. "She wants him to walk her down the aisle."

A real estate agent at the time in Toronto, as expected, he cancelled two months before the wedding.

"It will be summer. That's a peak time to make money. I can't go."

I could only shake my head. He had said it without a morsel of shame or regret.

Uncle Javed would step up and take his place being there for our family as he had on so many occasions in Trinidad.

I would never see Sony again. I spent the rest of that century meeting other women who never captured my heart. Finally, thirty-six years after her departure from TT, we would reconnect on Facebook. She would be a bit older and heavier with a daughter, happily married to a financial analyst.

As the eighties turned into the nineties Sunita and I found a common ground on which to meet, perhaps realizing that our past problems had more to do with the fallibility of our parents rather than with us.

She would continue to put up with her mother's parade of men and her evolving alcoholism. She would marry in the late nineties, banning Neelam from the wedding, afraid of being embarrassed by an alcoholic mother.

Just six months later, Neelam would die of lung cancer, aged 48.

Told that she would not be able to conceive and that if she did, she would probably not carry to a full term, she did do so in 2004 only to lose the baby in the second trimester.

Her Muslim mother-in-law, fed up of no grandchild after thirteen years of marriage, travelled to South Trinidad and prayed to a statue of Mary. This statue cried milk and had attracted worshippers from all parts of the country. She prayed fervently and was rewarded with a grandchild just ten months later, a boy, exactly on my birthday.

Sunita was a loving mother and sadly was only able to celebrate his first birthday with him.

One morning she awoke complaining of a pain in her side. She continued through the day and after lunch showed her husband how their eighteen-month-old son should be bathed. Just fifteen minutes later, she walked into the bedroom, groaned and collapsed. An ambulance was called but she was pronounced dead upon arrival at the hospital, the result of a blocked pulmonary artery. She was only 38 years old.

Neelam never saw her daughter get married nor her grandchild born. Sunita after years of struggle, could not even enjoy two years with her child, dying at an even younger age than her mother.

Ironically, it would be my mother and I who would befriend my nephew, she, playing with him and giving him gifts for Christmas – watching him grow up to be a handsome, intelligent young man. I sometimes wondered if this turn of events was some kind of karma for what Neelam and my father had put us through during our childhood.

I had always had a fondness for sports, graduating with a Journalism Degree from Humber College, I became a Sports Reporter of note in Toronto, contributing articles to the TT Press.

My relationship with both parents never recovered from the dysfunctionality of the previous years. I would pay them attention at my convenience. Having a few friends who did the same, it gave me some scant solace that my family was not a solitary freak show.

I looked at the Northern Range, my mind focused elsewhere. However, years later, I would look at it again through the eyes of a foreigner and realize how lucky I had been to live in the shadow of such beauty for eighteen years of my life.

CPSIA information can be obtained
at www.ICGtesting.com
Printed in the USA
BVHW091240160921
616891BV00013B/1265

9 781777 681616